Preserving Popular Music Heritage

There is a growing awareness around the world of a pressing need to archive the material remnants of popular music to safeguard the national and local histories of this cultural form. Current research suggests that over the past 20 or so years, there has been an expansion of DIY heritage practice, with the founding of numerous DIY popular music institutions, archives and museums.

This edited collection seeks to explore the role of DIY or pro-am (professional-amateur) practitioners of popular music archiving and preservation. It looks critically at ideas around DIY preservationism, self-authorised and unauthorised heritage practice, and the DIY institution, while also unpacking the potentialities of bottom-up, community-based interventions into the archiving and preservation of popular music's material history. With an international scope and an interdisciplinary approach, this is an important reference for scholars of popular music, heritage studies and cultural studies.

Sarah Baker is an Associate Professor in Cultural Sociology at Griffith University, Queensland, Australia.

Routledge Research in Music

Preserving Popular Music Heritage

Do-it-Yourself, Do-it-Together

Edited by Sarah Baker

Routledge
Taylor & Francis Group

LONDON AND NEW YORK

First published 2015 by Routledge

2 Park Square, Milton Park, Abingdon, Oxfordshire OX14 4RN

52 Vanderbilt Avenue, New York, NY 10017

Routledge is an imprint of the Taylor & Francis Group, an informa business

First issued in paperback 2019

Library of Congress Cataloging in Publication Data

    Preserving popular music heritage : do-it-yourself, do-it-together / edited by Sarah Baker.
      pages cm. — (Routledge research in music ; 11)
    Includes bibliographical references and index.
      1. Popular music—Historiography. I. Baker, Sarah, 1977-
    ML3470.P75 2015
    781.64028'8—dc23   2014049474

ISBN: 978-1-138-78143-6 (hbk)
ISBN: 978-0-367-23195-8 (pbk)

Typeset in Sabon
by codeMantra

For Alison Huber, in celebration of our collaboration from which this book was born

Contents

List of Figures and Tables

FIGURES

TABLES

Acknowledgements

My interest in enthusiast-founded and volunteer-run popular music archives and museums began during the Australian Research Council (ARC)-funded project Popular Music and Cultural Memory (2010–12, DP1092910), part of which involved working closely with the wonderful Alison Huber to look at a small number of community-based popular music archives and museums. This research with Alison produced a typology of the DIY institution (*European Journal of Cultural Studies* 2013), as well as a co-authored article on the Victorian Jazz Archive (*Popular Music History* 2012) and a chapter on "saving rubbish" that appeared in the book *Sites of Popular Music Heritage* (Routledge, 2015). Ultimately our work together led to a second grant funded by the ARC, *Do-It-Yourself Popular Music Archives and Museums* (2012–15, DP130100317). Although Alison was unable to continue working with me on this second project, the research and its outputs – including this edited collection – continue to be underpinned by the ideas we cooked up together during our three-year collaboration. I therefore owe Alison a huge debt of gratitude and dedicate this book to her.

The book has benefited enormously from participation at the following conferences: Sites of Popular Music Heritage (Liverpool, 2011); Popular Music Heritage, Cultural Memory and Cultural Identity (Rotterdam, 2013); Pop-Life: The Value of Popular Music in the 21st Century (Northampton, 2014); and On Collecting: Music, Materiality and Ownership (Edinburgh, 2014). I made contact with a number of the contributors to this collection during these conferences. Thanks especially to Paul Long and Lisa Busby, who came to the collection late after I heard them presenting their fascinating work on popular music heritage at a panel I co-organised with Jez Collins at Pop-Life. Jez, in particular, deserves to be singled out for thanks. Our many conversations, at conferences and by email, have helped shape the book, as well as the research more broadly.

I am also very grateful to the practitioners in Part II of this collection, who embraced the idea of showcasing their archives, museums, and heritage practices alongside the more academic work presented in Part I. These authors have all dealt with the production of the volume with great patience and good humour, and I sincerely appreciate the time each one has put into this enterprise. It is an absolute pleasure to be able to include the stories of their organisations here.

I would like to acknowledge the support of the Griffith Centre for Cultural Research, Griffith University and their assistance with the production of this volume. In particular, thanks go to copy editor Sue Jarvis for her meticulous work. Thanks also to Andrew Weckenmann and his colleagues at Routledge for their sound advice and assistance at all stages of the production of this book.

To friends and family who have supported me along the way, thank you – especially Vuk and his red pen.

Most importantly, to all the volunteers and enthusiasts whose work is documented in this volume, thank you for the love and care you happily bring to your role as custodians of popular music's material past.

Sarah Baker
Scenic Rim, Queensland

1 Identifying Do-it-Yourself Places of Popular Music Preservation

Sarah Baker

There is increasing recognition across the globe of the pressing need to archive the remnants of popular music's material past so as to safeguard the national and local histories of this important cultural form. Traditionally, popular music cultures were not regarded as heritage. As Bennett (2009, 477) argues, "Their mass-produced, commercial and global properties rendered them the antithesis of authentic cultural value as conceived in conventional heritage discourse." There has been a gradual shift in the heritage sector that now balances the preservation and showcasing of formal evidence of statehood, modernity and other central aspects of regional or national life with a fiscal and administrative responsibility for the preservation of popular culture (Baker, Doyle and Homan 2015). National archives and museums have thus become key institutions for the preservation of the material aspects of popular music heritage. Many countries now have national institutions dedicated to the collection, preservation and display of popular music, and they often seek to provide a level of public access to these collections. In Australia, for example, the National Film and Sound Archive (NFSA) houses sound and visual recordings as well as some ephemera related to popular music's material history. Comparable institutions include the British Library Sound Archive in the United Kingdom and the National Sound Archive at the National Library of Israel. As repositories for national heritage, institutions like the NFSA are accordingly supported by federal funding and an institutional structure designed to meet the aims of collection, preservation, promotion and access. But in the recognition that it is virtually impossible for institutions to collect everything and to function as comprehensive repositories of the nation, collecting strategies often lean towards the pursuit of selective narratives of particular national significance. As a result, the selection of materials and sounds of popular music in national institutions tends to follow established narratives in written and oral histories, reinforcing existing canons (Baker, Doyle and Homan 2015).

Brandellero and Janssen (2014, 225) note, "In recent years, spurred by the growing status and recognition of intangible heritage, bottom-up approaches to heritage identification have emerged, legitimating the role of communities as bestowers of heritage status." As a result, alongside prestigious national institutions such as those mentioned above, there exist a range of community-led, grassroots, specialist archives, museums and halls of fame, manifested physically and/or online, which are equally important to the preservation of popular music's material past. While some of these places have developed broad collection remits (e.g. Sarasota Music Archive, United States; Lippmann+Rau-Musikarchiv, Germany), others are dedicated to specific genres (e.g. SwissJazzOrama, Switzerland; Hector Country Music Heritage Museum, New Zealand), artists (e.g. Ramones Museum, Germany; Rokkheimur Rúnars Júlíussonar, Iceland) or locales (e.g. Rhode Island Music Hall of Fame, United States; Birmingham Music Archive, United Kingdom), which are marginalised, or at least not the focus of national collections, and which operate largely without any form of significant government support. Such institutions tend to have limited paid staff and rely for their operation sometimes entirely on the work of volunteers (e.g. National Jazz Archive, United Kingdom; Nederlands Jazz Archief, Netherlands) or interns (e.g. The ARChive of Contemporary Music, United States; SR-Archiv österreichischer Popularmusik, Austria). Indeed, many such institutions have no paid work-force whatsoever and no workers with training in the areas of archiving and curating (e.g. Sound Preservation Association of Tasmania, Australia; South Australian Jazz Archive, Australia). These archives, museums and halls of fame are therefore important in epistemological terms because the parameters of their heritage practices are determined by the volunteers and enthusiasts involved, enabling archival records and museal exhibitions to be created other than those that are governed by the policies and fiscal constraints of national institutions. The development of these grassroots archives and museums is "suggestive of broader trends in the ways in which communities and individuals within those communities show interest in asserting ownership over, and expertise in, the cultural history of popular music, which leads them to acts of preservation and display that contribute to our collective memory of these musics" (Baker and Huber 2013a, 514). Such places therefore have the potential to democratise popular music heritage, "contributing to a national archive that exists beyond the National Archives" (Flinn 2010, n.p.).

This book offers some insights into the ways in which these enthusiast-founded, volunteer-led, community-based archives and museums are contributing to the public record of popular music's material past. The chapters contained within its pages confirm that the desire of individuals and communities take on the role of custodians of popular music heritage is prevalent rather than isolated; they produce archives and museums that are distinct and specific, but reside on a continuum of popular music heritage practice at the community level; and "they have a history; and that they relate to an identifiable set of concerns, making themselves public through the practices of communities and individuals wishing to participate in the management of music heritage" (Baker and Huber 2013a, 526). This is a book about the ways in which popular music heritage is managed by ordinary people in extraordinary ways (Flinn 2007). As noted elsewhere, "If popular music culture is genuinely a culture of the people, then its preservation in the hands of the people seems appropriate" (Baker and Huber 2013a, 526).

The chapters in this book capture the extent to which popular music heritage, as a form of cultural heritage, is both practice and process, inasmuch as "its meanings and uses are socially, spatially and temporally enacted, and, as such, are constantly being remade and renegotiated" (Roberts, 2014, 267). Thus the question becomes not one of why it is important to amass the "junk" of pop culture in archives and museums (see Baker and Huber 2015) or revere canonic figures of the music industry in halls of fame (see Baker and Huber 2013b) but rather one concerning what this practice offers the enthusiasts involved and the networks and communities that form and are formed by these independent heritage enterprises. As Roberts puts it:

> Rather than attempting to sketch the manifold heritages that attach themselves – with varying degrees of coherence – to forms of popular music culture, it is more instructive to pay critical attention to the discursive and performative structures of meaning and practice by which they are constituted. ... By breaking down music heritage discourses into the spaces, practices and "acts of transfer" that play performative host to the cultures of popular music pasts, we can gain a better understanding of how these pasts, in all their colour, diversity and authenticity, are lived in the present (2014, 276–7).

The book demonstrates some of the ways in which popular music's past becomes enacted in the present in the space of community-based archives and museums.

This introductory chapter sets the scene for what follows by providing an overview of the small body of existing literature that has been adopted as a critical framework by a number of the authors in Part I. In particular, the reader's attention is drawn to the work of Roberts and Cohen (2014) on "self-authorized" and "unauthorized" popular music heritage practice, Bennett's (2009) notion of a "DIY preservationist sensibility" and Flinn's (2007) conception of the "community archive." The work of Baker and Huber (2013a) on "DIY institutions" is also outlined in the context of the professional-amateur "revolution" (Leadbeater and Miller 2004) and with reference to "communities of practice" (Wenger 1998). Throughout the chapter, these conceptual frameworks are illustrated, where practical, with reference to the twenty-three enthusiast-founded, volunteer-led, community-based archives, museums and halls of fame the book's editor visited between 2010 and 2014 as part of two consecutive projects funded by the Australian Research Council, *Popular Music and Cultural Memory* (DP1092910, 2010–12) and *Do-It-Yourself Popular Music Archives* (DP130100317, 2013–15). During this time, 125 workers were interviewed, most of whom were volunteers who gifted their time, and sometimes even their money, to these heritage enterprises. The sites of popular music heritage that are the focus of that research are located in ten countries: Australia,

Austria, the Czech Republic, Germany, Iceland, the Netherlands, New Zealand, Switzerland, the United Kingdom and the United States. Such a spread begins to show the breadth of this type of heritage activity, and this is confirmed further in the chapters that also draw attention to archiving being undertaken in Africa (Chapters 10, 14 and 15), South America (Chapter 16) and other European countries (Chapters 8 and 9). While the places of the editor's research are primarily physical collections of popular music (see Chapter 4), this book also emphasises online community archives dedicated to preserving popular music's material past (see Chapters 2, 5, 6, 10, 11, 13 and 16). Where possible, reference is also made in this chapter to other archives and museums that are not covered by the aforementioned research or the chapters contained in this collection so as to further demonstrate the extent of grassroots popular music heritage preservation practices around the world.

A CONTINUUM OF POPULAR MUSIC HERITAGE PRACTICE

This section considers at length the contribution of Roberts and Cohen (2014) to an understanding of popular music heritage as a continuum of practice. By focusing on commemorative plaque schemes in England, Roberts and Cohen draw on qualitative research to propose "a critical and analytical framework through which to explore popular music heritage" (2014, 242). This framework sets out to avoid a binarism that positions popular music heritage practice as either official (top down) or unofficial (bottom up). Rather, they put forward a more nuanced critical framework that highlights three types of interrelated discourse about popular music heritage: officially authorised, self-authorised and unauthorised. Such a typology, they argue, enables an exploration of the dynamics of popular music heritage "as a situated, relational practice involving various, often contested negotiations of the musical past" and the analysis of "the various ways in which popular music heritage is not simply practised but also authorised and ascribed with value, legitimacy and social and cultural capital" (2014, 243). In this typology, officially authorised popular music heritage – or "big H" Heritage – tends to be that which is sanctioned by and/or substantially sponsored by government bodies. However, the interest of contributors to this edited collection is primarily in Roberts and Cohen's (2014, 244) development of the other two categories in their critical framework that situate "heritage-as-praxis."

With self-authorised popular music heritage, there tends to be limited official government backing and an absence of the "gilt-edged symbolic capital" that is attached to prominent public institutions (Roberts and Cohen 2014, 248). Rather, self-authorised sites, organisations and activities are established alongside their more prestigious counterparts by way of the music and media industries and "by musicians, audiences, entrepreneurs and organisations who participate in particular musical cultures" (2014, 248).

Roberts and Cohen refer to these as "DIY, localised or vernacular popular music heritage discourses," which, though not officially authorised in the same way as prestigious public institutions, still make "claims to (or solicitations of) some form of official status" with regard to their "marketing and publicity, or ensuring the sustainability and development of the heritage initiative or resource in question" (2014, 248). Mechanisms through which self-authorised initiatives can build more influence and cultural clout include the endorsement or patronage of famous or influential people such as celebrities (as is the case with The ARChive of Contemporary Music, United States, which has the support of high-profile artists such as David Bowie, Keith Richards and Paul Simon); the capacity to secure grants and other forms of public funding, including local government or council funding such as that received by Tónlistarsafn Íslands, Iceland; and the ability to be granted charitable status such as the classical music-oriented organisation Music Preserved, all of which can assist in lending an air of professionalisation to the activities of the initiative and thus further blurring "the distinction between ideas of official and 'unofficial'" popular music heritage (2014, 250).

In addition, while self-authorised institutions and practices may represent a more democratised form of popular music heritage, this type of activity memorialises "the personal musical heritage and history of individuals," such as the founders of these initiatives, as much as "that which is claimed on behalf of a wider group or nation" (Roberts and Cohen 2014, 250). Take, for example, KD's Elvis Presley Museum located in Hawera on Aotearoa New Zealand's North Island. While the museum is most definitely focused on Elvis – or, more accurately, Elvis memorabilia – it also uses this memorabilia to tell the story of KD's engagement with rock 'n' roll throughout his life, with a particular emphasis on the 1950s and 1960s (see Figure 1.1). The collection demonstrates the development in music players across time by including the devices on which KD played music in his teenage and adult years, as well as providing insight into Aotearoa New Zealand's 1950s and 1960s rock 'n' roll scene through a display of boots and jackets from his days immersed in that scene. We can see in such an example how self-authorised popular music heritage practice concerns, to some degree, the enactment of memory. As Roberts and Cohen (2014, 252) explain, "One of the chief functions of self-authorising music heritage practices is, therefore, to furnish a means by which to give substance to the ritual and performative dimensions of cultural memory: the sites of popular music heritage as an (in)tangible place of pilgrimage" and also "the experiential, affective and embodied contours of musical memory."

The third category in Roberts and Cohen's typology is a variant of heritage practice that does not seek authorisation and in which the emphasis is on everyday practice, cultural bricolage, anti-heritage and individual and collective memory. This is unauthorised, "small h" heritage, a form of heritage practice that tends to exist "without even an awareness that it *is* heritage"

Figure 1.1 Kevin "KD" Wasley, founder of KD's Elvis Presley Museum, which is located in the garage of his home in Hawera, New Zealand. Photo by Sarah Baker.

(2014, 17). Artist fan sites might fall under this category, as might the taking, collecting, and circulating of offstage photos of a pop group like Take That (see Chapter 12).

The work of Roberts and Cohen (2014) highlights the importance of thinking about popular music heritage activities on a spectrum. Such thinking opens up rather than closes down our understanding of community-led heritage endeavours, enabling the inclusion of what might be described, using Roberts and Cohen's proposed framework, as the unauthorised heritage initiatives of someone like Yashiv Cohen in Israel, who founded a music history lecture series in Tel Aviv bars, to the self-authorised practices of organisations like the British Archive of Country Music, United Kingdom and the Klaus-Kuhnke-Archiv für Populäre Musik, Germany, to those that have amassed a level of authority that sees them on the verge of achieving a broader public acceptance comparable with that of esteemed public establishments. An example of this would be The ARChive of Contemporary Music, United States, which has established a partnership with Columbia University.

It should be pointed out that at least one of the most distinguished sound archives in the world began its life as a self-authorised institution. The British Library Sound Archive, the United Kingdom's national institution for collecting popular music recordings and artefacts, was first established in the 1950s as the British Institute of Recorded Sound. The institute was founded by a private individual, Patrick Saul, with financial support from a charitable trust and donations from the public and recording companies. It became part of the British Library in the 1980s. In an early account of those self-authorised roots, Trevor Fisher notes:

> Realising what unique records there have been and how many of them have been lost makes it the more regrettable that this country, so eminent in the field of recording, has not in good time founded an Institute. Even now it might exist only as an idea if it had not been for the enterprise and generosity of a group of distinguished enthusiasts and critics, backed by a few leading musicians (1957, 26).

The case of the British Institute of Recorded Sound highlights that enthusiast-led approaches to music heritage have a long history and demonstrate how unauthorised and self-authorised heritage endeavours have the capacity to become authorised, prestigious institutions.

DO-IT-YOURSELF, DO-IT-TOGETHER: THE DIY ETHIC IN HERITAGE PRACTICES

The sites involved in the collection, display and preservation of popular music's material past that are discussed in the pages of this book are examples of do-it-yourself (DIY) heritage practice. The ethos of DIY is a familiar one in popular music culture, particularly with regard to the often politicised practices associated with punk and post-punk cultures (Dale 2008). DIY characteristics have also been present in many other music cultures such as folk and country, making the term a valuable and recognisable signifier of the grassroots activities of the community-based archives and museums that are the focus of this book. In the spirit of DIY, the founders of the organisations discussed in this book have taken the initiative and started these enterprises themselves. In some cases, the DIY spirit that sparked the founding of these archives and museums is inherently rooted in punk, as can be observed in the case of the Ramones Museum in Germany and the founding story of SR-Archiv österreichischer Popularmusik in Austria (see also Chapter 8). The politics of DIY is present in, for example, the feminist music archives that are the subject of Chapter 7. The DIY approach to the recording industry and also the DIY craft aesthetic are obvious in the Editions of You archive (see Chapter 20). There is a degree of activism inherent in the work of all the independent heritage practitioners and their archives and museums discussed in this book. While a casual observer might question how the DIY spirit might be present in the preservation work of old-age pensioners in an archive devoted to jazz (see Chapter 17) or teenage girls collecting and sharing offstage photos of Take That (see Chapter 12), these can be understood to be manifestations of a DIY spirit at the level of everyday interventions by amateurs and enthusiasts keen to do archiving themselves.

Beyond its music-specific context, DIY is broadly defined as "when ordinary people build or repair the things in their daily lives without the aid of experts" (Wehr 2012, 1). While a useful nomenclature for the sites of independent popular music heritage practice discussed in this book, DIY is perhaps also a problematic descriptor in that it might be mistaken as referring to the work of an individual. In some instances this is the case, in the sense that a place is founded by one person and continues to operate as such. Examples might include KD's Elvis Presley Museum or, online, the Birmingham Music Archive. However, even when they are the work of an individual, these are places that rely on a network of contributors and other invested parties to operate. Sometimes they are underpinned by explicit collaborative frameworks, such as the Birmingham Music Archive (see Chapter 6), but even for KD, whose private museum can be found in the converted garage of his home, the running of the museum depends on the continuing support of his family as well as the generosity of enthusiasts from around the world who send artefacts to add to the collection. Wehr (2002, 67) distinguishes between "DIY individualists" who work in isolation and "DIY coordinators" who work with others collectively. Such a distinction suggests an orientation towards collaboration can be present in DIY practice in such a way that do-it-yourself can also be framed as do-it-together, hence the subtitle of this book. Plural versions of DIY – do-it-yourselves, do-it-ourselves, do-it-together (Chigley 2014; Jenkins 2010; Reilly 2014) – more accurately capture the collective preservation initiatives outlined in the chapters that follow.

Bennett (2009, 276) has observed the DIY ethos at work in the context of projects that aim to "reposition rock music as an aspect of late twentieth century cultural heritage." Trends in "heritage rock" emphasise "dominant, critical canons of rock music" on the one hand and "alternative, DIY (do-it-yourself) definitions of rock artistry and achievement" on the other (2009, 475). The latter trend is referred to by Bennett (2009, 475) as a form of "DIY preservationism," and he illustrates this mode of heritage work using the examples of the Canterbury Sound website and the small, independent record label Songworks. DIY preservationists are described by Bennett as:

> rock music enthusiasts who establish media such as internet fan sites or small, independent record labels to preserve and promote the music

of rock musicians who have, for a variety of reasons, fallen into obscurity and thus do not feature in established canons of rock achievement. The activities engaged in by DIY preservationists include the salvaging and re-mastering of old, unreleased music or the production of albums featuring new material by forgotten and obscure artists (2009, 475).

The "DIY preservationist sensibility" Bennett (2009, 483) identifies is concerned primarily with interested parties reclaiming lost material, often for commercial exploitation, albeit on a small scale, in order to rewrite the conventional histories of rock culture. Bennett (2009, 483) writes, "DIY preservationists concern themselves with representing the roots of the rock phenomenon, digging below accepted terrains of rock to expose those artists whose contribution to the field of rock have been lost or forgotten." As such, they are "actively engaged in the production of an alternative history" based on a "series of aesthetic judgements pertaining to issues of musical and cultural value" (2009, 483). In the case of those enthusiasts who establish small, independent record labels devoted to heritage rock, DIY preservationism involves "apply[ing] their own conventions of taste and distinction in rescuing particular songs, albums and artists from obscurity and reinserting them into the rock historical context" (2009, 483).

Bennett's consideration of the emergence of a DIY preservationist sensibility in heritage rock practice, while instructive, overlooks how such practice might operate in small, independent archives and museums, and the contributions these places might make to heritage rock discourse. The writings of Flinn (2007, 2010, 2011) and colleagues (Flinn and Stevens 2009; Flinn, Stevens and Shepherd 2009; Stevens, Flinn and Shepherd 2009) have become instrumental in providing a lens through which to understand the establishment of popular music archives and museums that operate at the community level. In relation to archives specifically, there has been increasing critical interest in such institutions that exist outside the purview of authorised projects of national collecting, and these alternatives to prestigious institutions have been referred to in a variety of ways, including "autonomous archives" (Moore and Pell 2010), "participatory archives" (Huvila 2008) and "Pro-Am [Professional Amateur]" or "popular archives" (McKee 2011a, 2011b). But the most cited of these conceptions is Flinn's (2007, 153) "community archive," which he defines as "the grassroots activities of documenting, recording and exploring community heritage in which community participation, control and ownership of the project are essential." Although members of the community may not always understand their collective work as "archiving," these independent archives are made up of collections of artefacts assembled predominantly by members of the community (Stevens, Flinn and Shepherd 2010, 59). Many of the community archives Flinn and others investigate are concerned with documenting minority or marginal communities and are forms of activism that declare ownership over a community's stories about their past

(Flinn 2007; Flinn, Stevens and Shepherd 2009). As such, they "often attempt to actively transform and intervene in otherwise partial and unbalanced histories," thus "contributing to a democratization of heritage and history making" (Flinn 2010, 40).

Two broad types of community archives have been identified by Flinn. The first is those archives that have been the primary focus of Flinn's research – that is, archives propelled by a "political agenda in which the preservation and use of historical materials might play a role in serving a set of political aims (be they educational, commemorative, empowering, or transformative)" (Flinn 2011, 8). The second type is "characterized as largely inspired by interest, or leisure, or even antiquarianism" (Flinn 2011, 8), and it might be said this space of community archiving is the one principally addressed in this book. This is not to suggest, however, that the community archives and museums referred to in the chapters contained here do not embody a form of activism, or that those working in these places are not activist archivists (Zinn 1997; see especially Chapters 6 and 10 in this volume). Archiving undertaken at the level of community is never "neutral or disinterested" (Flinn 2011, 12), and we might therefore think of the popular music heritage projects being discussed here as being located on a spectrum of activist archivism.

While the term "do-it-yourself" is never used by Flinn and colleagues to describe community archiving practice, the spirit of DIY is evident in the archives being used to illustrate their ideas around the development and practices of these bottom-up initiatives. In the context of community-based popular music archives and museums, Baker and Huber (2013) offer a typology of "DIY institutions" that are dedicated to the collection, preservation and display of popular music's material past. The term "DIY institution" was coined in order to identify collectively a group of popular music archives, museums and halls of fame that were founded by enthusiasts, run largely by volunteers and existed outside the frame of authorised projects of national collecting and display. These are informal cultural institutions, the creators of which did, quite literally, do it themselves by establishing their own self-managed archival and museum facilities after identifying the need for a repository for the vast collections of popular music artefacts in their communities. In a number of cases, including the Victorian Jazz Archive, Australia, and Heart of Texas Country Music Museum, United States, founders and volunteers went so far as to build or renovate the buildings that were to house and display the collections, thus adding a further dimension to the DIY-ness of these institutions (see, for example, Chapter 17).

These DIY institutions are part of the broader movement in community-based ownership over archival and historical material identified by Flinn (2007). While these archives and museums strive to replicate the professional standards of national institutions, they do so with scarce resources, usually obtained through grants, donations and membership fees, and rely on a volunteer labour force committed to the painstaking tasks associated with archiving and curating. While national collecting institutions like the NFSA and Sydney's Powerhouse Museum in Australia or the Victoria and Albert Museum in the United Kingdom recognise the national importance of popular music's material culture, the work of the DIY institution augments and builds upon national strategies at a community level and fills gaps they have identified in the public records collected at authorised institutions. However, what is at stake in the archiving of popular music at the community level is the inclusion of agendas that come from those communities themselves. DIY institutions set their own parameters for collection using criteria that emerge from within their own expertise. Under DIY control, these communities of volunteers and enthusiasts who assemble around a shared interest in popular music and/or its heritage are "able to strategically represent themselves rather than submitting their archives to be filtered through the words and space of state-based institutions" (Moore and Pell 2010, 261).

While this work on DIY institutions shares Bennett's (2009) concern with DIY in the context of popular music, the terrains of Baker and Huber's interest are slightly different. The DIY institutions of their research have not been focused so much on "conventions of taste and distinction" or an urge to make good the inaccurate historical record by recovering forgotten works (Bennett 2009, 483). Rather, the DIY institutions to be found in the pages of this book more often "aim for an inclusive, and thus 'taste-less' collection of material with limited or no interest in commercial opportunity" (Baker and Huber 2013a, 515). Rescuing artists from obscurity (2009, 483) is also of limited interest, and a number of these institutions focus attention on canonic artists such as The Beatles (see Chapter 11) and Elvis Presley (see Chapter 19). While there is an urge in these institutions to preserve material, and it is done by DIY practitioners, it has not so much of the "preservationist" impulse as defined by Bennett (2009). Rather, "it should be thought of as an indiscriminate desire to retain a material record of popular music's historical past, perhaps indicating a key difference between the cultural curation/connoisseurship described by Bennett, and the cultural archiving" of many archival and museal DIY institutions (Baker and Huber 2013a, 515).

The pairing of DIY with institution may at first seem antithetical. Often the archives and museums being described in this book replicate the organisational structures of national institutions, giving people titles like General Manager, Collections Manager, Archivist, Curator, Data Entry Clerk and so on. In most cases, especially once the preservation team expands beyond two or three individuals, DIY institutions "operate under and report to boards of management, follow expansive mission statements with aims that could be seen as comparable to national programs of collection and preservation, and strive to achieve industry standards in their practices" (Baker and Huber 2013a, 516). This can be seen in the case of the Australian Jazz Museum as outlined by its General Manager, Ray Sutton, in Chapter 17. Institutionalisation should not, therefore, be conceived of as undesirable or detrimental, or as something that will constrain the DIY spirit. Rather, the framework of the institution becomes, in many instances, enabling for the DIY archive or museum. Many DIY institutions desire to meet professional standards of practice and expertise. For example, the Australian Jazz Museum incorporating the Victorian Jazz Archive has had museum-standard accreditation for a number of years (see Chapter 17), and a volunteer at the Australian Country Music Hall of Fame in Tamworth, Australia, described that organisation as having a "professional approach as amateurs" (interview, 2 August 2011; see also Chapter 18). As such, these institutions also fit neatly into accounts of trends in professional-amateurism.

The influential report on the "Pro-am [professional-amateur] revolution" by Leadbeater and Miller (2004, 12) brought to wide attention the emerging cultural power of "amateurs who work to professional standards." Following decades of corporate and governmental control of resources, they argue, pro-ams can now "achieve things that until recently only large, professional organizations could achieve" (2004, 12) in areas as varied as coaching and sport, acting, computer programming and musical production, and in volunteer organisations such as ambulance services and surf lifesaving. These days, pro-ams are highly visible in a variety of contexts. DIY archives and museums add one more area to the list of pro-am expertise. However, many of the volunteers involved in DIY institutions did not necessarily begin with the intention of becoming professional amateurs. Rather, the DIY ethic of community involvement was the inspiration for much of their work, and their status as part of the so-called pro-am revolution is more or less a symptom of the archival impulse.

Further emphasising DIY is a do-it-together practice, the success of DIY institutions is in the formation of strong "communities of practice" (Wenger, 1998). These pro-am DIY practitioners constitute a group of people who form themselves around shared interests (popular music, volunteering and the preservation of cultural heritage) and learn the skills related to these interests (archiving, curation, and archival and museum management) through regular interaction. It is here that the connotations of the DIY ethic, so long associated with certain forms of popular music production and consumption, can help us think through exactly what it is that these community archives and museums are doing in and for their communities. In DIY institutions, community builds itself around the joint task of cultural preservation. The curatorial and archival work being undertaken in these places is done by volunteers who are learning these skills on the job, sometimes under ad hoc instruction from contacts at national institutions from whom they can obtain advice on matters related to conservation and other museal and archival practices (see Chapter 9). A term coined by Lave and Wenger (1991) and developed substantively by Wenger (1998), "communities of practice" are "groups of people who share a concern or passion for something they do and learn how to do it better as they interact regularly" (Wenger 2006, n.p.). This is a critical concept for understanding the environment that is being nurtured in DIY places of popular music preservation, given that the majority of volunteers in these institutions have next to no formal training in archiving or curating but rather rely on a form of situated learning (Lave 1991) in order to fulfill the preservation project they are undertaking.

OUTLINE OF THE BOOK

The above frameworks and understandings of community-based popular music heritage practice shape many of the chapters in this collection. Part I of the book presents new academic perspectives on DIY practitioners and institutions and the preservation of popular music's material past. The chapters are ordered in such a way that they guide the reader through a series of core concerns in current scholarship around enthusiast-led approaches to popular music preservation, beginning with a focus on the relationships between professional institutions and DIY practitioners (Chapters 2 and 3) and what makes DIY institutions distinctive (Chapter 4), before considering the specificities of online archiving and public history-making (Chapters 5 and 6). Attention then turns to the extent to which DIY archives and museums can offer alternative histories of popular music's past (Chapters 7 and 8), followed by a case study of how one independent archival project is breaking new ground in the archiving and preservation of CDs (Chapter 9). Part I ends with a consideration of fans as popular music heritage practitioners (Chapters 10–12). A number of the chapters in this first half of the book include extracts from qualitative interviews with DIY practitioners (Chapters 2, 3, 4, 7 and 12) or are written by authors who have worked closely with DIY institutions (Chapter 8) or have been involved in their founding (Chapters 6 and 9). Part I provides a lens through which the case studies offered in Part II might be considered.

Part II consists of a series of case studies of DIY institutions written by DIY practitioners who have founded or who volunteer in the kinds of popular music archives and museums discussed in Part I. Some of the sites discussed have only been founded very recently (see Chapter 16), while others are much older, having been established in the early to mid-1990s (see Chapters 15 and 17). The DIY practitioners contributing to this section of the book provide insights into the practicalities of founding and running archives and museums that have limited funding, too few hands on deck to assist in cataloguing and preservation projects and not enough space to house the volume of material being donated. These chapters were never intended to be read as scholarly, though some certainly are. Rather, they provide the reader with stories from the coalface. Part II privileges community-based, enthusiast expertise and creates a space for the exchange of this experience and vernacular knowledge. It ensures the book includes agendas that come from the communities under examination in Part I, and provides DIY practitioners with an opportunity to purposefully narrate their own activities as opposed to having their heritage practices presented in the language of academics. The inclusion of the voices of DIY practitioners could be described as a democratising manoeuvre, as it asks the volunteers and enthusiasts working at the community level to tell the story of their organisation in their own words. Sometimes these are provided as a chronological narrative (see Chapter 15), while others go much deeper, demonstrating the level of reflexivity inherent in the work of DIY practitioners (for example, Chapters 13, 18 and 20). As Derrida (1996, 4, n 1, emphasis added) famously argued, "There is no political power without control of the archive, if not memory. Effective democratisation can always be measured by this essential criterion: the participation in and access to the archive, its constitution, *and its interpretation.*"

As can be seen in what follows, the DIY version of popular music heritage management encapsulates a difference between the industry conventions of cultural preservation in national institutions and the more ad hoc, learning on-the-job, community-based preservation practices observed in community archives more broadly. As Brandellero and Janssen (2014, 237) observe, "Bottom-up, often amateur or fan-initiated practices have come to fill an institutional void of preservation and remembrance, becoming more institutionalised and professional in the process." DIY sites of popular music heritage are much more than unofficial versions of official institutions. Rather, they invoke a complex network of affect and sociality, and are sites where interested people, often enthusiasts, are able to assemble around shared goals related to the preservation of and ownership over the material histories of popular music culture.

REFERENCES

Baker, S., Doyle, P. and Homan, S. 2015 (forthcoming). Historical records, national constructions: the contemporary popular music archive. *Popular Music and Society.*
Baker, S. and Huber, A. 2013a. Notes towards a typology of the DIY Institution: Identifying do-it-yourself places of popular music preservation. *European Journal of Cultural Studies* 16(5): 513–30.
Baker, S. and Huber, A. 2013b. Locating the canon in Tamworth: Historical narratives, cultural memory and Australia's Country Music Capital. *Popular Music* 32(2): 223–40.
Baker, S. and Huber, A. 2015. Saving "rubbish:" Preserving popular music's material culture in amateur archives and museums. In S. Cohen, R. Knifton, M. Leonard and L. Roberts (eds.), *Sites of Popular Music Heritage: Memories, Histories, Places.* New York: Routledge, 112–24.
Bennett, A. 2009. Heritage rock: Rock music, representation and heritage discourse. *Poetics* 37(5–6): 474–89.
Brandellero, A. and Janssen, S. 2014. Popular music as cultural heritage: Scoping out the field of practice. *International Journal of Heritage Studies* 20(3): 224–40.
Chigley, R. 2014. Developing communities of resistance? Maker pedagogies, do-it-yourself feminism, and DIY citizenship. In M. Ratto and M. Boler (eds.), *DIY citizenship: Critical making and social media.* Cambridge, MA: MIT Press, 101–13.

Dale, P. 2008. It was easy, it was cheap, so what? Reconsidering the DIY principle of punk and indie music. *Popular Music History* 3(2): 171–93.

Derrida, J. 1996. *Archive fever: A Freudian impression.* Trans. E. Prenowitz. Chicago: University of Chicago Press.

Fisher, T. 1957. The British Institute of Recorded Sound. *Tempo* 45: 24–7.

Flinn, A. 2007. Community histories, community archives: Some opportunities and challenges. *Journal of the Society of Archivists*, 28(2): 151–76.

Flinn, A. 2010. An attack on professionalism and scholarship? Democratising archives and the production of knowledge. *Ariadne* 62. Accessed December 1, 2014. http://www.ariadne.ac.uk/issue62/flinn.

Flinn, A. 2011. Archival activism: independent and community-led archives, radical public history and the heritage professions. *InterActions: UCLA Journal of Education and Information Studies* 7(2): 1–20.

Flinn, A. and Stevens, M. 2009. "It is noh mistri, wi mekin histri": Telling our own story: Independent and community archives in the United Kingdom, challenging and subverting the mainstream. In J. Bastian and B. Alexander (eds.), *Community archives: The shaping of memory.* London: Facet, 3–27.

Flinn, A., Stevens, M. and Shepherd, E. 2009. Whose memories, whose archives? Independent community archives, autonomy and the mainstream. *Archival Science*, 9: 71–86.

Huvila, I. 2008. Participatory archive: Towards decentralised curation, radical user orientation, and broader contextualisation of records management. *Archival Science* 8: 15–36.

Jenkins, H. 2010. Afterword: Communities of readers, clusters of practices. In M. Knobel and C. Lankshear (eds.), *DIY media: Creating, sharing and learning with new technologies.* New York: Peter Lang, 231–53.

Lave, J. 1991. Situating learning in communities of practice. In L.B. Resnick, J.M. Levine and S.D. Teasley (eds.), *Perspectives on socially shared cognition.* Washington, DC: American Psychological Association, 63–82.

Lave, J. and Wenger, E. 1991. *Situated learning.* Cambridge: Cambridge University Press.

Leadbeater, C. and Miller, P. 2004. *The pro-am revolution: How enthusiasts are changing our economy and society.* London: Demos.

McKee, A. 2011a. YouTube versus the National Film and Sound Archive: Which is the more useful resource for historians of Australian television?, *Television and New Media* 12(2): 154–73.

McKee, A. 2011b. Alternative primary sources for studying Australian television history: An annotated list of online pro-am collections. *Screening the Past* 32. Accessed June 23, 2012. http://www.screeningthepast.com/2011/11/alternative-primary-sources-for-studying-australian- television-history-an-annotated-list-of-online-pro-am-collections.

Moore, S. and Pell, S. 2010. Autonomous archives. *International Journal of Heritage Studies* 16(4–5): 255–68.

Reilly, I. 2014. Just say yes: DIY-ing the yes men. In M. Ratto and M. Boler (eds.), *DIY citizenship: Critical making and social media.* Cambridge, MA: MIT Press, 125–36.

Roberts, L. 2014. Talkin' bout my generation: Popular music and the culture of heritage. *International Journal of Heritage Studies* 20(3): 262–80.

Roberts, L. and Cohen, S. 2014. Unauthorising popular music heritage: Outline of a critical framework. *International Journal of Heritage Studies* 20(3): 241–61.

Stevens, M., Flinn, A. and Shepherd, E. 2010. New frameworks for community engagement in the archive sector: From handing over to handing on. *International Journal of Heritage Studies* 16(1–2): 59–76.

Wehr, K. 2012. *DIY: The search for control and self-reliance in the 21st century*. New York: Routledge.

Wenger, E. 1998. *Communities of practice: Learning, meaning and identity*. New York: Cambridge University Press.

Wenger, E. 2006. Communities of practice: A brief introduction. Accessed August 14, 2012. http://wenger-trayner.com/wp-content/uploads/2013/10/06-Brief-introduction-to-communities-of-practice.pdf.

Zinn, H. 1997 (1970). Secrecy, archives and the public interest. In *The Zinn reader: Writings on disobedience and democracy*. New York: Seven Stories Press, 516–28.

Part I

Unpacking DIY Popular Music Heritage Practice

2 The Shaping of Heritage

Collaborations between Independent Popular Music Heritage Practitioners and the Museum Sector

Marion Leonard

Over the past twenty years, it has become increasingly common for museums to produce exhibitions celebrating, documenting and interpreting the cultures, sounds, histories and experiences of popular music. The scale of these presentations ranges from dedicated popular music museums and blockbuster shows through to smaller temporary exhibitions and displays within social-history galleries. Such initiatives within the professional museum sector have often involved working relationships with private collectors, music communities, external archives, and independent or DIY heritage projects and collectives, which have contributed content and expertise and influenced exhibition outcomes. This chapter explores the relationship between formal museums and independent heritage practitioners, examining both their separate activities and various collaborations as a way to understand how notions of heritage are constructed and shaped by the interaction of different agents. The term "independent practitioner" is used to indicate that these individuals and collectives are working outside formal institutional structures, often balancing their endeavours with other work. While these individuals do not have formal archival or museum training, I wish to avoid naming their activities as amateur, as they might present their work in very professional ways and often bring other skills and knowledge that contribute to how music is understood and produced as heritage.

In discussing this relationship, it is not intended that the division between museums and independent enterprises should be exaggerated. There are many different types of organisations operating within the museum sector, from those that receive the support of national or local authorities through to historic properties and independent museums run by volunteers. Indeed, some grassroots popular music heritage initiatives in the United Kingdom have resulted in the establishment of independent museums such as the Museum of Club Culture in Hull, Yorkshire, and the Coventry Music Museum in the English West Midlands. This chapter narrows its focus to examine the interactions between independent popular music practitioners and museums registered under the Accreditation Scheme, which confirms that they meet nationally agreed standards in management, collections care, and delivery of information and visitor services. Drawing on original interviews with United Kingdom-based museum professionals, collectors and representatives from independent heritage initiatives, the chapter considers the different motivations and priorities of these parties, examining the reasons for and the outcomes of their collaborations. Through a focused discussion of two case studies, the Manchester District Music Archive and Home of Metal, it raises wider questions about how music heritage is defined and given value, and who is active in preserving and publicly representing such heritages.

HERITAGE PRACTICE

A distinguishing feature of museums is the value they accord – and that is in turn given by others – to their collections and the material they exhibit. The agreed definition established in 1998 by the Museum Association, the professional organisation of the United Kingdom museum sector, serves as illustration: "Museums enable people to explore collections for inspiration, learning and enjoyment. They are institutions that collect, safeguard and make accessible artefacts and specimens, which they hold in trust for society" (Museum Association 2008, 8). The final part of this definition is significant, as it reinforces the presumption that the materials held within these institutions have importance for current and future generations and by enabling access, such bodies can stimulate the minds of their visitors in ways that are both entertaining and educational. Given the breadth of the material within museum collections, the ways in which importance might be accorded to individual objects will, of course, vary. Items might, for instance, be judged to have cultural, scientific, historic and perhaps also economic value, although the last of these is unlikely to be the primary reason for their inclusion within a museum collection. Yet key to this discussion is the fact that museums are understood to undertake a civic duty to protect selected materials for the greater good of society. In turn, the materials they select are invested with significance. As Pearce has observed:

> Museum objects have (at least in theory) been lifted out of the marketplace where commodities are exchanged and have become something else, to which a word like "heritage" is often attached. ... They share a perceived spiritual or intellectual worth and are guarded as such in a way which puts them in a special "otherworld" category.
>
> (Pearce 1992, 33)

While the social and cultural worth of museum objects is seemingly self-apparent because of where they are housed, independent heritage practitioners actively assert the value of the materials they collect and archive. As the case studies within this book attest, the range and work of what Baker and Huber (2013) term "DIY institutions" of popular music are very varied, existing "along a continuum that begins with the individual collector who seeks to establish a place to share their collection, all the way through to the DIY institution that might have found enough funding for a few staff members, and has become formalised to the extent that it is on the verge of official, national acceptance" (2013, 514). The following discussion focuses primarily on two case studies that involve numerous volunteers and offer insight into music practice and culture in two English cities. However, while they are akin to Bennett's (2009, 483) description of "DIY preservationists" concerned with "digging below accepted terrains ... to expose those artists whose contribution to the field ... have been lost or forgotten," the examples under discussion are concerned with more than recovering hidden histories about the previously uncelebrated. As the chapter discusses, independent popular music heritage projects can also seek to promote artists who have enjoyed commercial and/or critical success, but might not be given prominence within the heritage story of a given locale.

Independent popular music heritage initiatives such as websites, digitisation projects, archives and exhibitions may be thought of as challenging mainstream views of heritage, but they have not necessarily been conceived in opposition to existing heritage institutions. Instead, they have frequently been initiated by enthusiasts of a particular dimension of popular music they felt needed greater public recognition and should be carefully archived or documented. As Baker and Huber (2013) observe, the aims of many DIY popular music institutions can closely align with the statements of purpose of more traditional heritage organisations in that they have a broad mission to create and maintain collections and make them publicly accessible. By collaborating with the professional museum sector, such independent practitioners can reach a wider audience and ensure the contribution of popular music is more evident within public celebrations of culture. This can be a key motivation for working with such formal institutions. For example, Joolz Denby, a writer and artist who has designed numerous cover sleeves for post-punk/alternative band New Model Army, co-curated an exhibition about the music and art of the band at Cartwright Hall, Bradford in West Yorkshire. She commented:

> I think that these are the most important exhibitions for any gallery and any culture because they are the culture of the people. If you want to continue running galleries and museums, you have to step down from the ivory tower and understand that you need to get people in to your gallery and the only way you're going to do that is by acknowledging the people's art.
>
> (Denby, 25 October 2010)

The language some independent practitioners use to describe their activities directly engages with ideas about institutional authority and professional practice. For example, Gari Melville, a collector and guest co-curator of an exhibition on Welsh popular music at St Fagans National History Museum near Cardiff, commented he has always considered his collection of Welsh music to be an archive:

> simply because when I started, institutions such as the National Library [of Wales] and St Fagans weren't interested in that area. They were still stuck in a "local record library, three sections: jazz, brass, and classical" mode. That was something that has only recently been broken down.
> (Melville, 14 September 2010)

This nomenclature positions Gari not so much as an enthusiastic collector but as a custodian, and confers greater status to the material in his care, privileging it as worthy of preservation and scrutiny. Similarly, the founders of a user-led website that aims to "celebrate Greater Manchester music, protect its heritage and promote awareness of its cultural importance" chose to use the title Manchester District Music Archive (MDMA), despite the fact no one within the organisation had undertaken formal training (MDMA 2014c). The MDMA's Abigail Ward commented that this has had a mixed response, especially from the more established heritage organisations: "They are very suspicious of the fact that we use the word 'archive' when none of us in any remote way is qualified as archivists – that annoys people" (Ward, 21 October 2010). The MDMA claimed the authority of an archive and presented material that more usually was associated with fan collections (tickets, flyers and mementos) as public heritage. The initiative can be situated alongside other independent community-led archives that, as Flinn (2011, 5) discusses, exist "outside the framework of mainstream, publicly funded, professionally staffed institutions" in a way that "is both a reproach and a challenge to that mainstream."

The discussion in this chapter focuses on two independent initiatives concerned with the music heritages of two English cities. One of the case studies is the aforementioned MDMA, a not-for-profit organisation run by volunteers that aims to "protect vulnerable collections pertaining to Greater Manchester music, record and document the memories of fans, artists and industry alike and facilitate exhibitions and events about Greater Manchester music that target as broad an audience as possible" (MDMA 2014a). As part of this mission, the organisation has developed a substantial online resource that "contains 3135 bands, 560 DJs, 1052 venues and 10255 artefacts" (MDMA 2014b). The organisation has collaborated on a number of exhibition projects, including *Unknown Pleasures*, a Joy Division exhibition at Macclesfield Silk Museum in 2010 co-curated with Jon Savage, and *Defining Me – Musical Adventures in Manchester*, which opened at The Lowry, Salford in 2013. The other case study, Home of Metal (HoM), also developed a digital archive featuring images of stage wear, concert programs, ticket stubs and other objects related to selected rock artists from Birmingham. Organisers Capsule describes the project as "a celebration of the music that was born in the Black Country and

Birmingham" (Home of Metal 2014b), and it is one of a number of "activist archivist" music initiatives focused on the popular music heritage of this city (Collins, 2012). As part of this initiative, the organisers worked with eighty volunteers and numerous museums and galleries, staging events and exhibitions related to the Home of Metal theme. The following discussion focuses in particular on the development of a major exhibition at Birmingham Museum and Art Gallery in 2011 entitled *Home of Metal: 40 Years of Heavy Metal and Its Unique Birthplace* (hereafter referred to as HoM).

DEVELOPING THE HERITAGE NARRATIVE

MDMA and HoM are examples of how independent projects can sponsor and consolidate ideas of popular music as heritage. The projects were initiated because of a discrepancy between the public recognition of popular music heritage by official city institutions such as museums, libraries and city council authorities and the social importance given to popular music by individuals, for whom it was significant in terms of memory, emotion, social history, identity and place. The projects sought to address this discrepancy by engaging with the discourses and practices normally associated with official heritage bodies. Neither MDMA or HoM began with a collection of physical, or indeed digitised, objects. Instead, the foundation for the projects was motivated by a belief in the need to recognise and celebrate the cultural importance of their respective music cultures and to understand them as significant in heritage terms. For example, Abigail Ward of the MDMA explained the motivation for the project came from "quite a few conversations in the pub really about the story of Manchester music and particularly about the elements of it that aren't particularly celebrated or well known" (Ward, 21 October 2010). To progress this idea, those involved secured funding to establish an online site where users could upload images of related material, resulting in the production of a digital record of music activity in Manchester. Thus the belief in the cultural importance of this music heritage preceded and produced the archive in a singular digital location. This in turn was a digital record of a dispersed amount of material in the possession of numerous individuals. Once established, this digital record took on a symbolic power of its own as testament to the importance of this musical culture as heritage.

The HoM project had a similar genesis. It was conceived and developed by Capsule, music promoters with eleven years' experience in staging events in Birmingham. Lisa Meyer, the co-founder of Capsule, explained that when hosting bands and artists, Capsule was repeatedly asked about the city's heavy metal heritage:

> whether that band that we were putting on were a post-rock band or an experimental electronica band, they all knew that this was the birthplace of Black Sabbath, and we always felt a little bit embarrassed

that there was nowhere to take them. So I always talk about this idea
that there was no tea towel, so to speak, no visitor attraction.

(Meyer, 12 August 2011)

To begin to address this absence, Capsule organised a symposium discussion
and undertook a small research project to establish the extent of existing
holdings in museums, libraries and archives. Having found very little material within formal collections, Capsule decided, "We needed to create our
own collection, and we knew that we couldn't house a physical collection at
such early days, so that's when we looked at this idea of the digital archive"
(Meyer, 12 August 2011). The digital archive stood in for a physical collection and indicated the type and scope of material resources that could be
displayed within an exhibition.

In each instance, the development of the digital archive bolstered the
heritage claim and reproduced the material culture of the respective scenes
in a format that could readily be understood by more established heritage
organisations. This is indicated by the fact both organisations have been
successful in securing funds from the Heritage Lottery Fund, Arts Council
England and their respective city councils. In a sense, the digital content
within these archives was secondary to what the existence of the archive
itself represented. It produced each respective music culture in a way that
made it, within the bounds of the archive, knowable and quantifiable. It
offered a material, albeit digitally reproduced, anchor for a music heritage
that involved a much more extensive set of works, practices and events. The
content was, of course, crucial. However, the act of presenting the material in this format announced it as cultural heritage, demonstrated commitment to the conservation of memories, materials and other dimensions
of these musical worlds, and argued for the need and appetite for further
work to be undertaken to preserve the intangible and material dimensions
of these music cultures. While by no means definitive, the gathered material was indicative of the wider network of agents involved with a music
scene, including musicians, promoters, record labels, concert venues, managers and audience members. Moreover, various artefacts and mementos
within each archive provided a connection to lost dimensions or transient
moments, related perhaps to celebrated live performances or live venues
that have long since closed down. While these lost dimensions could not be
recovered, their archival remains could be put to work to stimulate memories and provide a way for museums to relate a music history narrative
through material culture.

The number of people involved in the production of each of the digital
archives is also significant. The content of each archive was crowdsourced
and acted as testimony to the emotional investment numerous individuals
have in the music of each particular locale. The creation of an archive from
the input of numerous individuals, rather than one or two specialist collectors, provided an argument to the established heritage sector that these

projects had broad appeal and could engage a considerable number of people. Lisa Meyer, a lead organiser of the HoM project, explained that Capsule initially developed the archive by inviting contributions from bands and by running a series of open days at three galleries in the West Midlands: the New Art Gallery in Walsall, Wolverhampton Art Gallery, and Birmingham Museum and Art Gallery. The open days "were almost like the *Antiques Roadshow* but for metal bands" (Meyer, 12 August 2011). Project volunteers photographed the items members of the public brought along to these events and these images were used to populate the archive. The events provided a way of developing the archive and winning over the confidence of the staff at each of the venues. As Lisa reflected:

> We had to do quite a bit of work to persuade museums that it wasn't just going to be 60-year-old white men coming along, because I think they were quite nervous that the audience would essentially be that and that it wouldn't attract families, and that it would be too risky, but actually on the open days you had everyone from grandpas right through to their kids.
>
> (Meyer, 12 August 2011)

In both instances, the online archives offer more than just a gallery of digitised material. They are documents of heritage work, offering insight into the significance of the uploaded material for contributors. As Smith (2006, 2) discusses, the "real sense of heritage, the real moment of heritage when our emotions and sense of self are truly engaged, is ... in the act of passing on and receiving memories and knowledge." These archives show this act in process. For example, contributors uploading an image of a ticket, flyer or poster to the MDMA also usually leave a short message of description and/or personal reflection. It might be a lament for the loss of a well-loved music venue, a snippet of detail about a gig or even a full list of the set played on a particular night. While most of the commentaries are brief, some are more detailed reflections on how personally significant a particular band or music culture has been over perhaps a twenty-year period. A facility on the site allows others to add further comment, with the potential to create a chain of stories or memories prompted by the digitised object. These commentaries confirm how popular music is valued as cultural heritage, how it has influenced personal trajectories and identity work, and how the dispersed contributors have an ongoing sense of belonging to a past or present music community.

PRODUCTIVE RELATIONS

Independent projects such as MDMA and HoM have drawn together dispersed materials as a digital collection, undertaken public engagement activities, enabled the capture of people's music-related memories and thus provided evidence of how music is integrated into people's histories, identities and sense of place. By doing so, they have presented and produced their particular subjects as heritage. Collaboration with museums strengthens the heritage claim of such projects. The institution of the museum can be seen to confer authority – even a certain form of validation – to the heritage narrative promoted from below by independent practitioners. This is not to suggest these enterprises *need* the endorsement of such institutions for their work to be judged as worthwhile or valid as heritage. Rather, it is to recognise that collaborations, co-curated exhibitions and consultation exercises between these different agents impact upon the profile and meaning-making of individual projects and enterprises.

The display of materials within a formal gallery brings them into an associative relationship with the museum, provoking a re-evaluation of their cultural meaning and importance. The HoM exhibition at Birmingham Museum and Art Gallery is an example. The institution, which now contains forty galleries, was established in 1885 with collections that were intended to provide "models of excellence to educate and inspire Birmingham's craftspeople and industrialists" (Birmingham Museum and Art Gallery 2014). The city museum service is described as "being vital to the promotion of the history and heritage of Birmingham" and as having played "a key role in enhancing a sense of pride and identity for local people" (Birmingham Museums Trust 2013, 3). The decision to hold the HoM exhibition in this venue, rather than in an independent art space, helps to register this music as part of the heritage of the city. As the museum exhibitions officer commented during the development of the project:

> It adds kudos to it, I suppose. The museum has world-class collections and we're at the cultural heart of Birmingham, as they like to quote on their marketing materials. So by having it here instantly lends it that authority – the authority of the museum – and that's what we want with these objects. Raising them to the level of – you know, saying that the Napalm Death fanzines are as important as your Rossetti painting. So that's why it's important that it's at the museum.
>
> (Tom Grosvenor, Birmingham Museum and
> Art Gallery, 12 May 2011)

This comment is a provocation, arguing the ephemeral media of popular music and a prized example of fine art should be given equal regard, but it also points to the ways in which museums shape cultural meaning. The exhibited popular music items do not have the privilege of being accessioned museum objects. Nevertheless, their display within the museum space affords them a particular, additional cultural weight. The exhibited items are displayed with the same care and presentation as an example of fine art, suggesting an equivalence of value.

In turn, the input of independent practitioners brings advantages to the museums with which they collaborate. They can help to shift the profile of an institution that might not have a strong track history in exhibitions of popular culture or contemporary collecting. As Birmingham Museum and Art Gallery exhibitions officer Tom Grosvenor commented, the decision to stage HoM would benefit the image of the museum: "It's important for the museum to do it. It's important for the project and it's important for us because we're going to get a lot out of it as well in raising our profile" (Grosvenor, 12 May 2011). The museum is well known for its collection of Pre-Raphaelite paintings, so the development of a major exhibition dedicated to popular music serves to indicate it is also committed to contemporary art and culture. Moreover, it was hoped the subject would help in the museum's audience-development efforts by attracting people with lower socioeconomic status who are under-represented within the audience profile of the museum (Birmingham City Council 2009, 63). The topic of the exhibition was a good fit with the museum strategy of targeting under-represented audiences "through particular interests or points of identity e.g. culture, faith, or experience" (2009, 4).

Such collaborations also encourage a re-examination of the idea of the expert. Most museums in the United Kingdom do not have the luxury of having a subject specialist in music as part of their curatorial staff. In addition, museums have been relatively slow to include popular music objects within their acquisitions, so the work of collecting and caring for such materials has more often been undertaken by individual collectors, libraries, specialist archives and commercial organisations (Leonard 2007). The involvement of external practitioners as guest curators allows museums to access subject expertise, which in turn gives such projects greater credibility. As one of the HoM curators reflected, Capsule's track record of marketing music events enabled the organisation to work effectively with music journalists. By communicating directly with the press, Capsule promoted an understanding of the project as authentic, driven by musicians, promoters and enthusiasts rather than being a City Council initiative. This recognition of the expertise of external contributors must, however, be balanced by an understanding that they might not have full control over the process of interpreting exhibition content. Tensions have the potential to arise where there are differences of opinion about selection of material or display decisions. As co-producers of these exhibition projects, external contributors and guest curators are not necessarily key decision-makers (Davies 2010), and their independent practice is at risk of being somewhat overtaken by the patterns and work structures of formal museums (Morse, Macpherson and Robinson 2013).

Nevertheless, by working with museums, independent practitioners can raise the public profile of their projects or collections, receive the endorsement of formal heritage institutions and further cement an understanding of popular music as heritage. The HoM project is a good illustration, as over 200 000 people attended the events and activities badged as part of the project, the exhibition received a positive media response and feedback indicated that 92 per cent of visitors felt their overall experience of the exhibition was either "very good" or "good" (Home of Metal 2014a). The success of the exhibition, along with the presence of other grassroots music heritage initiatives in the city, prompted Birmingham City Council to investigate the possibility of marketing Birmingham as a "music city" (Collins 2012). A key recommendation of the resulting report was "That the Cabinet Member for Leisure, Sport and Culture (and partners) support efforts … to find a temporary exhibition space for a music heritage exhibition in Birmingham which focuses on the local roots of heavy metal music" (Birmingham City Council 2012, 8). While this recommendation has not yet been implemented, the proposal illustrates how independent heritage projects can actively shape the way heritage is understood. However, although independent practitioners, museum professionals and city council representatives have all discussed heavy metal as part of city heritage, their motivations for doing so have varied. Capsule initiated the project because it was personally and professionally invested in this music culture and wanted it to have greater public prominence. The museum understood the project as helping with audience development and the council viewed it as a tool to attract tourists, which in turn would generate revenue. Thus, while Capsule has been effective in championing an understanding of popular music as heritage, the takeup of this idea by official bodies might have less to do with a recognition of the merit of this argument for its own sake and more with how it can aid the pursuit of other strategic priorities for the agents involved.

CONCLUSION

Collaborations between independent heritage practitioners and museums highlight how the meaning of heritage is negotiated and illustrate the impact that independent organisations can have as advocates for particular dimensions of popular culture. The chapter has discussed how the work undertaken by independent practitioners to construct, present and materialise popular music as heritage can enable a dialogue with the professional heritage sector. The fact that established museums wish to collaborate with such projects illustrates that independent popular music heritage practitioners are judged to be undertaking valuable archival work, which museums may not have the capacity, resources or expertise to develop themselves. The receptivity of museums to approaches from such bodies, along with instances where museums have initiated contact, also demonstrates the concern these institutions have with recognising the social values people ascribe to material and intangible culture, social practices and experiences. Exhibitions that explore how dimensions of the musical past are made meaningful in the present allow museums to engage with and represent public interpretations of heritage. Such collaborations should also be set within the broader context of contemporary museum culture, which emphasises participation and democracy, and working with communities (Golding and Modest 2013; Peers and Brown 2003).

While this chapter has focused on research within the United Kingdom, it has raised broader issues about how popular music heritage is conceptualised, promoted and struggled over by different agents. By working with independent heritage projects such as those under discussion, museums are augmenting traditional conceptions of heritage and museum practice. The concept of heritage is, of course, a complicated one, provoking questions about how it is defined, what it represents, who has authority to speak for it and what ideas are privileged within its discourses (Hall 1999; Smith 2006). Engagements between museums and independent practitioners can mean forgotten or overlooked histories are brought to public attention for the first time, ideas about place and identity are re-examined through a different prism and conceptions of cultural value are reappraised. Yet the narratives that are produced are also in need of critique – for instance, because certain dimensions of popular music may be afforded greater prominence and significance due to having effective and motivated supporters. How popular music comes to be understood as heritage is therefore in need of careful examination in order to register the investments, biases and motivations of the agents active in effecting this process.

ACKNOWLEDGEMENT

This chapter draws on interviews conducted by Robert Knifton and Marion Leonard for the research project "Collecting and Curating Popular Music Histories," funded by the Arts and Humanities Research Council as part of the Beyond Text program (ref: AI I/H013237/1).

REFERENCES

Baker, S. and Huber, A. 2013. Notes towards a typology of the DIY institution: Identifying do-it-yourself places of popular music preservation. *European Journal of Cultural Studies* 16(5): 513–30.

Bennett, A. 2009. Heritage rock: Rock music, representation and heritage discourse. *Poetics* 37: 474–89.

Birmingham City Council. 2009. *Birmingham Museums & Art Gallery: Audience Development Strategy 2009–2013*. Accessed November 9, 2014. http://www.bmag.org.uk/uploads/fck/file/Audience%20Development%20Strategy%20&%20Plan%202009-13.pdf.

Birmingham City Council. 2012. *Destination Birmingham: Birmingham, a Music City*. Report of the Leisure, Sport & Culture Overview and Scrutiny Committee, 7 February. Accessed November 9, 2014. http://birminghammusicnetwork.com/wp-content/uploads/2011/09/destinationbhamreportblog.pdf.

Birmingham Museum and Art Gallery. 2014. History of Birmingham Museum and Art Gallery. Accessed November 9, 2014. http://www.bmag.org.uk/about/history.

Birmingham Museums Trust. 2013. *Birmingham Museums Trust Review 2012–13.* Accessed November 9, 2014. http://www.bmag.org.uk/uploads/fck/file/Birmingham%20Museums%20Review%202012-13.pdf.

Collins, J. 2012. Multiple voices, multiple memories: Public history-making and activist archivism in online popular music archives. Unpublished MA thesis, Birmingham City University.

Flinn, A. 2011. Archival activism: Independent and community-led archives, radical public history and the heritage professions. *InterActions: UCLA Journal of Education and Information Studies* 7(2), Article 6.

Davies, S.M. 2010. The co-production of temporary museum exhibitions. *Museum Management and Curatorship* 25(3): 305–21.

Golding, V. and Modest, W. 2013. *Museums and communities: Curators, collections and collaboration.* London: Bloomsbury.

Hall, S. 1999. Whose heritage? Un-settling the heritage, re-imagining the post-nation. *Third Text* 13(49): 3–13.

Home of Metal 2014a. Website. Accessed October 17, 2014. http://homeofmetal.com/the-project.

Home of Metal 2014b. Capsule. Accessed October 17, 2014. http://www.capsule.org.uk/project/home-of-metal-2.

Leonard, M. 2007. Constructing histories through material culture: Popular music, museums and collecting. *Popular Music History* 2(2): 147–67.

MDMA 2014a. Aims. Accessed October 17, 2014. http://www.mdmarchive.co.uk/about_us.php.

MDMA 2014b. Homepage. Accessed October 17, 2014. http://www.mdmarchive.co.uk.

MDMA 2014c. Mission statement. Accessed October 17, 2014. http://www.mdmarchive.co.uk/about_us.php.

Morse, N., Macpherson, M. and Robinson, S. 2013. Developing dialogue in co-produced exhibitions: Between rhetoric, intentions and realities. *Museum Management and Curatorship* 28(1): 91–106.

Museum Association. 2008. *Code of ethics for museums.* London: Museums Association.

Pearce, S.M. 1992. *Museums, objects, and collections.* Washington, DC: Smithsonian Institution Press.

Peers, L. and Brown, A.K., eds. 2003. *Museums and source communities: A Routledge reader.* Abingdon: Routledge.

Smith, L. 2006. *Uses of heritage.* Abingdon: Routledge.

3 Valuing Popular Music Heritage

Exploring Amateur and Fan-Based Preservation Practices in Museums and Archives in the Netherlands

Amanda Brandellero, Arno van der Hoeven and Susanne Janssen

The institutional context for the preservation of popular music-related heritage in the Netherlands has changed dramatically in recent years. On the one hand, this is related to major cuts in government support for all kinds of culture-related initiatives (OCW 2011). On the other, it reflects a shift in priorities and a redistribution of functions across the institutional landscape. In the field of music, this resulted in the closure in early 2013 of dedicated institutions such as the Muziek Centrum Nederland (Music Centre Netherlands) and the Nederlands Muziek Instituut (Dutch Music Institute) and the fragmentation of their collections across a number of institutions, including the Nederlands Instituut voor Beeld en Geluid (Netherlands Institute for Sound and Vision) and the University of Amsterdam.

While by far the most visible, these institutions were not the only ones taking an active role in the preservation of Dutch music heritage (Brandellero and Janssen, 2014). In fact, a number of primarily amateur and fan-run museums and archives populate the landscape of popular music preservation in the Netherlands. As examples of do-it-yourself (DIY) heritage, these bottom-up initiatives (Baker and Huber 2013) generally focus on symbolic events in the history of Dutch popular music history or zoom onto a specific time, place or musical act. Such initiatives are not new. Popular collecting and community archives in wide-ranging areas, from recording the history of localities to the documentation of the struggle of marginalised communities, are well documented globally (Flinn, Stevens and Shepherd 2009; Kaplan 2000; Ketelaar 2005).

What makes DIY popular music-archiving initiatives interesting is their articulation of meanings and values of cultural products intended for mass consumption, which is generally the case with popular music products. These initiatives are therefore representative of a shift from sacred to vernacular in collecting (Belk 1995), but also of a "qualitative difference between objects in circulation and objects in collection" (Pearce 1994a: 2). An example of this difference is that between a CD in a record shop and one in a glass case at a rock museum. Moreover, these meanings and values are contested in the event of partnerships with formal heritage institutions when often highly contrasting custodial models come into contact (Stevens, Flinn and

Shepherd 2010). More generally, popular music provides a highly relevant case study of heritage practices due to the specific nature of its material culture, which strongly mediates and mobilises individual and shared identities while leaving few palpable vestiges beyond the performance (Born 2011). This chapter therefore considers how values and meaning are attributed to collections in the heritage practices of amateur and fan-based popular music museums and archives in the Netherlands. We also explore how these values are put to the test in collaborations with formal heritage institutions.

First, we will look at amateur and fan-run heritage practices theoretically, in the context of writings on collecting and associated values and meanings. Here we turn to existing typologies of DIY preservationism in the field of popular music, critically assessing their democratising potential by relating them to debates in media studies on the limitations of the participatory potential of the online realm. We then discuss our research methodology and data collection and analysis, centred on interviews with staff at popular music archives and museums in the Netherlands. Finally, we present our results and conclude by offering a typology of amateur and fan-run popular music heritage "projects" (Dannefer 1980). We use this to assess how these initiatives are participating in and contributing to changing conceptualisations of cultural heritage in the Netherlands.

THEORETICAL FRAMEWORK

Initiatives collecting and documenting the history of Dutch popular music can be positioned within a broader trend whereby communities record and make accessible their history "on their own terms" (Flinn, Stevens and Shepherd 2009, 73). Examples of these include community-based archives (Flinn, Stevens and Shepherd 2009) and autonomous archives (Moore and Pell 2010). Such initiatives play a transformative role in terms of putting more marginal or excluded communities and their histories on the map (Flinn 2007). Formal heritage institutions have also embraced more inclusive and dissonant practices, moving away from a unitary vision of the past towards one that incorporates multiple pasts (Merriman 1991). Such initiatives have focused on a number of purposes and objectives but they are primarily centred on the collection and preservation of objects or knowledge within a specific field of human and social activity.

Research on collecting has highlighted multiple layers of meaning and value in its associated practices, both for the collectors and for the people who may view and use the collection. First, the act of collection and preservation has the connotations of "a genuine and intense subjective attraction that can accurately be described as a passion" (Dannefer 1980, 392). As a special type of consumption, collection also evokes personal involvement, acquisitiveness and possessiveness (Belk 1995). While the nature of a collector's commitment might be perceived as "eccentric" by some, such levels of commitment would not be questioned in, for instance, religious devotion (Dannefer 1980). More generally, the attraction to objects and their potential to define and shape personal identities are contextualised as part of late capitalist society's commodity culture of consumption (Martin 1999).

Collected objects pertaining to the material realm of popular music are removed from their ordinary, utilitarian use and acquire new meanings as part of a wider, actively selected and categorised set (Belk 1995; Pearce 1994b, 1994c, 1994d). In their biographies, these objects can cross the boundary between commodity and singularity (Appadurai 1994; Kopytoff 1986), leading to their sacralisation, following which they are "treated with reverence, and revered with passion" (Dannefer 1980, 395). Vinyl records, for instance, may be purchased but never listened to in order to preserve their immaculate state. The object is perceived to carry meaning that goes beyond the life of the individual collector. It "bears an 'eternal' relationship to the receding past" (Belk 1995, 25). These objects also participate in a process of self-definition of the individuals to whom they belong, tracing their environment and roots (Morin 1969) and becoming markers of social position (Pearce 1994d).

Types of collections can be distinguished on the basis of whether they centre on "souvenirs," "fetish objects" or "systematics" (Pearce, 1994b, 194). Souvenirs are usually constituted by memorabilia or personalia relating to individuals or groups and intrinsic to past experiences. Fetish collecting refers to a passionate form of accumulation of the same type of pieces, where the concern is on the object rather than its social relations. Finally, systematic collecting strives to relate to an external reality that goes beyond the boundaries of the object itself. It is but a specimen, an example in a wider system of classification and a tool to communicate a pedagogic message to an audience. While the first two forms of collecting are more widespread among individual and bottom-up archivists, systematic collecting has been privileged by museums and formal heritage institutions. Nonetheless, the distinction between private and public practices of collection should not be overstated. The dynamics of legitimation of collections and attribution of value work similarly in the private and public realms while the differences lie in the actors involved (Martin 1999).

The personal attachment to the retrieval and preservation of objects and knowledge becomes problematic in instances when such collections are shared or publicly displayed, insofar as an intensely individual value is often of little interest to others (Pearce 1994d). DIY preservation initiatives generally fall within the first two collecting categories described above. They are bottom-up activities, driven by the desire of particular individuals to retain records of the past in an indiscriminate rather than selective fashion (Baker and Huber 2013, 515). They combine this with a desire to redress conventional music histories through connoisseurship and expertise (Bennett 2009, 483), and a range of attitudes are noted in relation to national heritage strategies and official heritage institutions (Baker and Huber 2013, 517; Roberts and Cohen 2013).

Various authors observe how bottom-up preservation practices benefit from developments in the online sphere (Cohen 2013; Long and Collins 2012;

van der Hoeven 2012). New digital media such as social networking sites and blogs have enabled the emergence of "micro or hidden musical histories" (Cohen 2013, 589). These online media facilitate not just the collection of physical objects but also information and audio-visual material related to local music scenes and communities. From a media and cultural studies perspective, it has been argued that Web 2.0 tools for online interaction and collaboration democratise processes of cultural production and blur distinctions between producers and consumers of cultural content, enabling the latter to become "amateur experts" (Baym and Burnett 2009). Following on from these trends towards audience participation, public and private institutions develop more consumer-oriented platforms (Livingstone 2013). One example is a crowd-sourcing project of The Netherlands Institute for Sound and Vision in which online users were asked to improve and share information on forty years of rock 'n' roll video footage recorded during a festival (Snoek et al. 2010).

However, such celebratory accounts of the democratising potential of Web 2.0 have also been extensively criticised (Van Dijck and Nieborg 2009; Scholz 2008). In his book on the "cult of the amateur," Keen (2007) raises awareness of the importance of professional standards and expertise in processes of cultural production. The outsourcing of tasks to audiences has even been described as a form of exploitation of their free labour (Scholz 2008). These debates in the fields of media and cultural studies carry important implications for the study of both online and offline bottom-up preservation practices, demonstrating that fans actively use digital tools to initiate heritage projects and audience participation is increasingly becoming central to the ways in which cultural and heritage institutions operate. However, the potentially conflicting aims, interests and work practices of amateurs and professionals should not be neglected.

METHOD

This chapter discusses sixteen different projects, including archives, exhibitions and museums (see Table 3.1). We focus on those initiatives that are publicly visible, either through an online presence (e.g. web archive) or physical presence (e.g. archive or museum). The majority of the projects are initiated by fans and collectors or involve some form of collaboration with collectors. However, we also interviewed several professional curators at museums and archives to glean insights into collaboration practices and contrasting definitions of the value and meaning of collections. In these semi-structured interviews, which typically lasted around one hour, we discussed the rationale for establishing the project, preservation practices, the organisational setting and respondents' understandings of heritage. Each interview was attributed a code, ranging from A1 to A15 (one interviewee was in charge of two projects). These codes are used in the empirical section below to anonymise the interviews.

For the purpose of our research, we defined amateur and fan-run archives and museums as a set of practices around the collection and preservation of popular music histories and material culture set up by people with no formal training or background in archiving or museology. We conceive of these initiatives as non-professional in terms of how the organisations position themselves in relation to: whether it is a (paid) job or, as in some cases, a hobby or personal collection that turns into a bigger project; the extent to which they adopt formal institutional structures (e.g. job titles); the division of tasks; formal classification of material; and the quality of what is delivered (whether there are set standards for collection, such as categorical ways of collecting information on materials). While individuals may lack formal training in heritage practices, all initiatives share a strong curatorial imprint, driven by one or a few individuals acting selectively as gatekeepers, with clearly stated aims and objectives. We thus excluded blogs or online forums where communities of individuals share knowledge and information sporadically, allowing us to distinguish an active act of collection from a less coherent expression of accumulation (Pearce 1994e).

Table 3.1 Overview of the initiatives analysed for this study. Year indicates year of exhibition or, in the case of archives, year of establishment.

Project	Focus	Organisation	Outputs	Year
Museum RockArt (Hoek van Holland)	The history of Dutch popular music from 1950 to today	Private museum initiated by a music enthusiast and supported by several volunteers	Permanent and temporary exhibitions on prominent national and international artists and movements	1994
Streektaalzang	Dutch dialect music	Online archive on Dutch dialect music, organised by region, curated by a private individual	Online archive	1996
Poparchive Achterhoek/ Liemers	The music history of the Achterhoek en Liemers region	Group of music experts and fans, connected to a local heritage organisation	Several books. These publications led to reunions of some bands and a list of dialect music from the region which was broadcast by a local radio station.	1998

(Continued)

Project	Focus	Organisation	Outputs	Year
Stichting Norderney	The cultural heritage of offshore radio station Radio Veronica, from 1959–74	Run by several volunteers, who used to work for Radio Veronica. Donors get access to a members-only section of the website.	Physical archive, online archive and annual events organised in collaboration with Museum RockArt	1999
Offshore Radio Club	Offshore radio	The website is run by volunteers and has a restricted section for members only.	Online archive	2001
Zaanse pophistorie	Bands and music venues of the Zaanstreek region located north of Amsterdam, from 1958 to today	This project is run by volunteers involved in the local music scene.	Online archive	2005
'Geef mij maar Amsterdam' (Amsterdam Museum)	The history of the city of Amsterdam through song from the seventeenth century to today	Hosted by the city museum of Amsterdam	Temporary exhibition	2006/ 07
Europopmusic	European pop music	Run by two collectors	Online archive	2008
Music Center the Netherlands	Dutch music	Closed in December 2012 due to its public subsidies being cut. MCN was formed in 2008 following the merger of a number of genre-specific institutes, including the National Pop Institute, set up in 1975. This institute was run by paid employees.	Library, physical archive and online archive	2008
POPstudio (Sound and Vision Institute, Hilversum)	Dutch popular music	POPstudio is housed in the Institute for Sound and Vision. It is a permanent exhibition of audio-visual material on Dutch popular music.	Permanent exhibition	2010

Project	Focus	Organisation	Outputs	Year
Het Geluid van Rotterdam	Music from Rotterdam	A local foundation supported by subsidies	Online archive	2011
Stempel Broodje	The punk movement	Private collection. One of the founders is involved in the Offshore Radio Archive. In 2013 they stopped their collaboration.	Their material was used in the travelling exhibition 'Europunk'.	2011
Golden Earring – Back Home (Historical Museum, The Hague)	The band Golden Earring, which originated in The Hague.	Showcased material from the archives of Museum RockArt, as well as from other collectors.	Temporary exhibition	2011/ 12
Drents Museum (Assen)	This museum acquired a private collection on the Dutch blues band Cuby & the Blizzards.	Museum of Drenthe, a rural province located in the North-East of the Netherlands.	Physical archive	2012
God Save the Queen – Art, Squatting, Punk: 1977– 84 (Centraal Museum, Utrecht)	The visual arts, music and social movements of the late seventies – early eighties.	This exhibition used materials from the Stempel Broodje collection (see above).	Temporary exhibition	2012
Special request – Cuby & the Blizzards in the 1960s (Centraal Museum, Utrecht)	Dutch blues band Cuby & the Blizzards.	Curated by an art handler of the Utrecht Centraal Museum in honour of 25 years in service. The exhibition is primarily based on collector loans and material from the Cuby & the Blizzards museum in Grolloo.	Temporary exhibition	2012

PERSONAL MOTIVATION AND MEANING-MAKING

Collectors and enthusiasts have been known to structure their passion for specific objects around "projects" (Dannefer 1980), through which their experience and passion are ordered and collectively shared. In our fieldwork, we found these projects to be structured around four practices: retrieving, cataloguing, sharing and displaying. The four are not mutually exclusive, and some projects can combine several of these practices. Sharing and displaying were particularly rich in formats, ranging from temporary museum exhibitions, public presentations and debates to web-based archives and publications. Moreover, a number of initiatives interacted with local media (radio stations and press), at times as an outlet for their activities but also as a means of crowdsourcing knowledge and expertise from other collectors.

Frequently, collections started as personal souvenirs – memories of the time when collectors were active in the music industry, for instance, or avid fans of a band or genre who treasured items of clothing, correspondence of known musicians and memories of concert-going years. We found Pearce's second category of fetish collecting to correspond to cases where collectors attempt to retrieve and catalogue knowledge about the musicians active in specific locations or the collection of all releases from a band. We noted this in particular in archives focusing on specific locations, as with the Zaanse poparchief, focusing on the Zaanstreek-region, and Streektaalzang, concentrating on dialect music in the Netherlands. Finally, we found several instances of systematic collecting in the form of recent exhibitions focusing on popular music or bands – for instance, the Golden Earring exhibition at the Historical Museum in The Hague in 2011 – which serve to tell something about the social history of a locality through music.

PERSONAL BACKGROUNDS

The DIY archivists with whom we spoke had different professional backgrounds. The majority had a background in the music industry, some worked in other sectors but most respondents shared the commonality of having no directly transferable skills in terms of collecting and archiving. Learning by doing and the development of networks reaching out to people with complementary skills predominated (A1, A3, A12, A6). Archivists also found inspiration not only from friends and family but also from fellow archivists, highlighting the "affective" qualities of DIY institutions (Baker and Huber 2013, 522). The process of discovery of other, similar activities was a source of inspiration and encouragement, and provided frames of reference for how to pursue and manage one's own collection (A1, A8).

DIY archivists expressed personal motivation for starting their collection and preservation activities as arising from a pressing need. In the words of one interviewee, "The only motivation was that something should be done" (A1). The discourse of cultural heritage appears fully internalised by many of the respondents (A1, A2, A8, A14, A15): "Well ... objectives ... the main objective is to make sure that what is still there, that that rises to the surface and that it is preserved for posterity. That's my core" (A14). Objectives and goals can change over time, as new interests come to inspire further collecting (A15).

Becoming more visible as collectors – for example, by setting up a private museum or an association – was an important step towards gaining the trust of other collectors and potential donors of materials: "As a foundation, you can make requests, it's also an easier platform. Anyone who knows me knows that I am not just collecting things to be better off myself, but as a foundation ... it's more reliable" (A1). Institutionalising bottom-up practices generates greater collective trust, or at least the perception thereof. Moreover, as word spread that "someone is taking up this giant kind of work" (A8), archivists noted people would get in touch to volunteer information and material for the cause.

The reliance on one's own resources, particularly time and finances, and the invaluable support provided by family and friends were widely acknowledged. The financial arrangements of the initiatives draw on the support of family and friends, or indeed, in some cases, of fans as donors. The non-publicly funded initiatives we surveyed generally struggled to break even, and personal investment was often necessary – for example, the use of one's own property or land. As one archivist put it, "It doesn't have to become a millionaire business, we find it terribly fun, it's a real hobby project" (A1). Indeed, collecting practices that have a more commercial intent and approach were scorned for "trading" and selling "copies of copies of copies [of radio recordings]. And then they would calmly ask for 25 euro per hour" (A6). Capitalising on collections was frowned upon, and DIY archivists felt the need to ensure they were not seen to be doing this. This was also noticeable when DIY archivists were reliant on membership arrangements, as in the case of a web-based recordings archive. When members complained about pages not getting updated regularly, they were reminded that "the 20 euro you pay are not just for the extra pages, but also to support us" (A1).

SETTING THE RECORD STRAIGHT

Straddling the line between personal and collective memories, many archivists were also motivated by a desire to set the record straight as far as the factual history of Dutch popular music went. For some, this meant ending discussions over the facts – finding the real version of events among hearsay and oral histories, and a tendency to romanticise the past somewhat (A12, A3, A6). Other respondents (A4, A6, A8, A12) signalled that a more accurate version of popular music history was one that was more truthful to the lived experience of individuals rather than mediated by present-day collective memory or narratives about the past. Two underlying purposes can be gleaned from the data. The first is about filling gaps in the more widely recognised music canons, giving space to smaller names. In the words of one archivist, "I want a complete history, with all the names, also the unimportant names" (A8). Second, there are attempts to promote a particular reading of the musical past. For example, when curating a museum exhibition on music, the arts and squatting movements in the late 1970s and early 1980s, a curator explained the intention behind highlighting the openness of the Netherlands to foreign influences was motivated by a desire to counter "private" readings of history where "you are here and that's your world and then there is nothing around it" (A4). This was seen as significant in the context of the rise of populist tendencies in Dutch politics and in the discourse on immigration.

When assessing the wider context of collecting and preserving popular music in the Netherlands, many archivists expressed concerns. Two perspectives were frequently shared: first, a lack of pride in Dutch popular music history translated to privileging the preservation of items relating to foreign bands and acts (A14, A13), signalling a perceived lack of interest or attention among audiences. Many shared the feeling that the government was not supportive of popular music and people in general were not proud of Dutch popular music (A1, A14). Second, Dutch frugality meant some materials, such as film reels, were reused or simply thrown away in order to cut down on preservation costs (A1, A6), pointing to the scarcity – and rarity – of materials to preserve.

EXTERNAL USE OF COLLECTION

While often being a desired goal of DIY archivists, making collections accessible also contributes to adding meaning to the collection practice. When asked what made organising a museum exhibition on his favourite band meaningful to him, a curator explained, "I can show to people who Cuby is" (referring to the 1960s Dutch blues band Cuby + the Blizzards) (A12). The desire to share an interest can have wider pedagogical undertones. Similarly to what Pearce (1994b) noted for systematic collectors, for many DIY preservationists the experience of music, via all its related material culture, should become part of a collective consciousness of that particular time and place (A8, A11). Staging exhibitions also has a pedagogical objective. As one curator stated, "My intention was … not only to amuse and inform the public, [the] broad public, but also make a start with serious research in this period, on this time" (A4). The public of such initiatives can be characterised broadly as containing music-industry employees, fans, music lovers and people searching for specialised knowledge – students and journalists, for instance.

At times, archivists experience some frustration when complex requests for information cannot be met due to understaffing. For example, one DIY archivist noted, "Obviously, this isn't an institute such as Beeld en Geluid with 100 staff" (A1). Moreover, some frustration could be detected when archivists discussed instances of media articles on local music histories for which their expertise was not utilised (A3, A6). An archivist refused to provide information to a journalist researching local punk bands because the journalist would not agree to acknowledge the archivist's assistance in the article: "If he'd received the whole lot from me, he would have been able to write a much, much nicer story" (A3).

Individuals connected to publicly and privately funded initiatives pointed to similar issues relating the external use of the collections. Collecting was seen as binding people together on an emotional level, creating a convivial sphere where like-minded people could come together (A1). It also binds family members together as memories and tastes are transmitted from generation to generation. Yet collecting can become quite cliquey, as archivists focusing on the same materials also highlight instances of competition among themselves over rights and access (A6).

INTER-INSTITUTIONAL COLLABORATIONS

Institutional collaborations reveal different collecting practices and valuations of popular music. The growing recognition of bottom-up practices in mainstream heritage practices has been noted elsewhere (Moore 2000). We observe a combination of complementarity and tensions in the relationships between DIY preservationists and formal heritage institutions, as exemplified in a number of collaborations at Dutch historical museums. The complementarity of missions and roles was generally expressed as a mutual reliance on resources and collections. Particularly for the more specialised collections, museum curators noted the reliance on external sources, with a reasoning echoing the "we can't keep everything but others can" attitude. One of the key areas of tension pertained to the definition of uniqueness and how this varies according to whether or not audiences are fan-based.

This tension comes to the fore in a number of ways. Putting together an exhibition raised questions about the differential appreciation of objects by fans and collectors and more general audiences. Professionalising and formalising DIY preservation initiatives by making the transition from personal collection to online archives or physical museums, for instance, provides preservationists with an opportunity to widen their potential audiences and boost the collective effort of gathering and cataloguing materials. Yet connecting fans and amateur collectors with wider audiences raises the challenge of how to communicate value to a diverse audience, as the curator of a temporary exhibition pointed out:

> I got a lot from other people, and I must make a choice because it was so much ... there were also a lot of things that were the same, so you see then different kinds of designs of covers ... sometimes you look at

the same cover and you think, but then "it's the one from Holland and the other one is from Chile." So collectors focus on the special pressings of the records. But you can't … I can show two versions of the record, but sometimes you have five or six, but people don't see this, they see the same cover (A12).

On the other hand, unique can also mean less accessible and known. As the editor of a public multimedia collection stated, when selecting clips for a TV-recordings installation, it was important to focus on items that "don't show up on YouTube or something, it has to be unique" (A5).

SUSTAINING COLLECTIONS

While the personal motivation of DIY preservationists is strong, they also refer to being inspired by the activities of other preservationists through personal connection or friendship as well as through the realisation that others are actively pursuing similar goals. This is also the case when thinking about the future and sustainability of initiatives (Baker and Huber 2012). When discussing whether he thought someone would continue his documentation of local music history in the future, an archivist stated, "I get a lot of reactions, they are very positive. There are more people like me who are interested in cultivating this heritage," while also admitting this was possibly more his hope than a realistic perspective (A8). Interestingly, the guaranteeing of the future of collections was generally interpreted as being reliant on the continuity of the collecting process, rather than ensuring a continued external interest in the initiatives.

Although some of the DIY projects applied for external funding or collaborated with local heritage institutions, public subsidies generally were not considered a viable option when assessing the financial sustainability of initiatives. Funding cuts for culture, the perception that popular music is not valued in the public realm, and the lengthy and time-consuming application procedures were mentioned as discouraging attempts to apply for such resources. Additionally, independence from both private advertising and public funding was highly prized.

CONCLUSION

DIY preservation of popular music in the Netherlands comes in a variety of forms. Many of the initiatives we examined told us as much about that the richness and variety of Dutch popular music as about the personal histories and passionate commitment of a generation of music lovers. The archivists' active preservation of music illustrated their desire to leave a trace and keep the memory of a time and place alive, often aiming to achieve recognition of the music heritage of particular communities, genres or media. In many cases, these practices of DIY preservationists went beyond mere collecting, as they provided an impetus for nostalgic concerts, radio shows and local encyclopaedias.

Privately led and funded DIY preservationism appeared to be more sustainable than public institutions in the Netherlands. One of the reasons is their relative independence from temporary subsidies or changing cultural policy priorities. However, DIY projects are vulnerable due to their reliance on the efforts of a few key individuals and their appeal to restricted communities of interest (Baker and Huber 2013). Furthermore, preservation and memory practices of public institutions can have more cultural legitimacy (Roberts and Cohen 2014) and a wider recognition in heritage communities. Nevertheless, we noted several collaborations in which established cultural institutions benefited from the meticulous collecting and archiving conducted by non-professionals.

With many new projects initiated since the mid-1990s, DIY preservationists and professional heritage practitioners together have enriched the field of popular music heritage in the Netherlands. In so doing, they ensure that the preservation of popular music's past is steadily achieving a solid position in the Dutch cultural and heritage industries. One of the key challenges for DIY preservationists will be to find new ways and formats to engage with younger generations who do not share the personal memory of this popular music past, thus extending its value beyond the often autobiographical nature of collectors' endeavours.

REFERENCES

Appadurai, A. 1994 (1986). Commodities and the politics of value. In S.M. Pearce (ed.), *Interpreting objects and collections*. London: Routledge, 76–91.

Baker, S. and Huber, A. 2012. Masters of our own destiny: Cultures of preservation at the Victorian Jazz Archive in Melbourne, Australia. *Popular Music History* 7(3): 263–82.

Baker, S. and Huber, A. 2013. Notes towards a typology of the DIY institution: Identifying do-it-yourself places of popular music preservation. *European Journal of Cultural Studies* 16(5): 513–30.

Baym, N.K. and Burnett, R. 2009. Amateur experts international fan labour in Swedish independent music. *International Journal of Cultural Studies* 12(5): 433–49.

Belk, R.W. 1995. Collecting as luxury consumption: Effects on individuals and households. *Journal of Economic Psychology* 16(3): 477–90.

Bennett, A. 2009. Heritage rock: Rock music, representation and heritage discourses. *Poetics* 37(5): 474.

Born, G. 2011. Music and the materialization of identities. *Journal of Material Culture* 16(4): 376–88.

Brandellero, A. and Janssen, S. 2014. Popular music as cultural heritage: Scoping the field of practice. *International Journal of Heritage Studies* 30(3): 224–40.

Cohen, S. 2013. Musical memory, heritage and local identity: Remembering the popular music past in a European capital of culture. *International Journal of Cultural Policy* 19(5): 576–94.

Dannefer, D. 1980. Rationality and passion in private experience: Modern consciousness and the social world of old-car collectors. *Social Problems* 27(4): 392–412.

Flinn, A. 2007. Community histories, community archives: Some opportunities and challenges. *Journal of the Society of Archivists* 28(2): 151–76.

Flinn, A., Stevens, M. and Shepherd, E. 2009. Whose memories, whose archives? Independent community archives, autonomy and the mainstream. *Archival Science* 9(1–2), 71–86.

Kaplan, E. 2000. We are what we collect, we collect what we are: Archives and the construction of identity. *American Archivist* 63(1): 126–51.

Keen, A. 2007. *The cult of the amateur: How the democratization of the digital world is assaulting our economy, our culture, and our values*. New York: Doubleday Currency.

Ketelaar, E. 2005. Sharing: Collected memories in communities of records. *Archives and Manuscripts* 33: 44–61.

Kopytoff, I. 1986. The cultural biography of things: commoditization as process. In A. Appadurai (ed.), *The social life of things: Commodities in cultural perspective*. Cambridge: Cambridge University Press, 64–91.

Livingstone, S. 2013. The participation paradigm in audience research. *The Communication Review* 16(1–2): 21–30.

Long, P. and Collins, J. 2012. Mapping the soundscapes of popular music heritage. In L. Roberts (ed.), *Mapping cultures: Place, practice, performance*. Basingstoke: Palgrave Macmillan, 144–59.

Martin, P. 1999. *Popular collecting and the everyday self: The reinvention of museums?* London: Leicester University Press.

Merriman, N. 1991. *Beyond the glass case: The past, the heritage and the public in Britain*. London: Leicester University Press.

Moore, K. 2000. *Museums and popular culture*. London: Bloomsbury.

Moore, S. and Pell, S. 2010. Autonomous archives. *International Journal of Heritage Studies* 16(4–5), 255–68.

Morin, V. 1969. L'objet biographique. *Communications* 13(1): 131–9.

OCW 2011. *Meer dan kwaliteit: Een nieuwe visie op cultuurbeleid*. Den Haag: OCW.

Pearce, S.M. 1994a. Introduction. In S.M. Pearce (ed.), *Interpreting objects and collections*. London: Routledge, 1–6.

Pearce, S.M., 1994b. Collecting reconsidered. In S.M. Pearce (ed.), *Interpreting objects and collections*. London: Routledge, 193–204.

Pearce, S.M. 1994c. Objects as meaning; or narrating the past. In S.M. Pearce (ed.), *Interpreting objects and collections*. London: Routledge, 19–29.

Pearce, S.M. 1994d. Thinking about things. In S.M. Pearce (ed.), *Interpreting objects and collections*. London: Routledge, 125–32.

Pearce, S.M. 1994e. The urge to collect. In S.M. Pearce (ed.), *Interpreting objects and collections*. London: Routledge, 157–59.

Roberts, L. and Cohen, S. 2014. Unauthorising popular music heritage: Outline of a critical framework. *International Journal of Heritage Studies* 30(3): 241–61.

Scholz, T. 2008. Market ideology and the myths of Web 2.0. *First Monday* 13(3). Accessed March 22, 2015. http://firstmonday.org/article/view/2138/1945.

Snoek, C.G., Freiburg, B., Oomen, J. and Ordelman, R. 2010. Crowdsourcing rock 'n' roll multimedia retrieval. In *Proceedings of the International Conference on Multimedia 2010*, ACM, 1535–8.

Stevens, M., Flinn, A. and Shepherd, E. 2010. New frameworks for community engagement in the archive sector: From handing over to handing on. *International Journal of Heritage Studies*, 16(1–2): 59–76.

Van der Hoeven, A. 2012. The popular music heritage of the Dutch pirates: Illegal radio and cultural identity. *Media, Culture & Society* 34(8): 927–43.

Van Dijck, J. and Nieborg, D. 2009. Wikinomics and its discontents: A critical analysis of Web 2.0 business manifestos. *New Media & Society* 11(5): 855–74.

4 Affective Archiving and Collective Collecting in Do-it-Yourself Popular Music Archives and Museums

Sarah Baker

To archive effectively would be high on the agenda of every archivist, whether professionally trained and working in a national heritage institution or an untrained enthusiast volunteering in a community archive. This chapter contends that the value of amateur, do-it-yourself (DIY) archives perhaps lies not so much in the extent to which they are a place of effective archiving but rather in what their *affect*-led practice might offer the volunteers who run these institutions and, subsequently, the preservation of popular music's material culture. This is not to say the work being undertaken in the volunteer-run archives and museums discussed in this chapter is not also effective. Indeed, a number of these institutions have achieved or aspire to achieve museum accreditation standards. Rather, in these community-based heritage sites, archiving goes beyond the goal of collection and preservation. This work brings with it a range of personal impacts that reach into other areas of volunteers' lives, with the objects in the collection and their archival practice affecting them deeply. As such, archiving affectively is not just about archiving the material of popular music's past but also about what the practice of archiving this material gives to the individual in an emotional sense and, in turn, what the individual gives to the practice.

This chapter reflects on research undertaken for the Australian Research Council-funded projects "Popular Music and Cultural Memory" (2010–12) and "Do-It-Yourself Popular Music Archives" (2013–15).[1] In the course of these international comparative projects, I visited twenty-three archives, museums and halls of fame that were founded by music enthusiasts and rely for their continued operation on the assistance of volunteers who share a desire to collect and preserve artefacts and/or recordings of various popular music cultures. Places like the Lippmann+Rau-Musikarchiv in Germany, SwissJazzOrama in Switzerland and the Sarasota Music Archive in the United States all established themselves in parallel to national programs of cultural preservation. These are DIY institutions in the sense they are volunteer run, enthusiast established and community based (see Baker and Huber 2013). They are places that have emerged from within communities of music consumption, where groups of interested people have undertaken to do it themselves, establishing places to store, and in some cases display publicly, the material history of music culture. As what Roberts and Cohen

(2013, 8) would call "self-authorised" sites of popular music heritage – that is, "DIY, localised or vernacular" heritage sites with limited "official government endorsement" that lack the "gilt-edged symbolic capital" attached to "prestigious public institutions" – these DIY archives and museums share similar goals to national institutions with regard to preservation, collection, accessibility and the national interest. However, they do so with limited financial support, relying primarily on volunteer labour, grant funding, memberships and donations to continue running and are often dealing with significant space constraints.

In this chapter, I draw on semi-structured ethnographic interviews with 125 volunteer archivists and curators representing twenty-three fieldwork sites in ten countries[2] as a way of thinking through the affective atmospheres of DIY archives, museums and halls of fame and the extent to which a collective form of collecting, in which numerous volunteers contribute to the collecting efforts of an institution, shapes the affective dimension of these places. As I argue, collecting collectively helps foster a strong sense of community among workers and emotional connections between volunteers and objects in their care. The chapter considers how collective collecting is a central feature of the DIY practice of archiving affectively.

This focus on affect brings to light the presence of feelings in the way that popular music heritage volunteers talk, think and act. Music itself is thought of as significantly affective. As Bourdieu (1993) explains, music is felt as much as it is heard. An affective analysis considers how emotions such as love, fondness, excitement and pleasure can be imagined as existing in relation to things as much as they might be in relation to experiences. I draw here on Ahmed's (2010) concept of the power of things to influence how people feel, with affect offering a way to imagine what is going on between the material world of objects and the physical and emotional world of people.

While it would be a mistake to suggest professionally trained archivists and museum workers in authorised institutions of national or regional significance perform their work in ways that are not affective, or that prestigious public institutions are affect-free zones, I argue that there is something specific going on in volunteer-run enterprises that separates their archival practices from the work of trained professionals. In many community archives, the project of archiving can be understood to have begun because of feelings of love and care related to the custodianship of popular music's heritage, rather than because of an abstract concept related to saving material for the national interest. Whereas preservation in authorised institutions can be characterised primarily as an intellectual project, the establishment of the DIY institutions of this research is born from affective investments. Affective archiving capitalises on the connections between people and objects. The artefacts in the collections discussed in this chapter provide opportunities for volunteers to share knowledge and deploy expertise, an affective act based on a love and care for the music, the artefacts, the institution and its workers. Feelings of love, care and emotion between the volunteers and the things they are looking after result in a different kind of archival and/or museal space, one in which affect is fostered and, indeed, privileged. Thus affect itself makes a contribution to the enterprise of cultural preservation.

AFFECTIVE ARCHIVING IN THE DIY INSTITUTION

During the period 2010–12, I collaborated with Alison Huber to explore the heritage practices of six DIY archives in Australia, Austria, Iceland, the Netherlands and the United States (see Baker and Huber 2012, 2013, 2015). In our interviews and observations at these places, we were struck by a range of similarities across the examples that transcend nation and genre, and so were led to propose a typology outlining a number of common structural functions of DIY popular music heritage institutions (see Baker and Huber 2013). Broadly speaking, we identified specifically articulated cultural, social and affective functions across the fieldwork examples. On affect, we noted that DIY archives and museums can be thought of as "as places in which affect is produced and made possible through community and the process of remembering, and made again through encounters with objects [and people] that inspire both these things" (2013, 525).

In establishing the affective dimension of the DIY institution in our typology article, examples were provided of volunteer–visitor–object encounters at Tónlistarsafn Íslands, a music history museum in Iceland, and the Victorian Jazz Archive in Australia, where volunteers bring visitors into contact with artefacts from dead relatives, producing highly emotional encounters filled with a sense of wonder for both volunteer and visitor (Baker and Huber 2013, 524). These are not isolated cases of the affect generated by volunteers. In recounting visitor experiences, volunteers are articulating their own feelings towards the institution and the work they do there, as well as their love of music. The affective potentiality of the DIY institution can be seen again in this similar example from the Australian Country Music Hall of Fame (ACMHF), an archive and museum located in the regional city of Tamworth, New South Wales, Australia:

> We have some wonderful experiences. We had this young fellow ... he came in and he said, "Oh," he said, "I think I'm in the right place," he said. "I'm looking for some information on [a particular female country performer]." "Yes, you've come to the right place." He said, "She was actually my grandmother, but I never knew her..." She'd only ever recorded six sides of old 78s, so she was a real pioneering lady ... so we showed him her outfit, and when we were having the [Australian Country Music Hall of Fame Tribute to the Pioneering Ladies] concert, we rang him up and said, "Look, we're having a tribute concert to ... the pioneering ladies – would you like to come?" Well he came down ... they drove from Queensland, they got to the concert ... and then afterwards

they came back up here and they met ... Joy McKean, Geoff Mack, Lilly Connors, I can't think who else they met ... and ... then we allowed them to have their photo taken with [his grandmother's] display, and, it was a sad thing ... to think that that poor boy knew nothing, but ... after it was all over, he got in his car and drove back to Brisbane ... and if you'd have offered him a million dollars he would have taken the experience here rather than the million dollars, and it was, it was a wonderful, wonderful thing, you know, so we can do some nice things ...
(interview, Australian Country Music Hall of Fame, August 2011)

In describing the visit of this country performer's grandson and his family to the museum, this volunteer is also conveying her own connection to the ACMHF and the extent to which her identity is tied up in her work at the museum. She uses examples of visitors' experiences to both emphasise and solidify her affective investment in the ACMHF, the genre of country music and her position as a volunteer. Further, this example shows that objects in the collection are utilised as ways for this volunteer to introduce the cultural world of country music to others, resulting not only in an information exchange but an experiential exchange, folding visitors into the affective realm created in this DIY space of music heritage.

Ahmed (2010, 30) suggests the study of affect should be underpinned by a focus on "how we are touched by what we are near." For some of the volunteers, achieving nearness or proximity to objects in the DIY archive's collection is one of the pleasures of the work in which they are involved, and can be one of the benefits of volunteering in such an institution. A key interest for this project is in what Thrift (2010, 293) calls the "surges of affect." These swells of feeling can be observed in the experiences of volunteers in DIY popular music archives, museums and halls of fame as they carry out their work in close spatial and temporal proximity to music's material past, a past to which they are intimately connected.

The intensity of volunteers' affective connections to objects in the institution's collection can vary greatly. For some volunteers, the attraction is to work closely with the artefacts in a broad sense, such as volunteer George Wilkinson at the National Jazz Archive in Loughton, England, who, when asked about favourite objects in the collection, responded, "I just like it all because always a new book comes in, you can look at it, and some [objects] are terrific, like the photographs" (Wilkinson, February 2013). Other interviewees identified specific artefacts that were particularly meaningful or of interest to them. Lexa Guha, a volunteer at PopMuseum in the Czech Republic, nominated a record made from an old X-ray as the artefact that excited him most. There are five or six of these records in the collection, and the best examples of these were on loan to a Prague exhibition at the time of my visit. One remained on the wall of the museum and Lexa removed it from the display case, holding it up to the light so I could take a photo and identify it as a Chet Baker recording on an X-ray of a pelvis (see Figure 4.1).

[X-rays were] used as a material to produce records, something like vinyl records, but it was done especially during the '50s before the era of magnetaphones. People had at home [a] small machine for it and they were able to produce [their] own records with recordings from radio, or from other recordings, or also sometimes they recorded something on microphone, and it's very unique. We knew about it and finally we received some copies of that. Very often it was [a] real X-ray from leg or hand and they cut it to the round ... they didn't have money for other materials. One of those producers produced only for black market or for friends, and was the son of a doctor so he had quite a lot of material.

(Guha, July 2014)

Figure 4.1 Lexa Guha, a volunteer at Prague's PopMuseum, with an X-ray pressed record from the museum's collection. Photo by Sarah Baker.

The extent of volunteers' affective connections to objects varies considerably within and across the institutions, from those sparked by a keen intellectual interest, such as the case of Lexa and his X-ray pressed records, to more heartfelt expressions that really highlight the ways in which surges of affect are experienced in these DIY museal and archival spaces. Take, for example, the following extract from my interview with Sharon Jackson from the Heart of Texas Country Music Museum in the United States. I asked Sharon whether there were any items in the museum she really loved.

Each piece holds a special memory. The Hank Thompson room for a lot of personal reasons. Hank Thompson is very special to me. One of the things that's always caught my attention ... He has a gorgeous ceramic and gold soap dish that belonged to Dottie West. Did you know Dottie? ... She did this song for Coke, and then wrote "Here Comes my Baby." It had little heart soaps in it and I came in one day and it was sitting in a case. It just – because she had such tragic things in her life, the IRS where they confiscated everything, there's not a lot of her stuff. For him to have that small piece, I just, I love it, you know ... That I think about a lot and I tell people a lot about it, and then he's got a beautiful beaded purse that belonged to Patsy Cline and I just think that's beautiful. I just think it's neat.

(Jackson, April 2014)

The connection felt by volunteers in DIY institutions towards objects in their care – a connection that is enhanced by the possibility of increased proximity to those artefacts – indicates the power objects sometimes have over people (Ahmed 2010). And, as highlighted in the extract from Sharon's interview, this is perhaps especially so when those objects are associated with performers of whom one is a fan. This relationship between people and objects is central to affective archiving. A sense of custodianship over items of popular music's material past develops, based on feelings of love and care for the music and its performers. This is archiving from the heart.

Archiving from the heart produces, and is produced by, the "affective atmospheres" (Anderson 2009) of DIY institutions, which emerge from the interrelationship of workers, objects and the archival environment. Ahmed (2010) talks about affect being "sticky." It "is what sticks, or what sustains or preserves the connection between ideas, values, and objects" (2010, 29); it "align[s] individuals with communities ... by sticking figures together (adherence), a sticking that creates the very effect of a collective (coherence)" (2010, 119). The way in which this is felt, experienced and lived works to "actively constitute or produce place," making the DIY popular music archive and museum akin to what Casey (2001) may have described as a "thick place" in which "one's sense of meaning and belonging" is enhanced (Duff 2010, 882). This is important, because the success of DIY institutions are dependent on the formation of strong "communities of practice" that ultimately harness this sense of meaning and belonging (Wenger 1998).

In Wenger's (2006, 1) words, "Communities of practice are groups of people who share a concern or passion for something they do and learn how to do it better as they interact regularly." Very few of the volunteers in the DIY popular music archives and museums of this research have any formal training in curation or archiving, so communities form around the collective learning and enactment of tasks related to cultural preservation.

This situated learning necessarily involves forming social relationships with others who are similarly engaged. Such relationships are formed around the acquisition of skills and cemented, in most cases, by a shared enthusiasm for a genre of music, the act of volunteering and/or an interest in preserving cultural heritage.

The types of relationships that contribute to the community of practice are made possible by the affective atmosphere more broadly. As such, the feel of the place and its accompanying sociality are the glue that holds these DIY institutions together. The affective atmosphere contributes to and is the product of a social institution that

> is produced through relationships, creating an experience for volunteers ... that is not a tangible or quantifiable property of the institution and its aims [of cultural preservation], but nevertheless is essential to [the institution's] sustainability and survival, as people work together to achieve shared goals, sometimes under difficult material circumstances.
>
> (Baker and Huber 2013, 522)

And, of course, the affective connectivity produced in these sites of music heritage goes beyond the strong social bonds that are very often forged between volunteers. Rather, these feelings and emotions extend beyond the enactment of social collectivity to include volunteers' relationships with the artefacts and music in their care (2013, 522).

That affective practice can be communal is essential to an understanding of the potentialities of affective archiving in the preservation of popular music's material culture. The labour of many volunteers is bound up with feelings of love and care for the institution, for one another, for the objects in the collection. Take, for example, the following comments that in turn illustrate each of these affective dimensions:

> When we had a display two years ago in that big room, for me it was a really wonderful experience. I'd never been involved in such a creative combination of creativity and joy in getting it all together. I was astonished. I was not familiar with all this stuff but out it came. Don, in particular, drove it with lots of ideas, Ron also had a lot of ideas, they bounced off each other very well when Ron was president and Don the secretary/archivist and the team of people they got together. ... What I was doing mainly was labels. I learnt how to do a textbox and labels, I did hundreds of them, so I'd do this and other stuff. Little skills but it was great and [the event] went over two days, it was quite wonderful.
>
> (Jane Shoebridge, South Australian Jazz Archive, June 2013)

> Well it's like when I said Frank was the oldest [at 88]. ... I said to Maria ... "Do you think you could bake a cake for Frank's birthday?" Well she made him a beautiful birthday cake with "Happy Birthday

Frank" on it and ... he didn't hear us all tiptoeing in the back and we suddenly burst into song "Happy Birthday" and he was so surprised. ... Frank is the eldest and he deserved a special cake.

(Gretel Jones, Victorian Jazz Archive, June 2012)

This year we put up ... a little outfit of Troy [Cassar-Daley][3] out there, and I deliberately put that near [the] Brian Young [display]. The reason for that was that Troy did an outback tour with Brian Young, and Brian Young was one of the last of the travelling show-men who did it the old-style way, travelling round with cars and stuff like that, and Brian Young is only one of a few people who have been allowed into the Aboriginal missions ... and he took Troy – and he's taken other people as well – but Troy has the highest respect for Brian because of what he's – he took him out and showed him, and actually took him back to his ... roots, Troy, as well – so I deliberately put that near Brian because of the connection there.

(interview, Australian Country Music Hall of Fame, August 2011)

These extracts bring to mind Grossberg's (1992, 81) description of the role of affect in everyday life, in which he sees "affect is what gives 'colour', 'tone,' or 'texture' to the lived." For Grossberg (1992, 82), "affect identifies the strength of the investment which anchors people in particular experiences, practices, identities, meanings and pleasures, but it also determines how invigorated people feel at any moment of their lives, their level of energy and passion." The passion with which DIY archiving is undertaken and the pleasure it brings to volunteers are reflected in the examples provided here. This is a labour of love for the individuals concerned but one that always has the collective in mind.

FIVE FORMS OF COLLECTIVE COLLECTING IN DIY INSTITUTIONS

The ways in which the collecting, cataloguing and archiving of materials take place in DIY institutions contribute to the affect-rich archival ecologies of these places. The interview material suggests collecting in many of these institutions is a collective practice and collecting collectively has a part to play in the cultural, social and affective dimensions of DIY archives and museums. In this section, I explore five forms of collective collecting that have emerged from the data before considering the impact of collective collecting on the practice of archiving affectively.

Merging Private Collections

Many of the places in this research were founded by the bringing together of private collections. Take, for example, the case of the Sound Preservation

Association of Tasmania (SPAT), Australia. Lindsay McCarthy, one of SPAT's founders, explained:

> [Co-founder] Gwen started on about [how] she'd like to start this record club, because we all had collections of old 78s. I probably had four or five thousand, Gwen would have had ten or twelve thousand old 78s and that was the basis of our early collection. Most of them are now stored in the [shipping] container. ... They [members] would say we're not using these anymore, let's put them in the collection here so anyone who wants to get a copy can do so.
>
> (McCarthy, June 2014)

A significant number of the volunteers in my study, and especially founders of these DIY institutions, had long histories of involvement in music communities as collectors. Bringing together these collections ensured the archives started with a wealth of material even before any outside donations started trickling in.

Retaining Private Collections for Collective Use

Where the institutions are in their infancy, collections usually remain in the care of the individual collector until suitable collective spaces can be found. The Rhode Island Music Hall of Fame (RIMHF) in the United States, for example, has an exhibition space for informative plaques that draw on archival material but it does not yet have a building that can house the various collections. As Mederick Bellaire, head of the RIMHF's Archives Committee, explained:

> There are two other major collectors of Rhode Island music ... one is on the board and one is on my archive committee. [Mike] just happened to settle in Rhode Island and was amazed to find out that he's a Rhode Island music collector by default. ... Then there's another guy [Al] ... who ... used to be a radio consultant. He ran a very important record store in th '60s and '70s. ... He is one of the biggest record collectors in the entire world. ... He has a collection of Rhode Island music as well. It's actually bigger than mine. So we have a lot of resources [to draw on but] ... I have not donated my collection, nor has Al, nor has Mike. ... Ideally, I would love to see a place that was like a library where we had all of the artefacts.
>
> (Bellaire, April 2014)

Retaining private collections in this instance is only an interim measure until an appropriate storage space can be found in which the various private collections, or parts thereof, can be deposited. Indeed, in the case of the RIMHF, a growing archive of new donations sits alongside the private collection as these acquisitions are housed not in a central location but in the house of the head of the Archives Committee.

Individual Volunteers Buying Items to Loan or Donate to the Collection

At the Heart of Texas Country Music Museum (HoTCMM) in the United States, volunteers have at times sought out items to purchase and donate to the museum, using their own funds as a way to help build the collection. Connie Edmiston, a volunteer at HoTCMM, has added to the museum's collection through the purchase of a number of artefacts. She explains:

Figure 4.2 Heart of Texas Country Music Museum volunteer Connie Edmiston stands by the Bobby Flores exhibition. Photo by Sarah Baker.

[Loretta Lyn] donated a guitar to the Heart of Texas country music anniversary show, the auction. Well, see, my husband and I are in charge of the auction. ... She donated it, and so we bid on it and got it. Well Tracy [the museum founder] told her about us, said, "This couple, you know they bid $500 and got it," and so she sent a [autographed] picture ... of herself and it's upstairs [in the museum] and it has on there, "To Bob and Connie, thanks for buying the guitar, Love you, Loretta Lynn." So we donated the guitar and the picture to the museum. ... And I don't know if you've heard of the West Texas Rehab. ... They have telethons every year. Well, Ronnie Milsap, he donated a keyboard, you know he's a blind artist ... and he'd autographed it and so we bid on it at the rehab sale and we got it and we put it in the museum. ... We asked Tracy you know, would he – it's not his to keep, but we asked him would he like to put it in the museum and he said, "Oh, I'd love to," so he never turns us down.

(Edmiston, April 2014)

Connie doesn't have a private collection. Rather, the project of collecting is tied up with eighteen years of personal investment in a museum devoted to something she loves – traditional country music, a genre with which she has engaged since childhood. In Figure 4.2, Connie can be seen standing in front of a glass cabinet in the museum that displays yet another of the items she and her husband purchased for the exhibit, a fiddle and bow that belonged to Bobby Flores.

Outposts for Collecting

Another example of collecting collectively is provided by Museum RockArt in the Netherlands. At the time of my visit in 2011, there were five core volunteers at the museum but a much larger network of approximately eighty spread throughout the country who, while not contributing to the daily running of the museum site on the outskirts of Hoek van Holland, acted as outposts for collecting. As one volunteer explained:

We have some people who are going through the country, looking. If they see something – "Oh is that something for the museum?" – they call me up and they get in contact ... (interview, September 2011).

This is akin to a "collective intelligence" (Levy 1997) strategy for building a collection, one that draws on vernacular knowledges across a nation. A network connected by mass communication technologies, this knowledge community is akin to those fan communities that Jenkins (2002, 155) has observed emerging online, which are "voluntary, temporary, and tactical affiliations, defined through common intellectual enterprises and emotional investments." For an archive that isn't centrally located in the Netherlands, the strategy of collective intelligence expands its capacity to build the collection by "enabl[ing] the group to act upon a broader range of expertise" (Jenkins 2002, 156) and access that isn't fixed to any specific geographic location. Even if these remote volunteers are unable to obtain or deliver the artefact themselves, they are able to alert the site-based volunteers to the material. They then travel around the country to assess the potential new acquisitions.

Collectively Deciding on Acquisitions

As a final example, we have the collective process of deciding what donated artefacts have a place in an archive's collection. Gretel Jones, a volunteer at Australia's Victorian Jazz Archive, described witnessing this process in action:

> Mel and Ralph [in the collection team] sort the [donations] out and I see them get put on the big table in the next room and there they sort them out. Somebody came in with … that many cassettes in this box. … But they get all sorted out, they take out what are jazz and what aren't jazz and what they need and what they don't.
>
> (Jones, June 2012)

The Victorian Jazz Archive has a significant volunteer workforce of about sixty (see Chapter 17) and ten or twelve of these volunteers are in the collections team, working under the direction of the Collections Manager, Mel Blachford. Decisions are not made in isolation at the Victorian Jazz Archive and volunteers often work together to sort, arrange and organise aspects of the collection. For example, in Figure 4.3 we see volunteers Richard Church and Jim Lightwood working together on transferring photograph donations into preservation-quality files.

This collaborative approach at the Victorian Jazz Archive extends beyond the process of sorting donations, which is just one example of a community of practice at work. Rather than being a solitary activity at a computer terminal, the cataloguing of the sorted artefacts can be a communal practice. When it comes to photographic entries, for example, another of the Archive's volunteers describes how, on occasions where she is unable to put a name to a face in an image from the archive's photograph collection, she will "just scan a photo … to my source in Sydney [and] nine times out of ten he can identify [it] for me" (Margaret Anderson, Victorian Jazz Archive, July 2011; see also Baker and Huber 2012, 273). This is also an example of the collective intelligence strategy observed in the previous section, demonstrating that none of the forms of collective collecting discussed in this chapter should be thought of as operating in isolation. The collecting practices of DIY institutions can involve all of the above, often operating simultaneously.

Figure 4.3 Volunteers Richard Church and Jim Lightwood work at sorting the
Victorian Jazz Archive's photographic collection. Photo by Sarah Baker.

FINAL THOUGHTS

The aforementioned activities around collective collecting undoubtedly contribute to the affective atmospheres of DIY institutions, enabling them to
be places where affective archiving flourishes. In these places, volunteers
work together in various ways to create a collection of value. While this is
obviously an aim for all forms of collecting, collective collecting in the DIY
institution is not just about "the nature of the value assigned to the objects"
(Durost, cited in Pearce 1999, 20) but is as much about the value of the
activity of collecting to the individual and their community of practice. In
a number of ways, collective collecting in the DIY institution is a form of
affective volunteer labour (see Baker and Huber 2013, 523). This mutual
engagement in a cooperative labouring activity becomes a significant source

of meaning in the lives of volunteers. In the register of affective institution we see volunteers' feelings and emotions towards things and people bound up in their daily experiences and the spaces they produce with their labour, including the communal approach to collecting.

Collective collecting in the DIY institution is perhaps less about the object being collected and more about what that object offers the community of volunteers as collectors and custodians of music heritage. In DIY archives, museums and halls of fame, the value of the object is in the affect it generates. While the object is also important in its own right – these are, after all, institutions of cultural preservation, regardless of the extent to which volunteers might be considered amateur or "pro-am" (Leadbeater and Miller 2004) – the artefacts in these places are not necessarily collected for their own object-ness. In some cases, items become part of a collection because they make a connection in a materialised form to the people they represent and can even stand in for the people themselves. While objects in these collections might be considered auratic, their aura comes from their association with the people who once touched them. As the archivist at the Australian Country Music Hall of Fame emphasised, "We are a people collection organisation" (interview, Australian Country Music Hall of Fame, August 2011).

Being an affective institution is not an overt aim of the DIY institutions of my study, in the sense that affect does not form part of the explicit mission statements of these establishments. However, affect is enabled more easily in these places than more authorised sites of popular music heritage because of the room afforded for the emotional connections that exist between people and things, combined with a communal urge to collect, preserve and archive that is generated by a love of music and performers. Indeed, it was these impulses generated at a community level and, notably in many cases from my fieldwork, an orientation towards collective collecting, that led to the founding of these grassroots, bottom-up sites of popular music heritage in the first place. Concerns that DIY archives and museums are compromised because they are not run by professionally trained archivists are misplaced. These are not compromised projects of preservation but rather projects with "differing priorities, competencies and motivations" (Baker and Huber 2012, 270). DIY archives and museums present "opportunities for 'personal enrichment' and a deepening of affective experience" (Duff 2010, 882) for the volunteers involved, and this in turn contributes to institutions that feel like the logical home for music's material past. These places are concerned with cultural heritage management and the preservation of artefacts, but they are also extensions of musical communities in the present in which activities around music preservation have personal, community and heritage benefits. It is by way of a tacit yet experiential emphasis on affect that the DIY institutions of my study might be seen to have an advantage over authorised sites of popular music heritage.

60   *Sarah Baker*

ACKNOWLEDGEMENTS

This chapter has as its foundation unpublished writing from collaborations with Alison Huber during the project "Popular Music and Cultural Memory."

NOTES

1. "Popular Music and Cultural Memory: Localised Popular Music Histories and Their Significance for National Music Industries" was funded under the Australian Research Council's (ARC) Discovery Project scheme for three years (2010–12, DP1092910). Chief Investigators on the project were Andy Bennett (Griffith University), Shane Homan (Monash University), Sarah Baker (Griffith University) and Peter Doyle (Macquarie University), with Research Fellow Alison Huber (Griffith University). Additional funding for fieldwork in Austria and Iceland was provided by an Australian Academy of the Humanities ISL-HCA International Research Fellowship (2nd Round, 2010) awarded to Sarah Baker. "Do-It-Yourself Popular Music Archives: An International Comparative Study of Volunteer-Run Institutions that Preserve Popular Music's Material Culture" was funded under the ARC's Discovery Project scheme for three years (2013–15, DP130100317). Chief Investigator on the project was Sarah Baker (Griffith University).
2. The ten countries are Australia, Austria, the Czech Republic, England, Germany, Iceland, the Netherlands, New Zealand, Switzerland and the United States. A music collector with hopes of establishing a DIY archive in Israel was also interviewed.
3. Troy Cassar-Daley is a well-known Australian Indigenous country music performer.

REFERENCES

Ahmed, S. 2010. Happy objects. In M. Gregg and G.J. Seigworth, eds., *The affect theory reader*. Durham, NC: Duke University Press, 29–51.

Anderson, B. 2009. Affective atmospheres. *Emotion, Space and Society* 2: 77–81.

Baker, S. and Huber, A. 2012. Masters of our own destiny: Cultures of preservation at the Victorian Jazz Archive in Melbourne, Australia. *Popular Music History* 7(3): 263–82.

Baker, S. and Huber, A. 2013. Notes towards a typology of the DIY Institution: Identifying do-it-yourself places of popular music preservation. *European Journal of Cultural Studies* 16(5): 513–30.

Baker, S. and Huber, A. 2015. Saving "rubbish": Preserving popular music's material culture in amateur archives and museums. In S. Cohen, R. Knifton, M. Leonard and L. Roberts (eds.), *Sites of popular music heritage: Memories, histories, places*. New York: Routledge, 112–24.

Bourdieu, P. 1993. *Sociology in question*. London: Sage.

Casey, E. 2001. Between geography and philosophy: What does it mean to be in the place-world? *Annals of the Association of American Geographers* 91: 683–93.

Duff, C. 2010. On the role of affect and practice in the production of place. *Environment and Planning D: Society and Space* 28: 881–95.

Grossberg, L. 1992. *We gotta get out of this place: Popular conservatism and post-modern culture*. New York: Routledge.

Jenkins, H. 2002. Interactive audiences? The collective intelligence of media fans. In D. Harries (ed.), *The new media book*. London: British Film Institute, 157–70.

Leadbeater, C. and Miller, P. 2004. *The pro-am revolution: How enthusiasts are changing our economy and society*. London: Demos.

Levy, P. 1997. *Collective intelligence: Mankind's emerging world in cyberspace*. New York: Plenum.

Pearce, S. 1999. *On collecting: An investigation into collecting in the European tradition*. London: Routledge.

Roberts, L. and Cohen, S. 2013. Unauthorizing popular music heritage: Outline of a critical framework. *International Journal of Heritage Studies* 20(3): 241–61.

Thrift, N. 2010. Understanding the material practices of glamour. In M. Gregg and G.J. Seigworth (eds.), *The affect theory reader*. Durham, NC: Duke University Press, 289–308.

Wenger, E. 1998. *Communities of practice: Learning, meaning and identity*. New York: Cambridge University Press.

Wenger, E. 2006. Communities of practice: A brief introduction. Accessed August 14, 2014. http://wenger-trayner.com/wp-content/uploads/2013/10/06-Brief-introduction-to-communities-of-practice.pdf.

5 "Really Saying Something?" What Do We Talk About When We Talk About Popular Music Heritage, Memory, Archives and the Digital?

Paul Long

Reflecting on the nature of community archives, Andrew Flinn cites a 2006 survey of United Kingdom activity that estimates there might be up to three thousand such entities in existence, involving up to one million people in their maintenance (Flinn 2007, 164). As the work collected in this volume and explored elsewhere suggests (Baker and Huber 2013; Roberts and Cohen 2013; Roberts et al. 2014), a great deal of such activity – whether in the United Kingdom or around the world – is concerned with archiving aspects of popular music. Just as the general domain described by Flinn has prospered online, communities of practice concerned with the preservation of popular music sounds, ephemera, scenes and memories have been enabled by digital technology (Collins and Long 2014). Bespoke websites, blogs, pages and groups on social-media sites such as Facebook abound. Such is the extent of this activity that even if one were to consider sites devoted to United Kingdom artists and communities alone, their number might surpass the impressive figures above.

In the titles and rationale of online activities, there is a promiscuous deployment of terms such as "history," "heritage," "memory," "community," "curation," "archive" and "nostalgia." By way of illustration, examples from Facebook include North East Music History; Richmond upon Thames Music Heritage; I Remember the Music of the 50s, 60s, 70s and 80s; Reggae and Dancehall History and Music; Curators of Hip Hop; Can't Stand – The Midwest: Music Archive; and Nepa Hardcore/Punk Nostalgia. Likewise, there are overt value judgements about music of the past, of the past itself perhaps when compared with the present, expressed in the names of sites such as those on Facebook including Back in the Days of Great Music; Vinyl Days: When Rock and Roll was Good; or in the strapline for Retro and Vintage Music!!,[1] which announces it is concerned with "music of the better times." While the phenomenal growth and scope of this activity merit assessment, the intention here is to consider the materiality, structure and meaning of the practices such activity represents as historical work and to look at its role for those involved.

In the context of this book's questions, what insights might be gained about wider practices of heritage prompted by the digital in the examination of such sites? What is it about popular music that merits such prodigious activity? What is the nature of this online production and the communities that convene around popular music of the past? Indeed, what are the DIY qualities of such sites, and how are they archives in any conventional sense? For instance, as Flinn (2007) suggests, the terms employed in the conjunction of community and archive are not at all transparent; he notes that they "might go unused and unrecognised by many working in community projects and in mainstream archive and heritage institutions" (2007, 152). Likewise, it is helpful to bear in mind the distinctiveness of concepts such as memory, history and archive, even as there is slippage between them in online practice that is both productive and potentially obfuscating. Indeed, what kinds of heritage – what kinds of histories – are constructed or suggested by these sites? What kinds of resources do these sites represent, if they are indeed archives at all in any recognisable sense? Ultimately, what kinds of ideas about music itself do these practices reveal, and in what ways does music play a part in such sites?

In this chapter, I outline a context for thinking about the efflorescence of popular work devoted to music history, on and offline, with respect to the archival turn. Suggesting that online practice in particular constitutes a mode of democratic community archiving, I describe some of its dimensions, drawing in particular on the wealth of Facebook groups and pages. I then turn to consider how this archiving and memory work might be understood in relation to the way in which popular music is imbued with a broad historical sensibility. The penultimate section opens up some ways of thinking about a political economy of online music archives and memory work in the context of the digital turn that might also prompt reflections on the field opened up in these chapters.

THE ARCHIVAL TURN

Carolyn Steedman (2011) has suggested that some time soon, historians may well attend to the archival turn that has been noted across the humanities and social sciences. She suggests a historical purview of this historical work might be able to determine what that turn actually *was*, or *is*, as the nature of the archive and its uses appears to be an ongoing concern for scholars other than the historians who "were always already there" (Steedman 2011, 321). Whatever the nature of this turn, it appears to involve an exhaustion of a particular concept of the archive itself. Thus, while Steedman's remarks come under the suggestive title of "*After* the Archive," one explanation for this apparent turn to it comes from Lucille Schultz in a foreword to a collection that looks "*Beyond* the Archives." This interdisciplinary set of reflections is one that Schultz suggests marks "the change from reading an archive not just as a source but also as a subject ... in the words of anthropologist Ann Laura Stoler, not as 'things' but as 'epistemological experiments'; not as sites of 'knowledge retrieval' but as sites of 'knowledge production'" (Schultz 2008, vii).

One source for this contemporary turn and mode of analysis is Jacques Derrida's treatise *Archive Fever* (1995). Here Derrida is concerned with the shaping and role of the archive in the origins of law and power, particularly a power over history. In Derrida's psychoanalytic reading, the archive's status at the centre of power entails a recognition of a pull between a "death drive," in which history and its records might be forgotten, and a drive to preserve, even a yearning for a return to the past. Here "archivization produces as much as it records the event" (1995, 17).

While Derrida's title in the original French, *Mal d'archive*, might not be conveyed most effectively in the idea of a "fever," this translation is suggestive for connecting the so-called archival turn with a pronounced expansion in recent decades in public activities devoted to history, heritage and cultural memory (e.g. Ashton and Kean 2009; Hewison 1987; Huyssen 2003; Kean et al. 2000). Derrida's concerns remind us too of the political dynamics characterising such activities. As Flinn notes, we have been told, and tell others, that archives "are the very essence of our heritage" and "the foundation on which are built all our histories" (Viscount St Davids, quoted by Flinn 2007, 152). They are a starting point for articulations of collective identity, of claims to truth and so to power. Flinn is attuned also to the idea of the archive as a potential site of struggle over its use, one that is traditionally deemed to be (as Steedman 2011 notes) a guarded, specialised, preserved space and special preserve for scholars in which they might pursue serious research. The efflorescence of public history activities in recent decades has in part democratised archives, which have either been opened up or bypassed as ordinary people pursue a desire to find out more about personal or communal histories that have largely been ignored by official accounts. Thus such activities have entailed a challenge to what the archive has meant in theory and in practice, a situation accentuated by a turn of a further kind.

While sensitive to the material shaping of the archive and its role in forging knowledge, Steedman (2001) notes Derrida's analysis is based on little understanding of the actual experience and materiality of archives, or indeed the knowledge production that takes place therein. Furthermore, she finds Derrida's metaphoric approach to the archive to be "capacious enough to encompass the whole of modern information technology, its storage, retrieval, and communication" (Steedman 2001, 1161; for a discussion, see also Manoff 2004). It is certainly the case that modern information technology and another turn occasioned by digital production, circulation and consumption have given the expansive metaphor of the archive a material quality. In his history, Terry Cook (2013) notes a contemporary mindset around the archive born of new social and communications realities. In short, this alludes to the technological opportunities and challenges of the Internet and practices in which distinctions of producer and consumer – here, of archivist and the archived, the archive user perhaps – are potentially dissolved. As Cook (2013, 152) suggests, engaged in the building of online archives are a range of nongovernmental organisations, lobbying groups, community activists and individuals who join together across a variety of forums and platforms where they share their interests, which reflect "every possible colour, creed, locale, belief, and activity, actual or hoped for. And they are creating records to bind their communities together, foster their group identities, and carry out their business."

MUSIC ARCHIVES ONLINE

In fact, the archival impulse and the generation of memory exhibited by the actors listed by Cook might be integral to new media technology. Wendy Chun (2011), for instance, suggests this is a major feature of digital media. She notes the way in which so much online practice is devoted to preservation, and points out that whether the content found on the Internet is about it or not, it is infused with memory. In the technology of the computer, the metaphor of memory becomes essence (2011, 97). Such characteristics are underlined by and made manifest in the myriad online projects devoted to the past of popular music. Communities are built and interactions facilitated by the digital "technologies of memory" (Van House and Churchill 2008; Plate and Smelik 2009) that enable some to construct bespoke websites while others adapt web-log templates such as Blogger or WordPress. Particularly productive are social-media platforms such as Facebook, Tumblr, Pinterest, MySpace and the microblogging site Twitter, around which communities cohere and which crowdsource user-generated content and collective identity. Here the nature of each site is created from such frameworks, often involving the posting of digitised artefacts from popular music culture as well as the assembly of communities of interest whose interactions define the parameters of meaning and what matters as memory – and indeed, what counts as music worth remembering. One way in which such sites evince their informal, non-professional status is in the conventions of expression, which are reproduced verbatim hereafter, not to mention the nature of how materials are presented, cited or preserved.

   Across platforms, online practice generally emulates the conventions of popular music in terms of its organisation and understanding. There are sites dedicated to specific artists and groups, for instance, those whose activities are long past – perhaps due to the death of key individuals. There are online sites dedicated to artists who have maintained lengthy careers and who continue to create new material, where their catalogue of work is supported and promoted by a corporate presence alongside and sometimes in tension with those created by fans. On Facebook alone, the British musician Paul Weller has an official page sanctioned by his record company for his first band The Jam and one for continuing work. These sit alongside fan sites such as The Jam: the Early Years or The Jam Society, a group for his subsequent outing in The Style Council, as well as pages that take an overview of his career, such as Weller World, Paul Weller: A British Institution or The Changing-man Through The Years Paul Weller.

In tandem with sites devoted to artists are groups organised around the music of particular time periods such as the Facebook page READY STEADY GO! 60s Bands/Artists. The rationale of such sites is evinced at Remembering the 50s, 60s, 70s & 80s + Music, which announces that music "holds a special memory for those of us who grew up with it. It was music you could Sing along with, music you Fell in Love with, and music you could Dance to." Such sites serve to underline normative discourses that understand and organise music in terms of discrete periods, ideas endorsed by generic categorisations such as the post-Punk years or the Disco era.

Many groups might dedicate themselves to collections of ephemera such as badges, flyers and so on, as well as the historical technologies of popular music such as cassette tapes or vinyl formats such as 45s or 78s. Then there are pages and groups devoted to defunct retail stores, chains and independents. These encompass the general and the particular: Record Shop Archive; Friends and Memories of "Tuckers Record Shop" on Market Square; Birmingham Record Shops 1970–1990; or Syracuse Record Store Memories, "a place to tell stories about stores like Spectrum, Desertshore, Modern Records, Oliver's, Record Theater, and any other place you think of. Please tell anyone you think might be interested to join and post." In such instances, members are invited to map the places where their music was encountered and purchased, and where they engaged with other music consumers, understanding themselves to be a part of a wider cultural community. Recalled and recorded are the everyday practices that were once integral to the constitution and understanding of popular music, now virtually lost as a result of digital retail, streaming and downloads.

Histories of musical periods, genres, places and spaces come together in communities constructed by those who belonged to particular subcultures in their youth, expressed in sites such as Teddy Boys/Girls 1954–present day, and Original Modernists 1959–1966. Many sites reflect the way in which music identities are often tied to geographical specificity (e.g. see Connell and Gibson 2003). These are often dedicated to particular venues, towns or indeed nations. There is, for instance, a considerable amount of online activity organised around Northern Soul music, a term coined by journalist Dave Godsin to refer to a kind of American R&B music popular in regular specialised events that took place in nightclubs and other venues in the Midlands and North of England from the late 1960s (see Wall 2006). These places include the much-mythologised Wigan Casino, which closed its doors in 1981, Golden Torch Club in Stoke-on-Trent (closed 1973), Twisted Wheel, Manchester (closed 1971) and Mecca, Blackpool (closed 1979). Dedicated Facebook sites that reinforce the totemic status and reassemble the habitués of each venue include The official Golden Torch Soul Club; BlackPool Mecca Appreciation Society; and I Went to Wigan Casino.

Members of online groups produce a form of community archive by uploading digital images of record sleeves, concert tickets, their personal photographs and varieties of official images from record-company publicity or from the music press and other sources. In the accretion of artefacts, such sites elicit the posting of memories, and the structuring feature of interaction is reciprocity as individuals respond to invitations to remember, evaluate or comment further by posting their own materials, questions and links. Thus, while many sites involve the posting of some highly original historical evidence, it is the memories of the membership that are the characteristic and most prodigious feature of such communities. Recollections online involve sharing encounters with specific pieces of music, performances, videos and the elaboration of what such things have meant to individual lives, in both private and public events.

POPULAR MUSIC, HISTORY AND ARCHIVAL PRACTICE

I have suggested the practices represented by the snapshot of sites detailed above take their cue from existing conventions of popular music. Sites are organised with reference to genre, era, scenes, subcultures, artists, geography and so on. I would argue the conventions of popular music as culture and as industry are imbued with a sense of history, memory, curatorial and archival practice, which might partly explain this activity. One wonders, in fact, whether any other field of popular culture is so conspicuously marked by the weight of the past across production, circulation and consumption. Here we could first point to the central organising principle of popular music, those things habitually referred to as the record: vinyl, tape, CD and digital compression files such as the MP3, as well as the capturing of the sound and image of musical events in film, TV and radio programs. The concept that there is a record of something comes from the fact that the history of music production has, for the most part, involved the capturing of artists performing in the studio much as they would do in a concert hall. As Michael Chanan (1995, 137–55) describes it, so much music is originated by technology that may or may not be part of a studio environment, presenting what is in effect a simulacrum of performance – as Baudrillard (2003, 5) would have it, a copy with no original.

Many aspects of popular music culture are characterised by curatorial practices. These manifest most obviously in the traditional notion of the record collection or in the way in which consumers log their attendance at concerts and their allegiance to artists, often evinced in the accretion of related merchandise. An analogue of the uses of the record collection is apparent in the simplest of online practices devoted to music of the past. Here, activity does not involve much beyond the posting and sharing of classic tunes, often in the form of YouTube video recordings of old 45s or albums spun on a turntable. The music as artefact is stripped of any contextual qualification beyond its core function. Typical in this regard is Prestons Northern Soultime, a group "for members to post and comment on there favourite northern tunes, ITS ALL ABOUT THE MUSIC, AND NOTHING ELSE."

The primacy of record collecting is sometimes expressed in completism, an objective that might involve the acquisition of every release by an artist or of a particular label's catalogue. Collecting and preservation take the mass-produced artefact, traditionally disdained for its cultural ephemerality, and grant it a new privilege and auratic quality. The value of the record collection is manifest in the figure of the modern DJ, whose status has shifted from mere cultural intermediary or gatekeeper of taste to creative performer in their own right. As Simon Reynolds (2011, 52) argues, DJ practice "confounds standard notions about creativity and authorship in pop music. ... The romantic figure of the creator [is] displaced by the curator." It is in the ownership of particular records and their display – on a shelf at home or heard from a turntable in a club – that affords DJs and other music consumers the authority of the archivist.

Not unconnected with the authority embodied in the dimensions of the consumer's music collection, whether manifested in vinyl or MP3 files or indeed in associated ephemera, is the manner in which the authority of cultural intermediaries such as journalists or DJs, whether of radio stations or club performers, is asserted through their historical knowledge of music, artists, places and indeed the parameters of canons of taste. In the role of reviewer, the critic reports on recordings and the live event, a witness to scenes, to the discovery of particular records and sounds, recognising important moments as such, so relating them to a potential audience and mediating what they might anticipate in their own encounters with pop. Any number of examples might be cited here, but to give one instance, this quality is captured in Greil Marcus's (2011) book on Van Morrison. Here, Marcus's interpretative authority comes from referencing the published works of this artist – the recordings – as well as his witness to concerts, which are also captured in a set of illicit recordings to which only a small number of people are likely to be privy. In total, the interpretation of Morrison as artist comes from a historical understanding of and witness to his work, of the waxing and waning of his creative abilities and his place in a wider narrative of popular music's meaning and canon. This historical sensibility and knowledge are echoed, too, in the everyday practices of fans, in the nature of record collections and their own sense of witness or participation in having purchased records at particular moments and attended concerts or clubs at a certain time.

While one would not wish to overstate the case at the expense of other themes, music itself is often imbued with tropes evincing memory practice. This is evoked in songs such as "Let's Twist Again (Like We Did Last Summer)," "Do You Remember Rock and Roll Radio?," "Summer of '69," "December 1963 (Oh What a Night)" and "In My Life." Songs might even attempt a self-consciously historical perspective – "We Didn't Start the Fire" or "Enola Gay," for example. Of course, in popular music the song lyric is an obvious means of consciously referring to the past, of what happened, where it happened and the associations of events and places, whether in a fictional or personally realist portrait. Nonetheless, memory and history are not only conveyed in song lyrics but also in the soundscapes of music compositions and in direct quotation, samples, pastiche and of course in cover versions.

For some commentators, the materiality of music as cultural product instills itself into memory as a result of its very consumption. In his lyrical mediation on the subject, Geoffrey O'Brien (2004) explores "pop music, memory and the imagined life," explaining how this character is not simply a result of the citation of the past in song. His is a familiar position, as he reflects: "No matter where the connection started – with Elvis or Bo Diddley or the Beatles ... the history of rock and roll inscribed itself in the nervous system of whoever passed through it, to persist years later as a network of potential responses and unbidden flashbacks" (2004, 159). Based on his own experience, he explores how impressionistic recollections of the past are subjectively connected with musical events: concerts, TV appearances and so on. Sometimes these associations come from music records, which at the time of the first encounter and in the moment of memory, interact with "the intricacies of your latest personal crisis" (2004, 159).

O'Brien's reflection also suggests a sixth and final point about historical practice and music. He wryly observes popular music was often understood to be ephemeral, it was not built to last. He writes:

> In the retrospect of anyone's life, the elements of the music track accumulate as promiscuously as the heap of records on the rug after a party. What those who attended this particular party couldn't have guessed was that the playlist would repeat for the next thirty years, tempering nostalgia with an echo of the old line: "How can I miss you if you won't go away?" (2004, 160).

While pop's endurance and place in personal and collective memory might be explained by recognition of its cultural significance, here O'Brien is thinking of how the music of the past is always present as a result of its regurgitation by music and entertainment industries. Dedicated oldies radio stations proliferate alongside adverts and films that make use of soundtracks that plunder the past. Then there are endless TV documentaries and retrospectives, not to mention dedicated channels such as Vintage TV, "a destination channel for music of quality and longevity; a vital, unique offering for those who grew up with the many vintage artists still touring and recording, and for younger audiences whose musical appreciation includes the best sounds of any decade" (Vintage TV, 2014).

O'Brien's analysis anticipates elements of the retromania identified by Simon Reynolds. Reynolds draws attention to the endless repackaging of the music of the past by the music business, an exploitation echoed in a wider heritage industry that includes tours by reformed bands, music tourism and the wending of pop into the museum. Online, the presence of the past sits alongside the present, and the continuum suggested by sites devoted to artists like Paul Weller, for instance, presents a conceptual question about where the past ends and the present begins in the digital realm, with projects announcing themselves or implicitly constituted as archive, history or heritage sites. How is one to make sense of the role and perspective of memory in relation to time, its passing, and the distance of and from what is recalled and by and for whom? For instance, some of those contributing to online sites share artefacts and memories from their original participation in music cultures of the past and from the perspective of their history of consumption. Alongside those who were witness to the past, younger music consumers come to such sites, where available artefacts and memories constitute resources for their own sense of culture and the meanings that music has for them.

The co-presence of past and present in music production, circulation and consumption is not unlike that in other cultural spheres such as literature or film – although, to reiterate, one wonders whether the presence of the past is as overt as it is here. As a result, I would suggest the nature of DIY archives and heritage projects dedicated to the field of popular music invites some reflection in terms of the commercial demands of the industries that have produced, and indeed curate, the core of this culture.

THE ECONOMY OF ONLINE COMMUNITY MUSIC ARCHIVES AND HERITAGE

The acme of the music archive lies in the warehouses and vaults of labels, publishers, distributors and artists themselves, a resource intended to generate a profit. The purpose of this archive is fully realised in platforms and services such as Spotify or the Apple iTunes Store and the long-tail economic model described by Chris Anderson (2006). Alongside films and so on, the iTunes United Kingdom store offers "37 million high-quality, DRM-free songs on iTunes for just 59p, 79p or 99p each. ... Buy on any device and your songs are instantly accessible in your iTunes library on your Mac or PC" (Apple 2014). Nonetheless, such riches and apparent income streams for the industry from the archive belie the fact that a significant amount of music is simply not available. As Louis Barfe (2004) observes, while some material seems to have been available since its day of release, "many deleted gems are locked in archives, unheard and quite possibly deteriorating, while original vinyl copies change hands for obscene money."

Barfe's comments are useful for underlining the sense of the power of the archive and how power over it is exerted. What is available, obscured or discarded is the preserve of the industries that originated the majority of what has counted as the central objects and meanings of popular music culture. Nonetheless, while community archives are about many aspects of popular music culture, much online activity is devoted to sharing its sound. In the types of sites explored in this chapter, community members post links to recordings hosted by platforms such as YouTube, Soundcloud or Spotify. These recordings include official and unofficial releases – material only available on ancient vinyl, for instance, or even bootlegs of material from the vaults or captured in live performances.

Making use of file-sharing sites such as Rapidshare or Mediafire, online sites invite the wrath of the owners of the intellectual property they make available. Thus it is not unusual to come across statements such as "Attachment Unavailable. This attachment may have been removed or the person who shared it may not have permission to share it with you." At The Jam Society, one of the groups devoted to Paul Weller's work, an administrator advises, "I've been 'asked' by someone at Universal to point out that the uploading of bootlegs/recording from any source … is illegal and that it will prosecute anyone found participating. I'm just the friendly messenger."

In spite of potential injunctions, the nature of user activities evinces an ignorance and disregard for issues of intellectual property rights and the commodity status of music. As one bemused poster at a Facebook group for Birmingham Bogarts, a site devoted to a former club venue, complains to the group after being reprimanded and blocked from certain pages by Facebook: "the punishment seems rather hard – how can old songs from 30+ years ago upset anyone now in 2014?" Ultimately, such attitudes and the treatment of music as collective property emerge from the attachment to it felt by individuals. As Rodman and Vanderdonckt (2008, 246) note in their analysis of music file-sharing, arguments about illegality fail to comprehend how "music routinely circulates through the culture in myriad ways that have little (if anything) to do with commerce and capitalism." They suggest that what is circulated in such activities are not commodities or things understood to be someone's property but instead "a set of affectively charged social relationships" (2008, 248). A fan's impulse to buy music is closely linked in a circuit of reciprocity with others. What one purchases is what one tells others about; what others share in turn prompts one's own further purchases. To this one might add the impulse to share music of the past and the associated artefacts one has preserved, as well as one's memories about encounters with bands, venues, concerts and so on. Through the affective charge of the relationship of consumers with music, one can understand something of the particularity of online DIY work as heritage, history or archive, which might also speak to something of the world of offline community activity.

Archivists, museum curators and historians no doubt have a love of their work and may well be attached to the artefacts under their care or the objects of their studies. However, notwithstanding the issue of whether sharing is a vocational motivation, such is the rational nature of professional decorum that the emotional qualities of such work are rarely articulated, at least in official discourse. The opposite is the case among the communities of DIY popular music archives and heritage, where emotional attachments are the key feature of their origination, construction and engagement. Such sites are best described, as Ann Cvetkovich (2003, 244) notes, as "repositories of feelings." The essence of this quality is captured in one assessment of the Manchester District Music Archive, which suggests it is "exactly what the internet was made for, *a labour of love* that couldn't exist in any other medium" (Big Chip Awards 2014).

Alongside the democratic qualities of the communities outlined in this chapter, there is something about the value of the love evinced around the affective archive that in turn underwrites economic returns. Some of the characteristic activity I have in mind here is piecemeal, linked to another mode of DIY in the form of enterprises that serve to remind us of pop's status as product and the value of heritage as industry. For instance, a range of sites devoted to memorialising club venues advertise "revival" nights, bringing together original club-goers with the aim of recreating the ambience and authenticity of clubs through the provision of particular playlists (and sometimes even DJs) for a fee. As is evident in activity devoted to figures like Paul Weller, the myriad related "pro-am" (Leadbeater and Miller 2004) tribute bands fulfill a similar function (see Homan 2006). The heritage experience of such acts is apparent in online discussions of the memories they prompt, an experience that is in turn memorialised in the sharing of related materials with ticket stubs and live recordings attesting to the economic value of this activity.

Of course, long before digitisation, music fans shared their passion for vinyl, cassette or memorabilia for a price, as evidenced by the robust market for second-hand recordings. In fact, this market has created versions of digital archives in areas of online trading sites such as eBay, which offers organising categories that include Music; Cassettes; CDs; Digital Music Downloads; Records; Music Memorabilia; and "Other Formats." Enterprising income-generation sometimes connects with community archives in formal and informal ways, an interaction evidenced on the Facebook page "One Chord Wonders – The 1970s UK Punk & New Wave Archives." With over 1,500 individuals registering their "likes" for the page and several hundred posting comments on the past it represents – "the Graduating class of 76," as one post puts it – the site is linked to a trader of the same name at Discogs, where the page's owner sells and buys music and related ephemera.

Discogs, which began as a hobby project for its creator, may be the apotheosis of the historical impulse of popular music culture in relation to record collecting. A self-conscious sense of curation is invoked in the site's title and its deployment of a definition of discography: "The study and cataloguing of phonograph records. A comprehensive list of the recordings made by a particular performer or of a particular composer's works"

(Discogs, 2014). Primarily a marketplace, its aim is also to compile a user-generated music database of the entirety of recorded music, a project to be fulfilled by the kinds of crowdsourcing evinced across the online world and the particular interests and dedication demonstrated in the DIY sites of popular music archiving and memory. Such activities and the ambition to generate knowledge lie on a continuum with overtly commercial objectives illustrated by applications such as Songkick. Alongside its primary objective of selling concert tickets, Songkick is an enterprise that aims also to record the live music experiences of its users. Reaching back to the 1960s, it has thus far documented over one million events, which will "put every single concert or festival that's ever happened online" (Songkick 2014). Such examples point to a synergistic relationship between online archives – and other forms of online activities, of course – and the music industries and, most importantly, those entities that make available the platforms for both digital commerce and DIY activities. Wolfgang Ernst (2013, 11) suggests, for instance, the storage capabilities of the Internet, its accretion and recirculation of material, are "a part of a memory economy." This expression of the logic of late capitalism points to the fact that, however potentially transgressive affective DIY online activities might be in appropriating intellectual property, they are built in spaces belonging to vested interests and from an incredible amount of voluntary labour. Such labour contributes directly to the value of enterprises like Songkick and, to a degree yet to be quantified, to generating interest in the available music of the past and enduring artists. Of course, the quality and quantity of activity online, whatever its nature, are vital to the businesses behind the online infrastructure in generating demographic data and supporting advertising-driven models. As Facebook helpfully explains, "A business creates an ad. They choose the type of audience they'd like to reach. If you're in that audience, Facebook shows you the ad" (Facebook 2014). One is tempted to suggest that in this economy, there is something for everyone so none might escape.

CONCLUSIONS

Ernst (2013, 5) suggests, "What in public discourse … is frequently called the 'archive' turns out to be, in most cases, a most imprecise metaphor for all sorts of collections and memory." This is an apt description of the kinds of practices outlined in this chapter, which might cause some to question their status as anything meaningful at all. Self-identified and labeled as archives, history, heritage or memory sites, or overtly dealing in related practices, we might ask what kind of durable resources they offer. As is apparent from the thousands of people who participate in creating this prodigious array of sites, they offer something meaningful to them and something of significance is signaled by this variety. Yet, considered in terms of usability and in light of the informal, unsystematic manner in which they are often arranged and present themselves to users, these might prove to be challenging should scholars look to employ them for insights into fandom, consumption practices, lived experiences and so on.

These sites clearly suggest an interesting and dynamic relationship with the originators of popular music, which gives the community archive a potentially unstable status. Chun (2011), by way of Derrida, suggests that the association of the archive with law, command and social order, in terms of its transformation from private to public space, is key to understanding the impact of new media. For her, the digital has "made certain archives more accessible by increasing the 'domiciles' in which they – or copies of them – can be kept, spreading democracy by compromising privacy" (2011, 100). The owners of intellectual property might provide a different description of what happens to the circulation of music and, indeed, the appropriation of other materials and manipulation of the nature of the image of certain artists online. While such things might happen offline and certainly predate the digital age, the instant availability of a Facebook group to millions or the endless reproducibility of a sound file are of a different order to the analogue world. A struggle over the ownership of memory and the archive is signalled by every cease-and-desist notice and website or social-media page closed by order.

The issue of sustainability is further identified by Chun (2011), who highlights the way in which the nature of the digital needs to be scrutinised for its efficacy in generating and sustaining archival work. As she explains, digital media appear to offer the preservation of analog media, as witnessed across YouTube, for instance: "Many users, blind to the limitations of electromagnetic materials, assume that one can actually 'store' things in memory" (2011, 137). The assumption is data saved on DVDs, hard drives and the Cloud will endure, "that disk failure and the loss of memory it threatens are accidents instead of eventualities" (2011, 137). Thus, while the digital might offer a utopian vision of democracy and communality, any DIY – or, for that matter, any official preservation – activity online is also tasked with the perennial business of the archivist in evaluating what counts, what is to be stored and to what uses might be put such materials.

The thousands of sites hinted at here contain endless accounts of everyday lives lived with popular music, of personal and personalised artefacts – photographs, diaries, posters, fanzines, letters, ephemera – digitised and then shared. The affective relationships demonstrated by this preservation and sharing testify to the value of pop music for a great many people's personal and social sense of history. This collective endeavour demands further recognition and exploration, if only to ask how we might archive the archive itself.

NOTE

1. Titles and esoteric spellings are reproduced verbatim.

REFERENCES

Anderson, C. 2006. *The long tail: Why the future of business is selling less of more.* New York: Hyperion.

Apple 2014. iTunes features. Accessed December 1, 2014. https://www.apple.com/uk/itunes/features.

Ashton, P. and Kean, H., eds. 2009. *Public history and heritage today: People and their pasts.* Basingstoke: Palgrave.

Baker, S. and Huber, A. 2013. Notes towards a typology of the DIY institution: Identifying do-it-yourself places of popular music preservation. *European Journal of Cultural Studies* 16(5): 513–30.

Barfe, L. 2004. Head to head: Music copyright. Accessed December 1, 2014. http://news.bbc.co.uk/1/hi/3547788.stm.

Baudrillard, J. 2003 (1994). *Simulacra and simulation.* Trans. S. Glaser. Ann Arbor, MI: University of Michigan Press.

Big Chip Awards 2014. Best Not for Profit Project. Accessed December 1, 2014. http://www.bigchipawards.com/BNFPP2014.

Chanan, M. 1995. *Repeated takes: A short history of recording and its effects on music.* London: Verso.

Chun, W. 2011. *Programmed visions: Software and memory.* Cambridge, MA: MIT Press.

Collins, J. and Long, P. 2014. Online archival practice and virtual sites of musical memory. In L. Roberts, M. Leonard, S. Cohen and R. Knifton, eds., *Sites of popular music heritage.* Abingdon: Routledge, 81–96.

Connell, J. and Gibson, C. 2003. *Soundtracks: Popular music, identity and place.* London: Routledge.

Cook, T. 2013. Evidence, memory, identity, and community: Four shifting archival paradigms. *Archival Science* 13(2–3): 95–120.

Cvetkovich, A. 2003. *An archive of feelings.* Durham, NC: Duke University Press.

Derrida, J. 1995. *Archive fever: A Freudian impression.* Trans. Eric Prenowitz. Chicago: University of Chicago Press.

Discogs 2014. About. Accessed December 3, 2014. http://www.discogs.com/about.

Edgerton, G.R. and Rollins, P.C., eds. 2001. *Television histories: Shaping collective memory in the media age.* Lexington, KT: University Press of Kentucky.

Ernst, W. 2013. Aura and temporality: The insistence of the Archive. Text of the keynote lecture of the conference The Anarchival Impulse in the Uses of the Image in Contemporary Art, organized by the University of Barcelona. Accessed December 3, 2014. http://www.macba.cat/en/quaderns-portatils-wolfgang-ernst.

Facebook 2014. About Facebook ads. Accessed December 3, 2014. https://www.facebook.com/about/ads.

Flinn, A. 2007. Community histories, community archives: some opportunities and challenges. *Journal of the Society of Archivists* 28(2): 151–76.

Hewison, R. 1987. *The heritage industry: Britain in a climate of decline.* London: Methuen.

Homan, S. 2006. *Access all eras: Tribute bands and global pop culture.* Maidenhead: Open University Press.

Huyssen, A. 2003. *Present pasts: Urban palimpsests and the politics of memory.* Palo Alto, CA: Stanford University Press.

Kean, H., Martin, P. and Morgan, S., eds. 2000. *Seeing history: Public history now in Britain*. London: Francis Boutle.

Leadbeater, C. and Miller, P. 2004. *The pro-am revolution*. London: Demos.

Manoff, M. 2004. Theories of the archive from across the disciplines. *Portal: Libraries and the Academy* 4(1): 9–25.

Marcus, G. 2011. *Listening to Van Morrison*. London: Faber and Faber.

O'Brien, G. 2004. *Sonata for jukebox: Pop music, memory, and the imagined life*. New York: Counterpoint.

Plate, L. and Smelik, A. 2009. *Technologies of memory in the arts*. Basingstoke: Palgrave Macmillan.

Reynolds, S. 2011. *Retromania: Pop culture's addiction to its own past*. London: Faber and Faber.

Roberts, L. and Cohen, S. 2013. Unauthorising popular music heritage: Outline of a critical framework. *International Journal of Heritage Studies* 19(1), 1–21.

Roberts, L., Leonard, M., Cohen, S. and Knifton, R., eds. 2015. *Sites of popular music heritage*. London: Routledge.

Rodman, G.B. and Vanderdonckt, C. 2006. Music for nothing or, I want my MP3: The regulation and recirculation of affect. *Cultural Studies* 20(2–3): 245–61.

Schultz, L. 2008. Foreword. In G. Kirsch and E. Rohan, eds. *Beyond the archives: Research as a lived process*. Carbondale, IL: Southern Illinois University Press, vi–x.

Songkick 2014. About Songkick. Accessed December 1, 2014. http://www.songkick.com.

Steedman, C. 2001. Something she called a fever: Michelet, Derrida, and dust. *American Historical Review* 106(4): 1159–80.

Steedman, C. 2011. After the archive. *Comparative Critical Studies* 8 (2–3), 321–40.

Van House, N. and Churchill, E.F. 2008. Technologies of memory: Key issues and critical perspectives. *Memory Studies*, 1: 295–310.

Vintage TV 2014. About Vintage TV. Accessed December 1, 2014. http://www.vintage.tv/about.

Wall, T. 2006. Out on the floor: The politics of dancing on the Northern Soul scene. *Popular Music* 25: 431–45.

6 Doing-it-Together

Public History-Making and Activist Archiving in Online Popular Music Community Archives

Jez Collins

Websites relating to cultural heritage, community archives, and everyday histories are proliferating online, democratising our understanding, approach and access to traditional history and archive collections. The archives are created and curated by activist archivists who employ participatory methods such as crowdsourcing and user-generated content (UGC) to build, preserve and share collections. This chapter explores activist archiving and public history-making in a number of participatory popular music archive sites related to popular music histories of Birmingham in the United Kingdom, and argues the activities taking place online go beyond the notion of do-it-yourself (DIY). Rather, the practices of building and sustaining alternative popular music histories and archives explored here can more evocatively be thought of as doing-it-together (DIT).

In what follows, I present a definition of activist archivists, and look at how this idea has emerged from academic literature on social and public history and community archive disciplines. I examine how new technologies have disrupted the established archive profession and, through the prism of contemporary archival theory, I explore how scholars and practitioners are responding to these challenges and opportunities. Building on this analysis, I then explore how activist archiving and public history-making practices manifest themselves in a number of online sites that focus on the city of Birmingham in the United Kingdom. I conclude by suggesting that sites of self-authorised popular music heritage and unauthorised popular music heritage practices (Roberts and Cohen 2014) that employ a bottom-up, participatory approach can be seen to represent the emergence of a DIT model in the online construction of alternative music histories, heritage and archives.

THEORISING ACTIVIST ARCHIVISTS, PUBLIC HISTORY-MAKING AND COMMUNITY ARCHIVES

Archives and their attendant communities share a complex and interlinked relationship with ideas of history. Cook (2013) recently laid out a theoretical framework to analyse the evolution of the archival profession. Cook names these four evolutionary stages in terms of their individual characteristics:

evidence; memory; identity; and community. Of interest to me here is Cook's fourth evolutionary stage, community, which concerns the rapid growth in digital technologies and the advancement of the Internet. This, Cook states, is democratising archival practices, allowing for a broad range of individuals, communities and organisations to come together in order to document, preserve, share and promote community identity through shared histories and heritage. Cook (2013, 113) highlights the countless "lobbying groups, community archives and 'ordinary' citizens joining together" in online communities of practice (Wenger 1999) and interest (Castells 2002).

The word "community" has many different interpretations, connotations and meanings, but for the purpose of this chapter I draw on Flinn and Stevens's (2008) understanding of community in the context of the archive: "By community archives we mean any collection of material that documents one or many aspects of a community's heritage, collected in, by and for that community and looked after by its members." Community is thus understood in this chapter as those spaces inhabited by individuals who coalesce in and around online sites that are anchored by music activity and geographic location (and are thus specific to place), and how the originators of and contributors to such sites and activities define and identify themselves.

In his study of independent and community-led archives and more formal institutions, Flinn (2011, 1, 8) describes the approach to archiving and history-making as an active and activist practice that can be seen as a "reproach and challenge" to the mainstream. The characteristics Flinn notes lend support to the earlier work of Howard Zinn (1977), in which activist archivists were called on to "compile a whole new world of documentary material about the lives, desires and needs of the ordinary people" (Zinn, quoted in Johnson 2001, 213). This call has also been echoed by social and public historians (Kean and Ashton 2009; Lipstiz 2001; Rosenzweig and Thelen 1998). Samuel (1994) highlights a number of amateur individuals, groups, associations and clubs that have been instrumental in our understanding of historical practices. Samuel claims these amateurs and their work should cause us to rethink our approach to history-making, and argues (1994, 8, 17) that history is "a social form of knowledge, the work, in any given instance, of a thousand different hands," and if "history was thought of as an activity rather than a profession, then the number of practitioners would be legion." This approach challenges the "unspoken assumption that knowledge filters downwards" (2004, 4) by embracing the public and personal actions of everyday people into different histories, shared among themselves.

Participation is central. Theimer (2012), in unpacking the meaning of participatory archives and their role in the wider archive field, has stated that technology has blurred the barriers of the archive profession, thus allowing individuals and communities to move from being passive consumers to active agents in archival activities, whether in institutional archives or in the creation of their own archive sites. Theimer (2012) defines a participatory archive as an "organization, site or collection in which people other than the archive professionals contribute knowledge or resources resulting in increased appreciation and understanding of archival materials and archives, usually in an online environment." Theimer's discussion sits alongside those of Flinn, Cook and Samuel to demonstrate there is an ongoing, evolving working-through within the academy and profession about the terminology that is employed when describing such a broad range of activities relating to a wide constituency of practitioners. The ideas briefly touched on here encompass ideas of community, sharing and active participation in the construction of everyday histories, suggesting a slightly more subtle and nuanced definition of the DIY practices I will examine next, which I will define as doing-it-together (DIT).

DESTINATION BIRMINGHAM: A MUSIC CITY?

Birmingham is the United Kingdom's second most populous city. Lying at the geographical heart of the country, the city was built on heavy industry, manufacturing and light engineering. Because of its industrial heritage, a sizeable proportion of the population is made up of migrant communities who have introduced a broad range of cultures to the city. The city's musical output has garnered not only local and national attention but also global success. Notable among these musicians are Black Sabbath and Ozzy Osbourne, Duran Duran, Robert Plant and John Bonham, UB40, Steel Pulse, Joan Armatrading, The Streets, The Electric Light Orchestra, The Move and jazz musician Andy Hamilton.

Recent initiatives have led to an ongoing reappraisal of the city of Birmingham's music heritage by a wide range of interested parties, most noticeably Birmingham City Council, which instigated a policy scrutiny review of this field in 2012. The review asked the following questions: What role can and does popular music play in improving perceptions of Birmingham, both in attracting visitors to the city and in enhancing the quality of life of residents? And how can this role be strengthened in Birmingham? (Birmingham City Council 2012, 7). While the review spoke of the potential economic benefits that a vibrant and integrated music industry could bring to the city, it also highlighted the culturally diverse nature of the city's music and communities and the role music heritage could play "in terms of benefits to the community and building civic pride" (2012, 67).

One recent initiative was B-Side Brum, a campaign that sought to create a "virtual 20-track album which reflects the diversity of music that originates from the [West Midlands] region" (Visit Birmingham 2014). The campaign was initiated by Visit Birmingham, part of the city's strategic marketing partnership and run by the Liquid PR agency. The campaign sought the involvement of the public in voting for the song(s) they felt best represented Birmingham. To vote, individuals had to register their choice on the B-Side Brum website or on Twitter via the hashtag #BSideBrum. This long list was then discussed and debated by an expert panel (including this author), which whittled down the choices into a final top twenty. This crowdsourced campaign, "To celebrate the past, present and future," is just one small example of how institutions and organisations are using online capabilities to engage with communities around music heritage activities. While there is not an intention on behalf of the organisers to create an archive, respondents have posted pictures of themselves with record sleeves of their favourite artists, linking YouTube videos of their favourite songs and using other materials drawn from personal archives or from the vast amount of material recovered from the Internet that celebrates Birmingham music.

This latest interest in Birmingham's music heritage was reignited by a number of projects, some in the form of physical exhibitions, others in the digital environment. These projects include Soho Rd to the Punjab, Home of Metal (see Chapter 2, this volume); Birmingham Music Heritage; and the author's own Birmingham Popular Music Archive. While these projects have garnered differing levels of public attention and may be considered as authorised and/or self-authorised music heritage practices (Roberts and Cohen 2014), they sit alongside a plethora of unauthorised sites on social media and local interest and history forums. As I discuss below, there are a variety of approaches to building each archive and to addressing and building community across these sites.

AUTHORISED AND SELF-AUTHORISED BIRMINGHAM MUSIC HERITAGE AND ARCHIVE ONLINE SITES

In order to analyse my examples, I draw on Roberts's and Cohen's (2014, 242) recent work, which has developed a "critical and analytical framework through which to explore popular music heritage ... and the ways in which it is practised, discussed and understood." Roberts and Cohen (2014, 243, emphasis in original) highlight three types of popular music heritage activity that are closely related: "*officially authorized, self-authorized* and *unauthorized*." Officially authorised heritage tends to be that which is sanctioned and endorsed by government bodies and agencies that bestow legitimacy on such activities. Self-authorised heritage mirrors official practices but without recourse to the full support or sanction of government bodies and agencies. Roberts and Cohen (2014, 248) argue that these activities are developed "by musicians, audiences, entrepreneurs and organisations who participate in particular musical cultures." Finally, they state unauthorised popular music heritage practices are concerned with, among other things, everyday practice and individual and cultural memory. Furthermore, this type of practice "does not draw attention to itself; indeed, for the most part it gets by without even an awareness that it is heritage" (2014, 257). In this chapter, I argue that self-authorised and unauthorised online sites of popular music practice – sites that employ a variety of platforms, some purpose built, others characterised by a use of ready-made social media templates such as WordPress, Twitter and Facebook – are enabling a DIT model of popular music histories, heritage and archives to emerge.

Soho Road to the Punjab

Funded via the Heritage Lottery Fund (HLF), the national grant-giving organisation of Heritage in the United Kingdom (Heritage Lottery Fund n.d.), Soho Road to the Punjab centres on the documentation of music activity related to the genre of Bhangra but is simultaneously a response to the exclusion of migrant experiences from the official history and archive discourse that Hall (2001), Samuel (1994), Flinn and Stevens (2009) and other scholars have identified. The project does not fully engage with emerging participatory models for building communities online. Rather, the approach has been relatively conservative in that it has brought together a selection of significant artists and artefacts, underwritten by the perspectives of a set of nominated experts or "Champions" (e.g. see Dudrah, Chana and Talwar 2007) to provide a multiplicity of narratives. Soho Road to the Punjab, then, has elements of DIT in its focus on the celebration of the ethnic and music communities that identify with the genre of Bhangra. However, it could be argued it does so in a way that creates a canon of Birmingham Bhangra.

Birmingham Music Heritage

Also funded by the HLF, Birmingham Music Heritage (BMH) focuses on Birmingham music between the years 1965 and 1985. The site invites visitors to share and submit photographs of bands and venues from this period, and has sought the help of the community by soliciting volunteers to "capture the memories and stories from some of the actual people who helped pioneer Birmingham's music industry, the venues key to its success, and an insight into the musicians and music they produced with the influence from the city's culture on their sound" (BMH n.d.). Through a spin-off community project called Soho Melody: A Way of Life, BMH has sought to bring people together in order to tell the stories of music-making and activity, this time from the inner-city suburb of Handsworth. BMH focused on bringing together specific geographical and temporal communities, rather than any particular music genre, in order to explore aspects of Birmingham's music heritage.

Home of Metal

Home of Metal (HoM) is another HLF-funded project. It is an online archive of memorabilia and stories organised around the five bands who are synonymous with the heavy metal genre (Black Sabbath, Led Zeppelin, Judas Priest, Napalm Death, Godflesh) and were from Birmingham and the Black Country, the surrounding area more commonly known as the West

Midlands. The activities of the digital archive also supported the creation of a physical exhibition at the Birmingham Museum and Art Gallery in 2011. The HoM calls on the citizens of Birmingham and the Black Country to "celebrate what is rightfully theirs, to claim the city and the region as the birthplace of 'Heavy Metal'" (Home of Metal, n.d.). Invoking a spirit of DIT, HoM calls on the heavy-metal community from the city and further afield to help it build capacity and sustainability, and "to share their passion for Heavy Metal and contribute stories and memorabilia by uploading images, sound files and film footage. WE NEED YOU to contribute to the archive with your Heavy Metal related wares, playing a part in securing our identity as the Home of Metal" (Home of Metal n.d.). As a result, several hundred user-generated digitised contributions are listed, ranging from personal photographs and rare promotional shots of bands during their formative years through to fan memorabilia such as badges and T-shirts.

Birmingham Music Archive

Following a research and development grant from the Arts Council England, the Birmingham Music Archive (BMA) site was established by this author. It captures the established democratic potential of online culture in a way that attempts to portray the scope of the city's popular music heritage through a DIT philosophy. Addressing the people of Birmingham as a whole, it asks its users to "tell us what you know, tell us what you think" (BMA 2008), encouraging them to contribute to building and shaping the archive. The approach is an exploratory and open one, and there are no set parameters for what should or should not be included: "We aren't just interested in the 'star' names. We want to hear about ALL the music activity in the city" (BMA 2008). Nonetheless, the site does suggest a structure for popular music culture, with users asked to recall bands/musicians; DJs/club nights/promoters; exhibitions; fashion/shops; managers; press/fanzines; radio stations; record labels; record shops; recording studios/rehearsal spaces and venues. With a view to the kinds of artefact that capture music culture, BMA evinces an awareness of how

> music provides us with memories, individual and shared experiences and self-expression. For us, these memories and meanings can be stirred by a vast array of music ephemera, it could be a song, it might be a photograph or a ticket stub or it could be someone else's recollections that make a connection with you and trigger your music experiences (BMA 2008).

The BMA appeals to the broadest sense of community: to anyone who identifies with the city of Birmingham, eschewing boundaries such as genre, ethnicity or timelines. The response to this DIT approach to the archive has resulted in hundreds of digitised materials being generated on 613 entry pages, with 4,315 comments being posted on the site. Physical materials are also increasingly turning up on the author's doorstep.

Alongside the reproductions of physical things, it is ultimately the pro-digious volume of memories captured that gives breadth and depth to the archive and articulates the voice and concerns of the community. When taken in isolation, the posts on the BMA can often appear scrappy or throwaway in nature, seemingly written without care or consideration – for instance, posts like "Remember seeing Spear of Destiny here. Good live act" (Hardware 2014) or "SCREAMING LORD SUTCH"[1] (Gilbert 2014). A closer reading of such comments, though, reveals these posts can be under-stood as memory texts that prompt, and indeed answer, questions posed by the community on the site. And so "SCREAMING LORD SUTCH" is not merely a random evocation of the 1960s/1970s R&B/novelty act but a response to the appeal of the BMA on a page devoted to the live music events that took place at a particular venue: "Our aim is to build a complete list of gigs at Aston University. Here's a start but we need your help!" (BMA 2010). Alongside digital images of posters used to advertise gigs at the Guild of Students at Aston University, the community – anchored here around a physical space of popular music activity – has responded by listing over 150 live events, some with exact dates, others just recollections of bands seen. The community members, who comprise ex-students, student-union staff and assorted interlopers, enter into conversation with each other. For example, posters discuss the merits of bands like The Cure: "If I remember rightly, had just fallen out with their record label (Polydor?), so refused to do any of their songs, thrashing at their instruments in a kind of free-style jazz/thrash" (Tom 2012); or Blur: "Blur played in the Guild one Freshers week or possibly May Ball around 1994-ish. I thought they were toilet" (Sleight 2013). For all posters, recalling such events is revisiting their past: "I remember seeing Pink Floyd for free. A group of us Mothers regulars man-aged to sweet talk the bloke on the door. He must have pitied us penniless working class hippies from Handsworth" (Kay 2014).

On a page dedicated to another club, Barbarellas, individual histories are shared, creating what Ketelaar (2005, 54) calls a "community of memory." He goes on to say this common past is not something easily ignored but more "a moral imperative for one's belonging to a community … which involves an embeddedness in its past and, consequently, in the memory texts through which that past is mediated." Recalling the days of punk, one poster writes:

> Remember my good friend Graham "Banner" Bannister being dragged out of Barbs by the police. We were queuing up to get into some con-cert or other (there seemed to be a brilliant gig every week) and a crowd of bored lads decided it would be a good idea to walk over a car parked outside the club, banner included. The car was quickly dam-aged. It turns out it belonged to an employee of the club. The police were called and Banner, at 6 foot daft, was quickly pointed out. So many memories of the place.
>
> (Sean 2012)

In response to this, another poster claims:

> Jeepers, think that car walking escapade included me, If i recall also tried to smash the window of some tyre company on the corner of Cumbernauld st/broad st and later tried pulling over the statues we passed as we went into city centre – not proud now ... it was the zeitgeist ... anarchy n all that. of the time, well that's my excuse and i'm sticking to it.

(Robinson 2012)

The nature of authorship here is thus based upon autobiography structured by music culture ("I was there"), one seeking to connect the individual with a community that might confirm if not the subjective claim entirely at least the basis for the recollection ("I was there too"). References to the specifics of local and specialised knowledge – about also-rans, streets, scenes, sounds and sites – offer a layering and detailed texturing of activity in the city and the places in which music was sought out and experienced: the embeddedness in *their* community.

These funded and part-funded projects can be understood as authorised and self-authorised sites, intentionally created by activist archivists interested in the popular music of Birmingham. They call, with differing approaches and results, for individuals and communities to come together to populate, celebrate and share their popular music histories and heritage through the uploading of what Marion Leonard (2007) terms "the material objects of popular music" through crowdsourced and user-generated methods. This approach suggests a subtle difference from what have previously been labelled as DIY practices, instead pushing us to think in more collaborative terms of something we might call doing-it-together – the collective work of building alternate popular music histories, heritage and archives.

UNAUTHORISED BIRMINGHAM MUSIC SITES OF POPULAR MUSIC HERITAGE

If the above sites were created with a specific intention and sense of purpose, I now turn to sites that may be understood as unauthorised or informal sites of music archive and history formation where individuals come together, enter into discussion and share materials associated with popular music culture. I focus primarily on the activities taking place on Facebook, but I note popular music also features on a number of sites that have as their basis a broader approach to the construction and remembrance of community histories. Sites such as Retrowow, Grapevine Birmingham and Birmingham History Forum harvest a wealth of interest and contributions on popular music in the city.

Birmingham History Forum

Birmingham History Forum is organised around a set of defined categories: family, industrial, religion, transport and so on. One of these categories is dedicated to Birmingham Entertainment, and it has a sub-category entitled Birmingham Nightclubs. Here a sizeable community has formed that discusses and uploads material related to its members' own and others' musical and cultural activity in the city. In just one thread, a discussion was started with the question: "Anyone got any memories and information about nightclubs in Brum, from any time last century?" (Mazbeth 2005). Begun in 2005, nine years on the community continues to add to the 114 pages of comments. Over 1,700 people have engaged with this discussion, with respondents entering into a process of exploration and recollection with one another to create what van Dijck (2006, 369) calls "explicit memory narratives" that "directly bespeak musical memory as it relates to personal and group identity."

Facebook Groups

But it is Facebook, especially group pages, that best exemplifies how social media platforms enable users to create and share prodigious amounts of content relating to popular music through social networks and participatory online communities of interest. As Facebook announces, groups are "for people to share their common interests and express their opinion. Groups allow people to come together around a common cause, issue or activity to organize, express objectives, discuss issues, post photos and share related content" (Pineda 2010). Facebook groups concerned with Birmingham music and music culture are numerous, and take a broad focus. Groups have been created for artists, genres, club nights, record shops and the physical buildings of popular music activity, as well as the time periods of such activities. For example, Birmingham Night Clubs in the 70's & 80's (Facebook 2014d) echoes the example from the BHM. Below, I highlight just a small sample of the communities found on Facebook, and suggest that, through their actions, a model of DIT is manifested in their approach to building, celebrating and sharing popular music histories.

Alongside official musician and band Facebook groups, which are verified and identified by Facebook's blue badge logo (Facebook 2014a), are the unofficial groups created and populated by fans. Unsurprisingly, the groups associated with Black Sabbath and the individual musicians who constitute the group are manifold. Black Sabbath (Facebook's ONLY, COMPLETE BLACK SABBATH Page) (Facebook 2014f), a group with 69,657 members at the time of writing, makes the claim that it is *the* fan site for the band: "DO NOT BE FOOLED BY OTHER 'SABBATH' FACEBOOK PAGES." This exists, and is sustained, through the efforts of the community of "many other die-hard Sabbath fans." The Global Black Sabbath Convention (Facebook 2014h), a group with 6,533 members, states that its aims are "purely for fans to celebrate all the eras, which we know as Black Sabbath. Our intention is to hold conventions, where there will be events, concerts, and regular conventions throughout the globe. ... We envision a grand stage where all Sabbath Lovers can hang out have a good time and Jam!!!"

Other groups focus on the physical buildings that were home to music activity in the city. Birmingham Bogarts (Facebook 2014c), for example – a group of 513 members – is dedicated to a rock club in the city from the 1970s that played host to the Sex Pistols in 1976. This group focuses on "Memories of bands you saw, the music you listened to, the dj's and people. No place like it since." The 654 members of the group Birmingham Odeon Memorial (Facebook 2014e) celebrate the cinema and live-music venue that was located on the same street as Bogarts and that was for many years regarded as the major venue in Birmingham. The group describes itself with the following statement: "Ah, the Odeon. The best gig venue Birmingham ever had. ... So, reminisce, post your photos and thoughts related to the Odeon and maybe one day, someone will see sense and re open it as a theatre once again." Responding to the provocation to reminisce and post photographs, one member of the community has posted digital scans of four ticket stubs relating to Black Sabbath Odeon gigs (Michelson 2014). The scans act as a prompt for other members to then engage in a discussion around Sabbath, recalling details such as what support acts played, the lineup of the band, the layout of the venue and adding other Sabbath gig dates. While this is just one example, such exchanges are typical of the types of activities that take place across similar Facebook groups that my research suggests number into the hundreds and possibly thousands.

Across these unauthorised sites of Birmingham music heritage, there are familiar aims and approaches to the construction of group identity and community-building. Typically, this can be seen in the mission statements on sites such as Birmingham Night Clubs in the 70's & 80's (Facebook 2014b) ("It would be nice to share stories with people of my age group, and who had a great time Clubbing"). The site has 6,156 members. Or Crown Punks, Birmingham (Facebook 2014g), a group with 640 members ("For all old punks that frequented the Crown pub in Birmingham City Center from 1977 onwards. Pictures, history, music, memories or just want to try and find out what happened to someone and hope they'll show up for a chat"). Here, then, it is in the communal nature of the extended invitation to "share stories," "discuss" and "find out what happened to someone" that leads to the collective building of music histories through communities of interest. Above all, these communities are built on the sharing of digital materials and individual recollections and their encounters with music and its place in relation to their own lives. Alongside the posting of memories, there are links to YouTube videos, Soundcloud files and Spotify playlists. Individuals also upload digitised photographs, ticket stubs, posters, record sleeves and other memorabilia from their personal collections, which act as the "memory glue" (Bastian and Alexander 2009) for individuals and communities in recalling and sharing music-based experiences.

CONCLUSION: DO-IT-YOURSELF OR DO-IT-TOGETHER?

The examples I have highlighted in this chapter barely scratch the surface of online sites dedicated to salvaging popular music's histories, heritage and artefacts (see Collins and Long 2014; Long and Collins forthcoming for broader overviews). The breadth and depth of these activities are also echoed in the physical community archival projects mapped by Baker and Huber (2013), as well as in the pages of this book. Until now, these practices have most commonly been described and understood as a form of DIY popular music heritage activity. DIY is a commonly used term when describing aspects of independent and alternate popular music production and activity (see Dunn 2012; O'Connor 2008; Strachan 2007). Baker and Huber employ the term to characterise the practices they discovered when researching the relationship between popular music and cultural memory in Australia. They identified the "existence of Do-It-Yourself (DIY) institutions" that were actively collecting, preserving and exhibiting a range of popular music materials (2013, 514). For them, DIY is "a recognisable signifier of the 'bottom-up' activities" they apply to a range of physical archival and museum practices concerned with popular music collection and preservation (2013, 515).

While I agree with Baker and Huber's use of DIY in describing the physical archives they have researched, I want to suggest that a small, but important, nuance should be considered to define the practices discussed in this chapter. While sharing many traits with their physical counterparts, online popular music heritage sites have taken advantage of the democratic tendency of the online environment. The participatory approach taken by individuals – those I refer to as activist archivists – in building and sustaining popular music culture with communities of interest (Wenger 1999; Castells 2002) can, I suggest, best be described as doing-it-together.

Through their actions in doing-it-together – the uploading of digital materials, the exchanging and sharing of personal histories and knowledge – alternate popular music histories are being revealed. These histories and their associated artefacts highlight the important role popular music plays in the everyday lives of individuals and communities. I am not claiming the online environment has created a utopia for capturing and preserving all of popular music's history through DIT methods. Indeed, there are very real issues of long-term sustainability to be considered: materials at risk of being lost, technologies becoming redundant, founders, owners or administrators losing interest in their sites and copyright infringement are just a few issues that need to be considered seriously by activist archivists and their communities. But in adopting a DIT approach, in particular in self-authorised and unauthorised sites of popular music heritage, the websites and applications described in this chapter are enabling individuals and communities of interest to come together online and participate in the construction of alternate popular music histories. These sites and the crowdsourced and user-generated tools they employ signal a subtle distinction in how these practices are conducted not as DIY but rather as DIT.

ACKNOWLEDGEMENTS

Thanks is due to those who aided in the production of this chapter, in particular Sarah Baker (Griffith University) and Paul Long and Nick Webber (Centre for Media & Cultural Research, Birmingham City University).

NOTE

1. I have retained the spellings from online sites verbatim throughout this chapter.

REFERENCES

Baker, S. and Huber, A. 2013. Notes towards a typology of the DIY institution: Identifying do-it-yourself places of popular music preservation. *European Journal of Cultural Studies* 16: 513.

Bastian, J. and Alexander, B. 2009. Introduction: Communities and archives – a symbiotic relationship. In J.A. Bastian and B. Alexander, eds., *Community archives: The shaping of memory*. London: Facet, n.p.

Birmingham City Council. 2012. Destination Birmingham: Birmingham, a music city. Accessed December 4, 2014. https://www.birmingham.gov.uk/scrutiny.

Birmingham Music Archive. 2008. About Birmingham Music Archive. Blog. Accessed December 4, 2014. http://www.birminghammusicarchive.com/about-us.

Birmingham Music Archive. 2010. Aston University. Birmingham Music Archive. Blog. Accessed December 4, 2014. http://www.birminghammusicarchive.com/aston-university.

Birmingham Music Heritage. n.d. About Birmingham Music Heritage. Blog. Accessed December 4, 2014. http://www.birminghammusicheritage.org.uk.

Castells, M. 2002. *The internet galaxy: Reflections on the internet, business and society*. Oxford: Oxford University Press.

Collins, J. and Long, P. 2014. Fillin' in any blanks I can: Online archival practice and virtual sites of musical memory. In S. Cohen, R. Knifton, M. Leonard and R. Roberts, eds., *Sites of popular music heritage: Memories, histories, places*. London: Routledge, 81–96.

Cook, T. 2013. Evidence, memory, identity, and community: Four shifting archival paradigms. *Archival Science* 13: 95–120.

Dudrah, R., Chana, B. and Talwar, A. 2007. *Bhangra: Birmingham and beyond*. Birmingham: Birmingham City Council Library and Archive Service.

Dunn, K. 2012. "If it ain't cheap, it ain't punk" Walter Benjamin's progressive cultural production and DIY punk record labels. *Journal of Popular Music Studies* 24(2): 217–37.

Facebook 2014a. What's a verified profile or page? Blog. Accessed December 4, 2014. https://www.facebook.com/help/196050490547892.

Facebook 2014b. 60's, 70's & 80's Music Revival. Blog. Accessed December 4, 2014. https://www.facebook.com/groups/125821844151838.

Facebook 2014c. Birmingham Bogarts. Blog. Accessed December 4, 2014. https://www.facebook.com/groups/22536038106.

Facebook 2014d. Birmingham Night Clubs in the 70's & 80's. Blog. Accessed December 4, 2014. https://www.facebook.com/groups/birmingham.nite.clubs.

Facebook 2014e. BIRMINGHAM ODEON MEMORIAL. Blog. Accessed December 4, 2014. https://www.facebook.com/groups/odeon.birmingham.

Facebook 2014f. Black Sabbath (Facebook's ONLY, COMPLETE BLACK SABBATH Page). Blog. Accessed December 4, 2014. https://www.facebook.com/groups/Complete.Black.Sabbath/?ref=br_rs.

Facebook 2014g. Crown punks, Birmingham. Blog. Accessed December 4, 2014. https://www.facebook.com/groups/108486069179177.

Facebook 2014h. Global Black Sabbath Convention. Blog. Accessed December 4, 2014. https://www.facebook.com/groups/GlobalBlackSabbath.

Flinn, A. 2011. Archival activism: Independent and community-led archives, radical public history and the heritage professions. *InterActions* 7(2): 1–20.

Flinn, A. and Stevens, S. 2008. About. Archives and Identities. Blog. n.d. Accessed December 4, 2014. http://archivesandidentities.wordpress.com/about-2.

Flinn, A. and Stevens, S. 2009. "It is noh mistri, wi mekin histri": Telling our own story – independent and community archives in the U.K., challenging and subverting the mainstream. In J.A. Bastian and B. Alexander, eds., *Community archives: The shaping of memory*. London: Facet, n.p.

Gilbert, D. 2014. Aston University. Birmingham Music Archive. Blog. Accessed May 16, 2014. http://www.birminghammusicarchive.com/aston-university.

Hall, S. 2001. Constituting an archive. *Third Text* 15(54): 89–92.

Hardware, J. 2014. The Powerhouse. Birmingham Music Archive. Blog. Accessed June 10, 2014. http://www.birminghammusicarchive.com/the-powerhouse.

Home of Metal n.d. Background. Home of Metal. Blog. Accessed December 1, 2014. http://homeofmetal.com/the-project/about.

Johnson, L. 2001. Whose history is it anyway? *Journal of the Society of Archivists*, 22(2): 213–29.

Kay, B. 2014. Aston University. Birmingham Music Archive. Blog. Accessed March 16, 2014. http://www.birminghammusicarchive.com/aston-university.

Kean, H. and Ashton, P. 2009. Introduction: People and their pasts and public history today. In P. Ashton and H. Kean, eds., *People and their pasts: Public history today*. Basingstoke: Palgrave Macmillan, 1–20.

Ketelaar, E. 2005. Sharing: Collected memories in communities of records. *Archives and Manuscripts* 33(20): 44–6.

Leonard, M. 2007. Constructing histories through material culture: Popular music, museums and collecting. *Popular Music History* 2(2): 147–67.

Lipstiz, G. 2001. *Time passages: Collective memory and American popular culture*. Minneapolis, MN: University of Minnesota Press.

Long, P. and Collins, J. Forthcoming. Affective memories of music in online heritage practice In J. Brusila, B. Johnson and J. Richardson, eds., *Music, Memory and Space*. London: Intellect.

Mazbeth 2005. Birmingham nightclubs of the past—memories. Blog. November 28. Accessed December 4, 2014. http://birminghamhistory.co.uk/forum/showthread.php?t=4001.

Michelson, D. 2014. Black Sabbath @ the ODEON 14/12/1973–10/10/1975–11/01/1976–5/06/1978–24/25 /05/1980. Birmingham Odeon Memorial Group

Facebook. Blog. Accessed October 30, 2014. https://www.facebook.com/groups/odeon.birmingham.

Pineda. N. 2010. Facebook tips: What's the difference between a Facebook page and group? Facebook. Blog. n.d. Accessed December 1, 2014. https://www.facebook.com/notes/facebook/facebook-tips-whats-the-difference-between-a-facebook-page-and-group/324706977130.

O'Connor, A. 2008. *Punk record labels and the struggle for autonomy*. Lexington, KY: Lexington Books.

Roberts, L. and Cohen, S. 2014. Unauthorizing popular music heritage: Outline of a critical framework. *International Journal of Heritage Studies* 20(3): 241–61.

Robinson, A. 2012. Barbarellas. Birmingham Music Archive. Blog. November 16. Accessed November 30, 2014. http://www.birminghammusicarchive.com/barbarellas.

Rosenzweig, R. and Thelen, D. 1998. *The presence of the past: Popular uses of history in American life*. Chichester: Columbia University Press.

Samuel, R. 1994. *Theatres of memory: Past and present in contemporary culture Vol. 1.* London: Verso.

Sean 2012. Barbarellas. Birmingham Music Archive. Blog. June 9. Accessed November 30, 2014. http://www.birminghammusicarchive.com/barbarellas.

Sleight, C. 2013. Aston University. Birmingham Music Archive. Blog. November 16. Accessed November 30, 2014. http://www.birminghammusicarchive.com/aston-university.

Soho Road to the Punjab n.d. Soho Road to the Punjab. Blog. Accessed November 30, 2014. http://www.sohoroadtothepunjab.org/component/option,com_frontpage/Itemid,1.

Strachan, R. 2007. Micro-independent record labels in the UK: Discourse, DIY cultural production and the music industry. *European Journal of Cultural Studies* 10(2): 245–65.

Theimer, K. 2013. The future of archives is participatory: Archives as platform, or a new mission for archives. http://www.archivesnext.com/?p=3700.

Tom 2012. Aston University. Birmingham Music Archive. Blog. 8 June. Accessed December 1, 2014. http://www.birminghammusicarchive.com/aston-university.

van Dijck, J. 2006. Record and hold: Popular music between personal and collective memory. *Critical Studies in Media Communications* 23(5): 357–74.

Visit Birmingham 2014. Birmingham's B-side. Accessed December 1, 2014. http://visitbirmingham.com/bside.

Wenger, E. 1999. *Communities of practice: Learning meaning and identity*. Cambridge: Cambridge University Press.

Zinn, H. 1977 (1970). Secrecy, archives and the public interest. *Midwestern Archivist* 2(2): 14–27.

7 Alternative Histories and Counter-Memories

Feminist Music Archives in Europe

Rosa Reitsamer

The history of women's archives dates back to the founding of the World Center for Women's Archives in New York and the International Archives for the Women's Movement in Amsterdam in the 1930s (Hildenbrand 1986). These archives served as models for the establishment of feminist archives in the course of women's movements in the 1970s and 1980s, followed by an increase of physical and online archives from the mid-1990s. Recent archives, such as the Riot Grrrl Collection at New York University and the online archive Grassrootsfeminism.net, are primarily concerned with the archiving of cultural artefacts, mostly fanzines, relating to the riot grrrl movement in the 1990s and its various offshoots. Feminist archives dedicated to the production and preservation of women's, feminist and queer music-making are the exceptions in the history of women's archives and, as a result, they have hardly been explored. In this chapter, I therefore examine the following five feminist music archives in Europe:

1 *Archiv Frau und Musik (Women and Music Archive)*: a physical archive in Frankfurt am Main, Germany, mainly for women composers in classical music
2 *Her Noise Archive*: a physical archive in London, Great Britain, as well as an online archive of mainly electronic and electroacoustic music
3 *Dig Me Out*: discourses on popular music, gender and ethnicity; an online archive focusing on feminist-queer musicians and artists mainly based in Spain and Austria
4 *Women's Liberation Music Archive*: an online archive on music-making in the United Kingdom Women's Liberation Movement, c. 1970–89
5 *Jenny Woolworth Women in Punk Archive*: an online archive on female punk artists.

With the exception of the Archiv Frau und Musik, which was founded in the late 1970s, the other four archives were established after the turn of the millennium and make use of the possibilities afforded by the Internet and free web tools. This rise of feminist music archives reflects the "archival turn in feminism" (Eichhorn 2013) after the mid-1990s, as archives have become an important site and practice for women of different generations to disseminate alternative music memories and histories. These archives include the experiences and voices of musicians who have been marginalised by the dominant music histories and official heritage projects on the basis of gender, sexuality, class and race.

By taking the five feminist music archives as examples, this chapter addresses the participatory do-it-yourself (DIY) approach to the production and preservation of alternative music histories, and aims to contribute to the recent discussions of the archival turn in feminism. I first focus on the activist practices of feminist music archives in the context of DIY cultures and explore the various strategies of doing-it-yourself and doing-it-together (DIT) that are employed by the archivists to archive and preserve the diverse histories of women's, feminist and queer music-making. In the second part of the chapter, I examine how feminist music archives create alternative discourses to male-dominated popular music histories and heritage projects by analysing the feminist music archives' online collections. These collections shed light on the "counter-memories" (Lipsitz 2006) that supply new insights into the relationship between popular music history and gender, sexuality and race. For Lipsitz, counter-memory is expressed by various forms of popular culture that draw on oral traditions, vernacular speech and the ordinary concerns of everyday life, and reveal sources of "collective memory to identify the repressed and the suppressed traditions of resistance to oppression" (2006, 231). Collective memory and counter-memory are concepts that refer to both "a past that is *commonly shared* and a past that is *collectively commemorated*" (Misztal 2003, 13, emphasis in original) and, rather than directing our attention to the past, stress "a sense of the continual presence of the past" (Crane 1997, 1373). For Nora (1989, 8), memory is "in permanent evolution, open to the dialectic of remembering and forgetting" and "a bond tying us to the eternal present," while history is "the reconstruction, always problematic and incomplete, of what is no longer." Similarly, heritage in general, and music heritage in particular, operate as a bridge to the past because heritage is "created, shaped and managed by, and in response to, the demands of the present" (Graham and Howard 2008, 3). For "activist archivists" (Zinn 1997), however, the production of music heritage is often not the primary concern (Collins 2012). As I illustrate in this chapter, feminist music archives are concerned with the production and preservation of women's, feminist and queer music histories, and aim to create a "useable past" (Flinn 2011) that should sustain feminist projects and political struggles in the present and into the future.

The empirical data for this chapter consist of interviews and conversations with five volunteer archivists (one from each of the aforementioned feminist music archives), complemented by an analysis of the feminist music archives' online collections. The online collections primarily contain music, videos, images and texts by female musicians. However, two of the archives also include cultural artefacts by male and transgender musicians who have been involved in queer-feminist and anti-racist politics. The archivists, each of whom was interviewed in May 2014, are between twenty-six and sixty years of age and live in different European cities (London, Berlin, Madrid, Amsterdam). In the interviews, they were able to give important information about their participatory approaches to music preservation and the size, scope and vision of their archives, while the analysis of the online collections provides important insights into the construction and articulation of feminist counter-memories. This analysis brings into focus both the music cultures as they were lived and experienced by the musicians and cultural producers represented in the archives, and the challenges of the officially recognised, male-dominated popular music histories and the processes of heritage-making by the music and media industries.

FEMINIST MUSIC ARCHIVES: DOING-IT-YOURSELF, DOING-IT-TOGETHER

The beginnings of DIY culture are rooted in the avant-garde art movement of the 1950s and the emerging new social movements of the 1960s. Throughout the 1970s, the DIY ethos gained a greater currency with the hippies' cultural concept of alternative lifestyles (Hall 1968) and in punk scenes with self-produced fanzines, independent record labels and alternative distribution networks. Since the 1980s, DIY cultures have been developed further by the European dance-party cultures, the global spread of the riot grrrl movement in the 1990s and grassroots cultural producers of, for example, alternative and feminist media and queer-feminist music and art festivals, often called Ladyfests. George McKay (1996, 2) defines the 1990s DIY cultures as "youth-centred and directed clusters of interests and practices" characterised by self-empowerment, self-organisation, improvisation and initiative, and by positioning themselves against dominant ideologies. Andy Bennett (2009, 2013), as well as Sarah Baker and Alison Huber (2013), refer to the DIY ethos with their concepts "DIY preservationism" and "DIY institutions" respectively, which describe the bottom-up approaches of individuals and collectives who preserve and communicate alternative popular music histories and challenge the dominant discourses of popular music heritage. Bennett, however, detaches the DIY ethos from its inherent association with youth by describing DIYism as "a sensibility that remains with individuals for the duration of life course" (2013, 99) and this is reflected in the various rock heritage projects of aging fans of popular music genres. Baker and Huber (2013) ascribe the DIY ethos to the cultural, social and affective functions of DIY institutions such as non-profit archives and museum collections. These institutions exist outside official popular music heritage projects but are part of "a continuum that begins with the individual collector who seeks to establish a place to share their collection, all the way through to the DIY institutions that [have] become formalized to the extent that [they are] on the verge of official, national acceptance" (2013, 514). The five feminist music archives explored in this chapter can be regarded as DIY institutions in terms of their size, scope and archival activism.

An important activist practice of feminist music archives manifests itself in the preservation strategies and selection criteria for collecting music, texts, photos, letters, concert programs and other ephemera. The Jenny Woolworth Women in Punk Archive features around 580 female artists who were active in the punk and post-punk scenes of the 1970s and 1980s around the world. Nicole Emmenegger, the archive's founder, has been adding new artists constantly since she established the online archive in 2003. This archival practice is rooted in her interests in music counter-culture and DIY cultures, and the desire to "see more female fronted bands and musicians" as well as in her own involvement in the riot grrrl movement in the 1990s:

> I am interested in bands and female performers who worked independently to record, distribute and perform their music to a dedicated audience of fans for a love of the music and not necessarily in search of commercial success. But I add more or less whatever crosses my path. Bands often email me with material for inclusion or I get tips here and there. I don't leave anything out, unless it doesn't feel right. Totally subjective, just that it fits the sound, the era and feel of the punk aesthetic, but then again that's my role as curator. And as I continue with the archive, I will also include riot grrrl bands from the 1990s (Nicole Emmenegger, interview).

In this online archive, the criteria for collecting material in order to preserve the history of female (post-)punk musicians since the 1970s in the most extensive and detailed way possible are gender, a particular music genre and a specific time period.

Similar selection criteria are employed by the Archiv Frau und Musik. Its physical collection contains sheet music, books, films, letters, concert programs and other ephemera by women composers in classical music from the ninth to the twenty-first centuries, including smaller sections on rock, pop, jazz, chanson and world music. This collection is not an ad hoc online collection by an individual collector, such as is the case with the Jenny Woolworth Women in Punk Archive, but rather an authorised collection comprising around 23,000 physical and digital media items that found their home in an adapted building in Frankfurt am Main, Germany (Collins 2013). Established in 1979 by a small group of musicians, activists and scholars, women and men from different age groups and backgrounds have been involved as employees and volunteers in the activities of the archive, which include, among other duties, the research of lost and forgotten as well as known and contemporary female composers, the support of archive visitors, the publication of the print magazine *VivaVoce* and the recent endeavour to digitise handwritten sheet music.

With these comprehensive activities and its physical existence since the late 1970s, the Archiv Frau und Musik occupies an exceptional position in comparison to the size and scope of the Jenny Woolworth Women in Punk Archive and the other feminist online music archives, which focus primarily on collecting and archiving digital cultural artefacts. However, all these feminist music archives aim for an "inclusive, and thus 'taste-less' collection of material" (Baker and Huber 2013, 515) by including as many artefacts as possible in their collections in order to avoid the erasure of the pasts and presents of female, feminist and queer musicians. By so doing, their activist approach to collecting and archiving differs from the DIY preservationism of ageing (male) rock music enthusiasts. The feminist archivists do not focus on the "conventions of taste and distinction" (Bennett 2009, 483) exhibited by alternative forms of rock heritage projects, such as record (re-)releases with material by lost and forgotten (male) artists, and they have hardly any interest in commercial opportunities.

The preservation strategies of the feminist archivists often align with their desire to prevent their own local music scenes from being forgotten. Therefore the experiences of the archivists themselves become an important source for collecting material, not only from musicians but also from other small-scale cultural producers involved in feminist music scenes. The collective of six women who have been volunteering for the Women's Liberation Music Archive (WLMA) since its launch in 2011 adapts such an approach, which encourages participation:

> We have all been involved in grassroots campaigning in the Women's Liberation Movement and music-making during the 1970s and 80s and subsequently. So we are working from our own experiences within this scope of this geographical area and timeframe, which is where we perceived a risk of feminist activist history being lost. We see our roles as facilitators and curators, rather than owners, and we involve the people who donate material as much as possible in the working process (volunteer, interview, WLMA).

The knowledge and lived experiences of the archivists in and about past and present (trans)-local feminist music cultures play a significant role in the development of an archivist activism, as they considerably shape their self-understanding as curators and facilitators who challenge the conventional notions of authorship and ownership of archival collections and employ various collaborative archival practices.

One of these collaborative archival practices is reflected in the processes of selecting and editing the contributions to the collections together with other archivists and in dialogue with musicians. This participatory approach to archiving allows musicians and artists to tell and record their own stories and to decide for themselves how they wish to be represented in the archive, rather than have the archive claim the authority to speak for them.

In addition, this participatory approach enables archivists and musicians alike to engage in the sharing of memories and to participate in the collective and activists' processes of history-making. María José Belbel, who, together with myself, established the online archive Dig Me Out in 2009, describes in the following quote how memories are shared while discussing the archival contribution with an artist. The Dig Me Out archive is mainly concerned with the preservation of the pasts and presents of feminist-queer music scenes in Spain and Austria:

> I invited different people to take part in Dig Me Out through friendship, trust and sharing common interests. I included also long-term friends. … We share a common past because we've been into music, arts, fanzines and radical politics together since the early 70s [in Spain]. We sat together, discussing and laughing and selecting the recordings of their performances and images that we digitalised for the archive. … Dig Me Out has been an opportunity to remember this time … and to make visible how musicians and artists connected politics with the DIY spirit of punk, camp and style as resistance (María José Belbel, interview, Dig Me Out).

This story amounts to what Pickering and Keightley (2012, 117) describe as "the sharing of memory *in* time" (emphasis added), in which "shared senses of common pasts, presents and futures are actively negotiated and constructed" by people born at the same historical time, building a generational consciousness. Drawing on Mannheim's definition of generation, Pickering and Keightley (2012, 117) distinguish "transmission or sharing of memory *in* time" and "transmission of memory *over* time." The latter manifests itself in collaborative archival practices in which the various histories of female, feminist and queer music-making are drawn into the present and shared among different generations of archivists and musicians in face-to-face interactions and diverse online communications. As the WLMA collective notes: "We are pleased to be working with women from different generations … and the mutual learning processes involved in that" (volunteer, interview, WLMA). Hence feminist music archives allow for a dialogue among and between different generations of women, who are often labelled as protagonists of "Second Wave" or "Third Wave" feminism (Henry 2004) and seem to be separated by political differences rather than linked by common interests and collaborative cultural practices. Such collaborative practices for undoing the generational logic that underpins the very notion of feminist "waves" is rooted in the DIY ethos and embedded in (trans)-local and virtual feminist communities and music scenes, which foster networking, informal peer-to-peer pedagogies and varied, processual communication. Thus further collaborative archival practices are reflected in collective decision-making processes at the grassroots level, as Mary Ellen Kitchens from the Archiv Frau und Musik explains:

> The archive is a registered cultural initiative officially led by the editorial boards. ... But the board members, the employees and the volunteers ... we all have our tasks and we work together and try to find decisions accepted by everybody (Kitchens, interview).

However, the emphasis on "sharing" of memories and knowledge, flat hierarchies and collective history-making also involves differences and conflicts (Baker and Huber 2013, 520). As a consequence of the cutting of public subsidies, the Archiv Frau und Musik has recently been forced to rethink the archive's priorities, and this has "led to fierce debates between the women," with Kitchens explaining that these debates have not "come to a final decision until now" (Kitchens, interview).

Nevertheless, feminist music archives and DIY institutions share the priority of making both physical and online collections accessible by finding numerous strategies such as calls for contributions (WLMA, Jenny Woolworth in Punk Archive), translations of texts and documents in different languages (Dig Me Out), the organisation of concerts with musicians playing music from the archival collection (Archiv Frau und Musik, WLMA), curating physical exhibitions of material from the collection (WLMA) or inviting guest curators to comment on the cultural artefacts included in the online archive (Her Noise Archive).

FEMINIST COUNTER-MEMORIES: A RESOURCE FOR THE PRESENT AND THE FUTURE

With their participatory approach to archiving and history-making, feminist music archives are embedded in specific times and places, and within particular feminist and queer-feminist communities. At the same time, the archives communicate "counter-memories" (Lipsitz 2006) that create alternative discourses to the officially recognised, male-dominated popular music histories and heritage projects by highlighting the lived experiences and "post-identities" (Hall 2000) of feminist, queer and anti-racist musicians and artists, and stressing a different understanding of time.

By archiving the lost and forgotten history of feminist music-making in Great Britain and Ireland in the 1970s and 1980s, the WLMA communicates the counter-memory of a social group that experienced both the collective euphoric mood of the women's movement and marginalisation and exclusion from the male-dominated music industry. In a longer autobiographical entry in the WLMA's weblog, Frankie Green describes her experiences of playing in the London Women's Liberation Rock Band (1972–74):

> I was struck by a collective goodwill that often enabled the band and the support that came from women. ... Women cheered us on, danced and sang along. ... At that time, lesbian women musicians faced not

only sexism. ... Women transgressing hetero-normative boundaries, living openly as lesbians, prioritizing relationships with women and singing about them was risky – k.d. lang was a long way away (Green n.d.).

The local, immediate and personal experiences of the musicians are also
echoed in their song lyrics, which address such taboo subjects as lesbian-
ism, homophobia and violence against women, and reference the dynamics
of participating in the women's movement (Withers 2014). These counter-
memories direct our attention to the local feminist music culture of the
1970s and 1980s as it was lived and experienced by women from different
social and cultural backgrounds.

In her article on the Women's Liberation Music Archive, Withers (2014)
argues these feminist counter-memories are often invisible because dominant popular music histories focus on released records. Feminist musicians and bands active in the 1960s and 1970s often lacked the financial
resources to make a record, to record and distribute it or refused to cooperate
with the male-dominated music industry for political reasons. As a result,
they did not produce a concrete legacy of their musical activity that could
be included in the officially recognised popular music histories and canons (2013, 4). The canon of the golden age of rock music, for example, is
95 percent made up of records by white male British and American musicians from the period between 1965 and 1969 (von Appen and Doehring
2006, 22). From *The Encyclopedia of Record Producers* (1993) and the
documentaries *Modulations: Cinema for the Ear* (1998), on electronic music
in the twentieth century, and *Woodstock: The Director's Cut* (1994), we
learn female musicians in the past and present are rare exceptions. The dissemination, marketing and promotion of such officially recognised popular
music histories and canons illustrate the processes of heritage-making by
the music and media industries, which increasingly act as commemorative
institutions (Burgoyne 2003) by making use of popular music histories and
recorded records as "the raw material from which to sculpt, craft or fashion a tangible 'product'" (Roberts 2014, 269). These products mediate the
idea that the activity of music-making manifests itself necessarily in making,
recording and distributing a record, and posit male experiences as universal
experiences because they commemorate specific activities, dates and people,
and invent traditions to support the collective memory of the white (male)
middle classes while at the same time deliberately eliminating others from
representation.

Contrary to these popular music heritage products, feminist music
archives bring the processes and dynamics of history-making into focus
and document the counter-memories of female, feminist and queer musicians who raise questions about power relationships in popular music's
pasts and presents. An example from the Dig Me Out online archive is Fatih
Aydogdu's text "Dirty Tone – 'You Don't Care'" (n.d.), which discusses the
devaluation of black popular music genres as "the other" at the beginning

of the twentieth century. His graphic collages and music compositions, complementing the article, explore popular music's hybrid character by mixing various different music genres together and subverting the visual stereotypes of black and white, female and male musicians. This contribution to the archive negotiates the tensions between the dominant historical discourse on black popular music genres and localised artistic practice in the present, and sheds light on a subversive language for both the critique of racism and the celebration of the popular music genres of marginalised groups.

Archival entries such as these suggest feminist counter-memories communicate "post-identities" (Hall 2000), which stress "notions of identification that are multiple, fluid, and ever-changing (always becoming) in relation to both the past and the present" (Flinn 2011, 4). By so doing, feminist counter-memories leave behind fixed identity formations mobilised by, for example, the tradition of British guitar pop since the 1960s (Gilbert and Pearson 1999, 169) or the touristic promotion of Austria as a country for principally classical music and mountains (Reitsamer 2014). Such national music heritage discourses are fundamental to the idea of nation states, as they emphasise the origin, continuity, tradition and timelessness of music culture and history (Hall 1999). These discourses embody the logic of linear time. Feminist counter-memories, however, mediate a "queer time" (Halberstam 2005) by stressing different models of temporality.

An interesting example for a visual representation of queer time is the map "Tangled Cartography" (http://hernoise.org/her-noise-hernoise-heroines), included in the online collection of the Her Noise Archive. The map shows the names of women composers and musicians in classical, rock and electronic music genres from the twelfth to the twenty first centuries, grouped together into various boxes and linked by lines. Lina Džuverović and Anne Hilde Neset, the creators of the map, humourously describe it as a "connection [that] is not a linear connection, it is a natural network" because "in our minds, there is an instinctual connection between Hildegard Von Bingen, Steina Vasulka and Afri Rampo" (http://hernoise.org/tangled-cartography). By stressing rhizomatic connections instead of linear traditions and national music heritage, a different model of temporality is communicated in which "linear time is muddled, as past, present and future touch and rebound in unexpected ways" (Withers 2014, 2). Feminist counter-memories also capture non-normative representations of local experiences of musicians, as demonstrated in the self-representation of Marriage, a collaborative project by Math Bass and Wu Tsang included in the Dig Me Out collection:

> Marriage is an ongoing project about our lives, bodies, communities, and ability to communicate with each other and the audience. As two queer bodies, Marriage also becomes an investigation of shape shifting and transformation both in the digital and the real. In form, this work reflects our shared history of working in performance, video, music, and of living together (http://digmeout.org/de_neu/marriage.htm).

This self-representation on the part of the artists points to a queer model of temporality that strips away "the temporal framework of bourgeois reproduction and family, longevity, risk/safety, and inheritance" (Halberstam 2005, 5) as it brings the horizons of past and present possibilities of queer communities into view in the context of AIDS and in postmodern times. Hence feminist counter-memories communicate "the process of remembering [that] is so fundamental to our ability to conceive the world" (Misztal 2003, 1), but they suggest different ways of producing meaning through the use of the past as a resource for the present from the officially recognised popular music canons and heritage projects.

For the archivists themselves, who are concerned with the production and preservation of alternative and oppositional music histories, the feminist music archives should create a resource for feminist struggles, as expressed by the WLMA collective:

> WLMA hopes not to be an exercise in nostalgia, or of preserving the past in aspic, or a rosy-tinted view of the women's liberation movement, but a conduit through which ideas and activism of the women's liberation movement can be accessed and the continuity of the movement understood and developed. We are interested in exploring how such archives might best be developed and used as useful tools for current struggles and the ongoing quest for women's liberation (volunteer, interview, WLMA).

The archivists strongly reject the idea of producing myths about the women's movement in the 1970s and 1980s but stress the political feminist struggle in the past, present and future. By so doing, the archivists create what Andrew Flinn has dubbed a "useable past" – that is, the use of "archives and history ... to support the achievements of political objectives and mobilization, as a means of inspiring action and cementing solidarity" (Flinn 2011, 12). Hence continuity is a word often used by the archivists to relate the past activities and struggles of women, feminist and queer musicians to the present and future, and to position the archive as a resource for further projects, as an archivist involved in the Her Noise Archive notes: "Let it be the starting point for future work, whether that is directly related to the archive, in response to the archive, or just taking certain themes or ideas forward" (volunteer, interview, Her Noise Archive). The physical and online manifestations of the Her Noise Archive were established as part of the broader Her Noise project in London in 2005, consisting of an exhibition and a series of lectures and talks. Since their launch, the archives have fostered several smaller initiatives such as the Sound. Gender. Feminism. Activism. conferences in London in 2012 and 2014. Similarly, the Archiv Frau und Musik was the catalyst for the launch of Furore Verlag in 1986, a publisher for sheet music and books by and about female composers in classical music and the distribution of recordings of their works.

CONCLUSION

This chapter has illustrated, through the analysis of five feminist music archives, how individuals and collectives develop a participatory DIY approach to producing and preserving alternative music histories while at the same time challenging the dominant (popular) music histories and heritage projects. As we have seen, feminist music archives mediate counter-memories that draw attention to music cultures as they have been lived and experienced by women, feminists and queers, and make available multiple cultural identities that are embedded in specific localities but vary across space and time. Integral to these activist practices of archiving are the knowledge and experiences of the archivists in and about past and present music cultures, and the collaborative practices that give voice to the musicians and artists who are represented in the archival collections. These practices share various aspects with alternative and feminist media production as they question the established notions and standards of professionalism, competence and knowledge acquisition (Atton 2002, 28). Like alternative and feminist media producers, activist archivists perform several functions, such as collecting, editing and archiving cultural artefacts, that are usually separated in official music archives and music heritage institutions, and they reject the traditional notions of authorship and ownership of archival collections. As a result, activist archivists transform social relationships, roles and responsibilities, and produce new knowledge in relation to both archivist practices and music histories. However, the activist practices of feminist archivists also hold the potential to undo the generational logic that underpins the idea of feminist "waves" through the sharing of memories and knowledge among and between different generations and the production of archives that stress the continuity of feminist activism. Hence feminist music archives contribute substantially to the "archival turn in feminism" (Eichhorn 2013) that is not so much shaped by generational divides but by the collaborative archival practices employed by archivists of different generations who are inspired by feminist activism and ideas.

REFERENCES

Atton, C. 2002. *Alternative media*. London: Sage.

Aydogdu, F. n.d. Dirty tone—"You don't care." Dig Me Out. Accessed October 27, 2014. http://digmeout.org/de_neu/fatih.htm.

Baker, S. and Huber, A. 2013. Notes towards a typology of the DIY institution: Identifying do-it-yourself places of popular music preservation. *European Journal of Cultural Studies* 16(5): 513–30.

Bennett, A. 2009. Heritage rock: Rock music, representation and heritage discourse. *Poetics* 37(5–6): 474–89.

Bennett, A. 2013. *Music, style and aging: Growing old disgracefully?* Philadelphia, PA: Temple University Press.

Burgoyne, R. 2003. From contested to consensual memory: The Rock and Roll Hall of Fame and Museum. In S. Radstone and K. Hodgkin (eds.), *Frontiers of memory*. London: Routledge, 208–20.

Collins, J. 2012. Multiple voices, multiple memories: Public history-making and activist archivism in online popular music archives. Unpublished MA thesis, Birmingham City University.

Collins, J. 2013. The Music Archive Network. Accessed October 27, 2014. http://www.archivingmediaculture.org/the-music-archive-network.

Crane, S. 1997. Writing the individual back into collective memory. *The American Historical Review*, 102(5): 1372–1385.

Eichhorn, K. 2013. *The archival turn in feminism: Outrage in order*. Philadelphia, PA: Temple University Press.

Flinn, A. 2011. Archival activism: Independent and community-led archives, radical public history and the heritage professions. *InterActions* 7(2): 1–20.

Gilbert, J. and Pearson, E. 1999. *Discographies: Dance music, culture and the politics of sound*. New York: Routledge.

Graham, B. and Howard, P. 2008. Introduction: Heritage and identity. In B. Graham and P. Howard (eds.), *The Ashgate research companion of heritage and identity*. Aldershot: Ashgate, 1–15.

Green, F. n.d. The London Women's Liberation Rock Band: 1972–1974. Women's Liberation Music Archive. Accessed October 27, 2014. http://womensliberation-musicarchive.co.uk/l.

Halberstam, J. 2005. *In a queer time and place: Transgender bodies, subcultural lives*. New York: New York University Press.

Hall, S. 1968. *The hippies: An American "moment."* Birmingham: Centre for Contemporary Cultural Studies, University of Birmingham.

Hall, S. 1999. Un-settling "the heritage," re-imaging the post-nation. Whose heritage? *Third Text* 49: 3–13.

Hall, S. 2000. Cultural identity and diaspora. In N. Mirzoff (ed.), *Diaspora and visual culture: Representing Africans and Jews*. London: Routledge, 21–33.

Henry, A. 2004. *Not my mother's sister: Generational conflict and third-wave feminism*. Bloomington, IN: Indiana University Press.

Hildenbrand, S. 1986. Introduction: Women's collections today. In S. Hildenbrand (ed.), *Women's collections: Libraries, archives, and consciousness*. New York: Haworth Press, 1–12.

Lipsitz, G. 2006. *Time passages: Collective memory and American popular culture*, 8th ed. Minneapolis: University of Minnesota Press.

McKay, G. 1998. DIY culture: Notes towards an intro. In G. McKay (ed.), *DIY culture: Party and protest in nineties Britain*. London: Verso, 1–53.

Misztal, B, 2003. *Theories of Social Remembering*. Maidenhead, PA: Open University Press.

Nora, P. 1989. Between memory and history: Les lieux de memoire. *Representations* 26: 7–24.

Pickering, M. and Keightley, E. 2012. Communities of memory and the problem of transmission. *European Journal of Cultural Studies* 16(1): 115–31.

Reitsamer, R. 2014. Born in the Republic of Austria: The invention of rock heritage in Austria. *International Journal of Heritage Studies* 20(3): 331–42.

Roberts, L. and Cohen, S. 2014. Unauthorising popular music heritage: Outline of a critical framework. *International Journal of Heritage Studies* 20(3): 241–61.

Roberts, L. 2014. Talkin' bout my generation: Popular music and the culture of heritage. *International Journal of Heritage Studies* 20(3): 262–80.

Von Appen, R. and Doehring, A. 2006. Never mind The Beatles, here's Exil 61 and Nico: The top 100 records of all time—a canon of pop and rock albums from a sociological and an aesthetic perspective. *Popular Music* 25(1): 21–39.

Withers, D. 2014. Re-enacting process: Temporality, historicity and the Women's Liberation Music Archive. *International Journal of Heritage Studies*, forthcoming, DOI: 10.1080/13527258.2013.794745.

Zinn, H. 1997 (1970). *The Zinn Reader: Writings on disobedience and democracy.* New York: Seven Stories Press.

8 "When Folk Meets Pop"

DIY Archives in the Making of a Punk Rock DIY Community in Western France

Gérôme Guibert and Emmanuel Parent

Before a cultural domain or practice is considered worth conserving, it has to be seen as worthy of interest or worth being remarked upon. This simple observation explains why do-it-yourself (DIY) initiatives relating to the archiving of popular music are underdeveloped in France, a country where popular music is still not considered a cultural heritage, either from a public policy perspective or by the French people (Teillet 2003). The popular music/heritage pairing in France constitutes a paradox. On one hand, the lack of recognition by institutions of the history of this music, events that have marked it, and how and where it is performed are seen by music professionals as a glaring injustice in relation to other cultural forms (Touché 2007). On the other, on the rare occasions when popular music and its subcultures are framed in a commemoratory context, this is seen as going against the grain in terms of the supposedly subversive nature of the music, whether resulting from public initiatives (which kill spontaneity), the market (commoditisation) or the networks of those who actually produce the music, with their partial, biased and subjective take on the story (Le Guern 2013).

Independent of these struggles for recognition in the public sphere (Fraser 2001), museums would not seem to be at ease with popular musical cultures, particularly as they traditionally are focused on objects. As a result, they have been a target of criticism (Guibert 2013). Faced with a plethora of musical activity,[1] institutions lack awareness about what should be taken into account and documented, particularly during times of economic difficulty and restrictions on funding for culture (Tronquoy 2014). Other factors in the contemporary dynamic do, however, lead to the belief that the situation will change, with new debates being generated by EU policies and the development of the notion of "intangible cultural heritage" (Leimgruber 2011).

This chapter offers a counterpoint to the still prehistoric nature of the general movement on these subjects in France. First, it relates the experience of the collective dynamic of building an archive of popular music within one of the most underground traditions (DIY punk culture in rural areas). Second, it confirms that those involved – the Icroacoa[2] collective – have gradually been led to perceive the archive as a statement of empowerment, built by democratic means, and as a work in progress rather than a process of nostalgia or self-absorption.

What gives the situation we are describing here its specificity is that it has arisen from the meeting of two rather disparate worlds and their subsequent collaboration. Aware of the importance of memory as part of its alternative cultural project, the Icroacoa collective began, through the efforts of some of its members, to work with an association of specialised folk music activists (Ethnodoc) twenty years its senior. While Icroacoa seeks to put its written and recorded data and its members' memories into order, over time Ethnodoc has specialised in collecting and archiving, and is interested in the energy exerted by those involved in popular music from the generations that have succeeded them.

Both are from the same geographical area, the Vendée, a *department* in Western France with a rural and working-class history. Icroacoa works in the canton of Montaigu, in the east of the *department*, and Ethnodoc originates in the west. For almost forty years, Ethnodoc has carried out collection and reconstitution operations throughout the *department*.[3] Above and beyond any technical contribution, this seemingly improbable collaboration has led to a fruitful and productive exchange, particularly because, in contrast to what might be expected, Icroacoa continually calls to mind the importance of cultural factors in the conservation of music.

ICROACOA: A DIY PUNK ROCK COMMUNITY AND THE PUBLIC SPACE

Before going any further into the process involving Icroacoa, Ethnodoc and ourselves (the authors of this article) as researchers, we must say a few words about the interested parties, starting with the Icroacoa collective.

In 1991, after a handful of concerts in the bars and youth centres of Montaigu in the early 1990s, a group of the town's young people, born in the late 1960s and early 1970s, created Art Sonic, a non-profit organisation, to stage concerts. This initiative had a positive effect on the young people of Montaigu and the surrounding towns and villages. After attending the first concert organised by Art Sonic, a group of young people created further associations to program concerts such as Ond' de choc and Aïnu. In the mid-1990s, musicians from local groups, who themselves created associations to represent their increasingly numerous groups (e.g. Craft, 80 Planet of Trash, International Mandary), set up a self-managed rehearsal space in a warehouse located in the industrial area in the north of Montaigu (Carroussel). As Guibert (2006) observes, by the early 2000s – only one decade after its emergence – the music scene in Montaigu had reached an incomparably higher level of activity and number of participants than other municipalities in the *department*, both in relative terms (number of rock bands and number of concerts per capita) and absolute terms. Montaigu associations were by this time involved all the way down the independent rock music chain (rehearsal spaces, recording, labels, management, organisation of concerts and a festival attended by 7,000 people in July 2000) and included alternative media, including Kerosene, a fanzine of international stature with a run of 5,000 copies. In addition, associations invested in other artistic forms, including street art. Simultaneously, other musical worlds such as free techno parties also drew closer to this dynamic.

It was during this period that the associations formed around indie music or underground rock decided, regardless of their primary vocation, to come together in a collective named Icroacoa. Icroacoa existed informally at first before becoming a non-profit organisation, with the other non-profits as its members. At that time, the main objective of the collective was to find a venue of its own. Over a decade passed before the collective took over le Zinor, a depot located near the existing rehearsal space, leasing it from a private owner and converting it into a concert venue, with the work done by members of the associations. The collective still exists and, at the time of writing in November 2014, consisted of nineteen member associations.

To understand what took place and continues to take place in Montaigu, two aspects of its specificity need to be noted. The first is the intensity of the activity and the numbers of those involved: nearly one hundred active persons currently aged between eighteen and forty-five. This intensity has been maintained for more than twenty years, and is a phenomenon we are studying along with Sandrine Emin, a research colleague with a special interest in "durable collective entrepreneurship" (non-profit). One of our hypotheses is that the situation originates in a dual dynamic between community education and DIY punk, with people involved in popular education working on issues of governmentality and democracy within the collective and others favouring spontaneity and the present moment (Emin, Guibert and Parent 2014).

The second aspect concerns the collective's relationship with public policy. It should be remembered that the rise of amateur amplified music and its related organisation came to France in the 1980s, both for political and legal reasons. Thus throughout the country in the early 1990s, groups of musicians and people involved in the organisation of local concerts were lobbying for venues and the support of public bodies, as we have shown in several monographs (e.g. Guibert 2007). However, Montaigu is characterised by a specific situation, with almost systematic political opposition from the mayor and the *department* defending a conservative, right-wing, populist line and led for a long time by Philippe de Villiers (Martin and Suaud 1996). No attempt was made by the Vendéen local authorities to hide their refusal to support popular music. Cooperation between the two parties on the establishment of a cultural centre, as occurred in dozens of other towns, was never a possibility in Montaigu. We will not dwell here on the numerous episodes in the relationship between the collective and the town hall, which can be summarised by listing a succession of phases of open hostility and thwarted attempts at discussion.[4] We simply wish to emphasise this situation of constant conflict played a central role for the collective in terms of the issue of memory and archiving. Collective memory (Halbwachs 1997) is a crucial foundation for any group or community, including Icroacoa. With regard to archiving, in terms of the municipality's strategies, time was often used as a pretext to counter or control the collective. In response, the collective gradually learned to use documents providing proof of the results of its past actions and demonstrating their impact: professionalisation in the organisation of gigs, significant proportion and diversity of the population reached, and so on. The emphasis on collective memory and the need to archive went hand in hand.

ETHNODOC: UPDATING FOLK ACTIVISM IN TWENTY-FIRST-CENTURY FRANCE

Ethnodoc is a non-profit organisation based in western France that has been collecting an oral repertoire and discography of regional folk music since the beginning of the French folk revival in the early 1970s. Over the years, Ethnodoc has acquired professional-standard skills in music heritage, both in terms of the process of collecting music and songs and in archiving and digitising this material. By 2014, Ethnodoc members had built a solid online database of over 200,000 items: the Raddo database. Ethnodoc did not build its expertise in response to demand from public or private bodies. Rather, the enthusiasts who founded the project were simply, and still are, passionate people who wanted to tell the story of a local popular culture that had existed prior to industrialisation.

Over the past few years, Ethnodoc has turned its attention from folk to popular music, joining Le Pôle régional musiques actuelles des Pays de la Loire, an umbrella network of music professionals bringing together 125 indie music bodies in Pays de la Loire, the fifth largest region in France. As members of this network, the DIY preservationists of Ethnodoc have had some fruitful debates with musicians and other local actors involved in hip-hop, electronic music, indie pop and punk rock, discovering new creative worlds for preservation. Persuaded, as they were, of the importance of this new music and the cultures surrounding it, and realising those involved were facing the same challenges in terms of archiving and preservation of the past they had addressed four decades previously in regard to folk music, they decided to share their expertise. The president of Ethnodoc is convinced of the importance of musical practice in his region. He believes that tapping into new currents of contemporary music enables us to develop a better understanding of our society, and he is also interested in fostering inter-generational dialogue (Bertrand 2012). Thus, in an action of reciprocity, Ethnodoc invited members of the network of music professionals to feed Ethnodoc's Raddo database with popular music-related archives and material.

To get a grasp of what is going on here, we also need to highlight two aspects of Ethnodoc. First, it is important to understand the associations:

Ethnodoc and Arexpo (from which Ethnodoc grew, having been created in 1970 in the Vendée when its founder, J.-P. Bertrand, was twenty-three years old), long remained on the sidelines of French culture in terms of symbolic recognition. Although the Ethnodoc archivists call themselves ethnologists or musicologists, they are self-taught and their work, through which they have produced numerous reports on most geographical areas of the Vendée and various other places in France, wasn't paid much regard, either by French national research bodies and ministerially accredited cultural institutions (including museums) or music professionals from the world of contemporary folk. Ethnodoc did, however, achieve successes and some national recognition in the late 1990s, with a Parisian linguistics laboratory that specialised in song and that worked on the association's collections, creating a collection of books dedicated to intangible cultural heritage with French publisher L'Harmattan and organising major conferences with nationally recognised academics in ethnomusicology such as François Picard and André-Marie Despringre (Paris-Sorbonne University). Nevertheless, these accomplishments did not really alter the lack of esteem in which Ethnodoc was held by the Ministry of Culture, which continued to reject all requests for public support.

Moreover, above and beyond the fact that they were autodidacts, those involved in Ethnodoc suffered from being labelled as right-wing, especially since Jean-Pierre Bertrand worked with Philippe de Villiers, a separatist-inspired conservative Catholic politician who was president of the Vendée Departmental Council from 1988–2010. This has sometimes made Ethnodoc's position within the generally post-1968, left-wing French revivalist movement hard to negotiate (Guibert 2006). In fact, Ethnodoc does not have a specifically right-wing agenda. The association is active in the preservation of the aural history of a rural area. However, the Vendée's right-wing council finances it, and its leader, Bertrand, is seen as being compromised by this association with local authorities and is partially isolated from national networks in the folk movement for this reason.

Outside of such labelling, the association between Icroacoa and Ethnodoc is an encounter based on the sharing of a common cultural background: the Vendée, a love of music played by the local population and a territorial approach to memory. This approach takes place outside conventions and institutional frameworks. It is also interesting to note the heritage dimension of the work of those involved in the Montaigu music scene is finding new perspectives through the public financial support received via Ethnodoc.

DIY ARCHIVES IN THE MAKING: THE ROCK SCENE IN MONTAIGU

The issue of archiving and heritage is not new in Montaigu's rock scene. Associations in the collective store hard drives and hard-copy paper documents, ranging from minutes of section meetings to cuttings of photos and articles taken from the local press. They also conserve the albums and demos of groups in the area or those who have asked to play at the venue, as well as flyers and posters for concerts. As we have found in our investigations, the evocation of the past can be used to present the memory of happenings, and this has proven to be a cohesive force for the collective, notably in terms of the integration of newcomers and younger members. This type of evocation also helps to build a historical legitimacy and give a particular meaning to the process. It helps to highlight the values represented by the associations.

In 2010, the collective organised an annual exhibition of archival material – flyers, newspaper articles, posters of events, covers of locally produced discs, etc. – at the Is This the End? festival, telling the story and relating the work that had been accomplished, including political struggles and past events that had brought people together. However, this is also where the limitations of the collective were exposed in terms of management of the past, given the imperatives of daily activities, lack of time and methods of collection, storage and management of archives. The desire to master the process of preservation of documents has nevertheless been strong and, since coming together with Ethnodoc and benefiting from its expertise in terms of collections and conservation management, new opportunities have opened up for the Montaigu collective. This is where the collaboration between Ethnodoc and Icroacoa has been most successful. Thanks to its ability to network with local right-wing politicians, Ethnodoc has convinced the town hall to see Montaigu's rock history as an intangible heritage worthy of respect.

The collaborative work between Ethnodoc and Icroacoa operates at two levels: practical and political. In 2014, a student was hired under a civic service program to work on this archiving project for the non-profit collective. She began her training in the village of Le Perrier, at Ethnodoc, in the west of the *department*, near the Atlantic Ocean, gaining expertise in archiving and proceeding to archive the collective's documents, starting with a set of photographs taken in the practice spaces or at concerts organised in the 1990s. Other activists are working in parallel to develop a site that, in 2015, will make the digitisation of all this documentation available online.

As with any heritage enterprise, there are many technical challenges. We cannot dwell here on issues to do with lexicons or fields, or on the technical issues related to wanting to archive, for example, a punk rock title – recorded using a four-track tape recorder in a 1999 rehearsal space and stored on 500 pressed copies of a CD – using tools designed to inventory local melodies sung during weddings before World War I, of which Ethnodoc has hundreds on its hard drives. The Icroacoa/Ethnodoc collaboration obviously leads one to think about the fact that, beyond the aspect of audio conservation itself and in the same way that folklorists of the nineteenth and twentieth centuries developed appropriate lexicons for their collections, new terms are required to describe cultures originating in the twentieth century.

OUR POSITIONING AS RESEARCHERS: ETHNOGRAPHY COMBINED WITH PARTICIPATORY ACTION RESEARCH

We would be remiss if we did not reveal our research methodology, which is more one of research activism and immersion than of detached objectivity. Indeed, the authors of this article initially worked for the Pôle régional des musiques actuelles de la région Pays de la Loire, where the link up between Icroacoa and Ethnodoc took place. Moreover, while one of us (Gérôme Guibert) had already investigated the non-profit collective in 2001 as part of the research for his thesis, the other (Emmanuel Parent) had studied the Ethnodoc collection apparatus.

In our reflection on the question of the popular music heritage industry as well as that of collecting, conservation and exhibition, and having been approached in this context by the Cité de la musique in Paris for several projects, it seemed of interest to look into this collaboration between two musical cultures of popular music and folk, a collaboration that we had helped create through the organisation of workshops under the Pôle régional des musiques since 2008.

Greatly impressed by the discovery of research into DIY archiving, particularly by researchers at the Popular Music Heritage, Cultural Memory and Cultural Identity conference (POPID, Rotterdam, January 2013), the idea emerged of integrating this methodological dimension within our platform of observation and research.

THE INITIAL FINDINGS OF THIS RESEARCH

In our case, it is not popular music in general that is referred to when discussing efforts being made to preserve music's past for the future. Rather, it is popular music within a given context in a given community. That is what is exciting: how communities in late twentieth-century rural France became artistically, politically and personally fulfilled through rock music and its particular modes of organisation. Our involvement in preserving this history, as outlined below, has the following agenda:

- for the benefit of the community itself
- for the political uses it can be put to
- for the sociological and historical knowledge of musical practices in france
- for the near and distant future: transmission to younger generations and the distant future within a heritage context.

After two years' work, we are beginning to see how a community is built around a passion for rock music. To take a concrete example, after a series of discussions between Icroacoa, Ethnodoc and the authors, we decided to hold a collection session in August 2014 focusing on the year 1997 in

Montaigu. Our choice of year was somewhat random – there is a lot of available data from across the years to sift through – but also had purpose, as 1997 was a pivotal year in terms of public policies related to popular music in France. The Minister of Culture proposed at this time to classify certain venues with the SMAC label (*Scène de musiques actuelles*, venues for popular music). Outside Paris, the year saw the development of festivals and related activities such as street art and decoration. These were truly bottom-up initiatives. For Montaigu, this was the time when the associative enthusiasm for the organisation of concerts gave rise to the other links in the chain. The first concerts with large crowds were also organised at this time with, for example, more than 5,000 people attending the festival in June 1997.

On August 27, 2014, half a dozen members of the community gathered together to select the documents from 1997 that were thought appropriate for scanning. We had them talk about each of these archived pieces so these descriptions could enrich Ethnodoc's Raddo metadata. It transpired that now, as in the past, the series of concerts, debates and periods of collective creativity corresponded to a rather ritualised and Catholic annual calendar: Easter, Midsummer, autumn and Christmas. Whereas French intellectual Alain Finklekraut says rock concerts are not representative of any social fabric and reduce music events to nothing more than a commercial transaction, without any historical background or ritual dimension (Teillet 1991), the importance of the Montaigu rock archives is clear in terms of reconstructing the social embeddedness of rock practices in France in the late twentieth century.

Icroacoa and Ethnodoc, in collaboration with the student on the project and we researchers, also organised a more widely accessible workshop during an event at le Zinor (the venue shared by the non-profits) held two weeks later on September 13, 2014, the Zinor Day, in order to collect opinions and anecdotes about the collection process. The idea was to try to get beyond the fetishisation of objects in order to develop a perspective on a social configuration of heritage practices in line with the work of Jez Collins (2012), Sarah Baker and Alison Huber (2012, 2013, 2015) and others. In addition to the work with the community of activists in Montaigu, collection efforts would also take place through various tools, such as the moderation of comment threads on a dedicated Facebook page. This no doubt sounds radical compared with the standards of the French heritage industry and approach to intangible culture, but it emphasises the importance that needs to be attached to multiple modes of narration and prevents archives from being commoditised or reified and interpreted in just one way.

Moreover, this is the principal reproach that can be levelled at other heritage industry initiatives concerning rock music in France today. Other heritage initiatives do exist. The Fedelima (a pro network of 150 indie rock and jazz venues in France) lists over 50 local music-scene publications that have blossomed since the new millennium. However, these initiatives, undertaken by journalists and/or activists, are often solo modes of narration. Once made, these narratives of the local rock scene are no longer open to contestation, confirmation, continuation and rearrangement. There is no room for comment in these classical narratives, no other ways of assembling the pieces of the story. Like the despised books of philosophy in the oral era of Plato and Aristotle, these pieces of paper cannot answer the questions one puts to them nor tell a different story; they are not dialogic. In addition, this research is not stored for the future or scanned to be made accessible to others.

The work on music archives being undertaken in the Vendée originated with the intuition that it is crucial to document the popular cultural practices of the present rigorously, with the idea being not to interest ourselves in popular culture for suspect practical or political reasons once it no longer exists – what Michel de Certeau (1974) calls "the beauty of death." The challenge is to open and stimulate collective memory, to create archives that are truly dialogic, that bear traces of collective elaboration. DIY has been one of the most significant and decisive elements in rock culture since the second half of the 1970s, and also lies behind both the approach and the aesthetic – lo-fi sound, for example. The idea is to harness its political and creative force in the way we envisage heritage work, which is still very much at the margins of public policy in France, even where areas are given legitimising labels such as "creative district" or "innovative region."

NOTES

1. For example, the Centre National des Variétés (CNV – French national popular music and jazz organisation) lists 40,000 concerts each year.
2. The history, interpersonal dynamics, concerts and local background of which the Icroacoa collective and the associations that constitute it are part, as well as the venue, rehearsal space and social area it coordinates, and are the subject of a research study we have initiated within the framework of the regional research program "Valeur(s) dans la culture" (Cultural value(s)) (Pays de la Loire, France).
3. Ethnodoc even tried to register "*dariolage*," an ancient technique of local song combining percussive and melodic elements to drive cattle, with UNESCO. Variations were found in other parts of the world.
4. These included the disruption of a stage start of the Tour de France (1999) and the creation of a list of opposition candidates by the collective in the municipal elections (2001) entitled "Poil à Gratter" (Thorn in Your Side), which won 14 percent of the vote.

REFERENCES

Baker, S. and Huber, A. 2012. Masters of our own destiny: Cultures of preservation at the Victorian Jazz Archive in Melbourne, Australia. *Popular Music History* 7(3): 263–82.
Baker, S. and Huber, A. 2013. Notes towards a typology of the DIY Institution: identifying do-it-yourself places of popular music preservation. *European Journal of Cultural Studies* 16(5): 513–30.
Baker, S. and Huber, A. 2015. Saving "rubbish": Preserving popular music's material culture in amateur archives and museums. In S. Cohen, R. Knifton, M. Leonard

and L. Roberts (eds.), *Sites of Popular Music Heritage: Memories, Histories, Places*. New York: Routledge, 112–24.

Bertrand, J.-P. 2012. Entretien avec Léa Voineau et Emmanuel Parent. Unpublished interview, June.

Collins, J. 2012. Multiple voices, multiple memories: Public history-making and activist archivism in online popular music archives. Unpublished MA thesis, Birmingham City University.

De Certeau, M. 1974. *La Culture au Pluriel*. Paris: Seuil.

Emin, S., Guibert, G. and Parent, E. 2014. Les Punks de Montaigu ... Et après? Paper presented at the Scènes et Territoires, MSH Ange Guépin: questions de Valeur(s) conference, Nantes, June 11–13.

Ethnodoc 2014. Website. Accessed November 8, 2014. http://www.ethnodoc.fr.

Fraser, N. 1990. Rethinking the public sphere: A contribution to the critique of actually existing democracy. *Social Text* 25/26: 56–80.

Guibert, G. 2006. *La Production de la culture. Le cas des musiques amplifiées en France*. Paris: Seteun/Irma.

Guibert, G. 2007. Les musiques amplifiées en France. Phénomènes de surface et dynamiques invisibles. *Réseaux* 141/42: 297–325.

Guibert, G. 2011. Local music scenes in France. Definitions, stakes, particularities. In H. Dauncey and P. Le Guern (eds.), *Stereo: Comparative perspectives on the sociological study of popular music in France and Britain*. Farnham: Ashgate, 223–38.

Guibert, G. 2012. La notion de scène locale: Pour une approche renouvelée des courants musicaux. In S. Dorin (ed.), *Sound factory*. Saffré: Seteun, 93–124.

Guibert, G. 2013. The sound of the city: À Propos du Colloque Pop Music, Pop Musée, Un Nouveau Défi Patrimonial. *Musées et Collections Publiques de France* 268: 28–33.

Halbwachs, M. 1950. *La mémoire collective*. Paris: PUF.

Le Guern, P. 2012. Un spectre hante le rock ... l'obsession patrimoniale, les musiques populaires et actuelles et les enjeux de la muséomomification. *Questions de Communication* 22: 7–44.

Leimgruber, W. 2011. Patrimoine culturel immatériel et musées: un danger? In Marc-Oliver Gonseth et al. (eds.), *Bruits: Echos du patrimoine culturel immatériel*. Neuchâtel: Musée d'Ethnographie de Neuchâtel, 34–46.

Martin, J.-C. and Suaud, C. 1996. *Puy du fou en Vendée, l'Histoire mise en scène*. Paris: L'Harmattan.

Parent, E. 2012. *Le Projet Folk Archives*. Nantes: Pôle de coopération pour les musiques actuelles en Pays de la Loire. Accessed November 8, 2014. http://www.lepole.asso.fr/fichiers/chantiers/Projet_Folk_Archives_Sept2012.pdf.

POPID 2013. Popular Music Heritage, Cultural Memory & Cultural Identity conference program, Rotterdam, January 31–February 1. http://www.eshcc.eur.nl/fileadmin/ASSETS/eshcc/HERA/2013_Conference/POPID_Draft_Schedule_23Jan.pdf.

Raddo 2014. Raddo database. Accessed November 8, 2014. http://www.raddo-ethnodoc.com.

Teillet, P. 2003. Publics et politiques des musiques actuelles. In O. Donnat and P. Tolila (eds.), *Le(s) public(s) de la culture*. Paris: Presses de Sciences Po, 155–80.

Touché, M. 2007. Muséographier les musiques "électro-amplifiées": Pour une socio-histoire du sonore. *Réseaux* 141/42: 297–325.

Tronquoy, M. 2014. Quels financements pour la culture? *Cahiers Français* 382: 1.

Zinorday Festival 2014. Website. zinor.fr/evenements/13-09-2014-zinorday.

9 Creating a Comprehensive Archive of Maltese Music on CD

Toni Sant

The Malta Music Memory Project (M3P) was launched in 2010 to address the need for a cohesive multimedia database of Maltese music and associated arts. There are no large-scale collections of Maltese music anywhere in the world. Specialised collections containing elements of traditional folk music or a few types of popular mainstream releases exist, but these are either in stand-alone private collections or not fully accessible to the public. This chapter contains practical details and technical information about a specific sub-project conducted within the context of the M3P to create a comprehensive archive of Maltese music on CD. However, this carrier medium was identified as particularly fragile and in need of immediate preservation attention, mainly due to the approaching obsolescence of the format from popular use.

Along with collecting the metadata from the collection, it was also necessary to create a workflow for the preservation process of the actual data on the audio CDs. This involved the creation of an open-source tool to enable the cloning of CDs so they can be normalised and played even after CD players are no longer as readily available as they have been in previous decades. As this process raises issues normally associated with music piracy, it has to be conducted within a do-it-yourself (DIY) context. However, attention to issues pertaining to intellectual property rights is also embedded in the process, ensuring appropriate preservation of materials that may not be easily accessible within just another few years. Work on the archive cannot be fully completed as long as new CDs are being issued and circulated, and even then, it is likely specific pieces from private collections will continue to surface for some time in the foreseeable future.

THE MALTA MUSIC MEMORY PROJECT

I first proposed the Malta Music Memory Project through a position paper that appeared in the *Journal of Music Technology and Education* called "Addressing the Need for a Collaborative Multimedia Database of Maltese Music" (Sant 2009). At that point, I expected contributions to the collection would come from the same people and venues creating the original artefacts in collaboration with their admirers and private collectors. However, as things turned out, the main initial contributions came from a small group of individuals who were already trying to create similar personal collections on aspects of related work that interested each of them. While their contributions have now become the main initial holdings in the M3P collection, there is still more than enough room for anyone to contribute their own mediated memories to this open database.[1]

It is impossible to preserve everything, and countless unique memories have already been lost. While acknowledging this, the M3P has started capturing as much detailed information as possible about live performances and recordings from shows, studio sessions, public releases on CD and the Internet, along with photos, posters and other similar materials. The database also includes details of all the technologies used to create and document music, from the equipment used for recording and live performances to individual websites and social networking tools used by both artists and their fans. The data are being captured with as much concern as possible at this stage for the broader context within which they were created. This will serve as the basis for a more systematic development of the collection within a relatively short period of time over the coming years. It is also important to clarify here that the term "associated arts" opens up the field of interest to include a larger number of attention points within the cultural sphere, such as broadcasting, theatre, dance, visual arts, traditional rituals, sports and other related forms of popular entertainment and creative expression. This indicates that while music has been selected as the primary focus for the database, it is inclusive enough to not exclude any other aspect of everyday life directly or indirectly associated with music. Furthermore, the focus on memory implies the project is not only looking to gather hard facts but also personal perspectives on things that would previously have been recorded mainly through an institutional or official channel. In a time of ubiquitous digital media, it would be rather shortsighted not to give an appropriate value to whatever mediated memories are generated by those who experience any cultural phenomenon, whether actively or passively.

The lack of a substantial body of scholarly research on the preservation of intangible cultural heritage, coupled with an absence of long-term preservation strategies for Maltese music and associated arts, makes it possible for cultural memory, whether individual or collective, to fade into anecdotal legend at best or become obscured, forgotten or even lost forever. The problem is evident even without delving back into a distant past. The liberalisation of broadcasting in Malta in 1991 spawned a glut of uncollected documents and data. These have increased dramatically with the recent proliferation of digital media technologies and the Internet. The rise in output can be felt particularly through the amount of popular music being produced and recorded now compared with just twenty-five years ago, when Malta had only one radio station, one television channel, three or four record shops and a couple of multitrack recording studios.

The day-to-day activities around the M3P are driven by a small team of dedicated enthusiasts who have varying degrees of expertise and skills to contribute to the project. All of this is coordinated by the M3P Foundation, a Malta-registered voluntary organisation that acts as the legal entity responsible for the project's longevity and well-being. A number of postgraduate researchers at the University of Hull work on the project within the institution's Media and Memory Research Initiative (MaMRI).[2] This was designed to be an integral part of the M3P from the very beginning. While they provide a vibrant framework within which the research can develop and the project can attain longevity, all the M3P activities are also considerably sustained by the non-academic work of the volunteer contributors who embrace the project – or at least parts of it – as their own. The main example of this aspect of the M3P is embodied in the attempt to create a comprehensive archive of all Maltese music ever released on CD. This involves the collaborative efforts of a small group of the M3P contributors who are based across Malta, the United Kingdom and Australia. That nothing even close to this yet exists anywhere acts as a great incentive to drive this group of individual record collectors to do-it-together themselves without expecting any constituted institution to lead the way on such an undertaking. It is beyond the scope or capacity of the National Archives of Malta to do this work urgently. The National Library of Malta does not have the means, retroactively or otherwise, to expand the requirement for legal deposit to include non-paper-based works, and what is now Public Broadcasting Services (Malta) Ltd, the national broadcasting organisation that was originally established in 1935 under British colonial rule and ended up in Maltese hands after a hostile takeover in 1975, has a long history of mismanagement when it comes to its archival assets. In this infrastructural vacuum, the dedicated individual collectors associated with the M3P have better private holdings of Maltese music than any publicly funded institution.

PRESERVING AUDIO CDS

In 2013, the M3P started developing a workflow model for the preservation of audio CDs. Initial work on this project was enabled through grants from the British Academy, the Malta Council for the Voluntary Sector and the Jisc-funded Sustainable Preservation Using Community Engagement (SPRUCE) project, administered through the Digital Preservation Coalition from the University of Leeds and the University of Hull. Rather than focus on static preservation of the discs in their cases and any included printed matter, the need to preserve the digital data on CDs containing Maltese audio, rather than just the physical objects, was immediately seen as the more urgent point of focus. Audio CDs are much more fragile than previous marketing hype had led most people to believe. While the data stored on them are harder to damage by everyday use, as with vinyl records they are not only liable to scratches and heat but they also have a relatively short shelf life. Furthermore, very few electronic equipment manufacturers now produce high-quality audio CD players, and this media format is well on its way to obsolescence (Respers France 2010; Knight 2013).

In a publication aimed mainly at librarians and archivists, Byers (2003) provides a very comprehensive guide to caring for and handling CDs as objects. While emphasising ways to maximise the useful lifetime of optical discs (including DVD media along with CDs) in elaborate detail, there is little attention to the preservation of the data on the discs beyond the useful lifespan of the physical object itself, even if this is not completely overlooked. Additionally, Byers (2003, 1) points out that his document is "intended neither to represent nor imply a standard" but is rather a consensus of reliable sources. In other words, it is a compendium of best practice, even if not working directly with established standards. From a digital preservation perspective, this raises the essential need to establish standards for such work, including, of course, the M3P's own CD archiving efforts. An important point to take away from Byers (2003, 3, 12–13) in this preservation framework is that not all CDs have the same shelf life, and there are various factors that affect disc life expectancy. A *PCWorld* article published in 2006 was among the first attempts to draw public attention to the fact that "[u]nlike pressed original CDs, burned CDs have a relatively short life span of between two to five years, depending on the quality of the CD," while cool temperatures and darkness are also highlighted as ways to extend the life of a burned CD (Blau 2006).

Although there are two ways to place audio files onto a CD, there are actually three types of disc-burning processes. This outline is derived from Byers (2003, 27–8):

Disc-Burning Process

1 Commercially pressed CDs, which are produced on an industrial scale. Many thousands (in some cases, millions) of copies are produced through a process that has proven to provide the best possible longevity for the format.
2 Multiple copies of discs, usually hundreds (in some cases, thousands) of copies produced on less sophisticated CD duplication machines, which essentially use widely available writable CDs. These are not too different from the sort of CDs someone would burn on a PC at home, other than the fact they are produced through specifically designed hardware for CD duplication on a relatively small scale compared with the widely distributed commercially produced CDs.
3 Individual copies produced on personal computers or similar disc-burning devices. In some cases, this is done on rewriteable discs, which are designed to enable reuse or rather rerecording of different data a seemingly unlimited amount of times.

Before moving on to consider standards for audio CD data preservation, we should also distinguish the different types of data that are found on audio CDs. This is adapted from Chitode (2007, 24–37) and augmented with other observations made through direct experience working with such media.

Types of Data on Audio CDs

1 File formats playable on all audio CD players (mainly *.aiff but actually raw bitstream data/PCM).
2 File formats playable on specific types of audio CD players (mainly *.mp3 but also *.wma).
3 File formats playable only on personal computers running specific media players that support particular formats and codecs (such as *.wav, *.flac, *.ogg and others).
4 Non-audio files, including video files, image files, text files and others (such as *.cda index files).

RELIABILITY OF LONG-TERM DIGITAL STORAGE

Baker et al. (2006) identify ten threats to long-term digital storage and preservation: large-scale disaster, human error, component faults, media faults, media/hardware obsolescence, software/format obsolescence, loss of context, attack, organisational faults and economic faults. Of these, the most pertinent to the preservation of audio CDs are media faults and media/hardware obsolescence, as well as software/format obsolescence. These are to be expected for audio CDs as much as for other media, hardware, software and formats. It is striking to note that, according to this article, "the biggest threats to digital preservation are economic" but "detailed cost modeling of long-term storage will require much more real-world data to be meaningful" (Baker et al. 2006, section 4.3).

Media faults with CDs are not rare, even if they are not common with discs that have been handled carefully and not exposed to extreme temperatures and/or excessive friction on the data surface. As noted earlier, media/hardware obsolescence is a very evident problem for audio CDs. Fewer CD players are available now, as other types of music players have superseded CDs. For some time – mostly throughout the 1990s and the first decade of the twenty-first century – CDs were a common feature of personal computers, including laptops. This was how most CDs were played, aside from hi-fi systems, in cars and on portable CD-playing devices such as the Sony Discman.

Software/format obsolescence can, however, be overstated with regard to audio CDs. For example, at the turn of this century, Cohen (2001) believed that "within three years MP3 will be an obsolete format, compression will be a thing of the past, and costs of converting to digital format and migrating data into the future will drop significantly." While it is not entirely clear why MP3 has survived and even thrived as a format, except for the rise of its acceptance as a standard format in mobile/portable music-playing devices such as iPods and other such MP3 players, it was not entirely unreasonable for Cohen to make that prediction because MP3s are in what is known as a lossy format,[3] which instantly degrades the quality of audio files from the much higher bit rates found on audio CDs as uncompressed sound. Furthermore, the format has a patent associated with it that, from a financial perspective, makes it a less desirable format than Ogg Vobis (.ogg), which provides a similar lossy compression through an open source codec.

Despite this, there was another relatively popular format at the time Cohen predicted the demise of the MP3, and this was the RealAudio codec used for live web streaming. The once ubiquitous RealPlayer, which for some time was one of the two main ways to stream audio and video online, has now receded into a specialist format and it is unlikely it will regain popularity as it has been superseded by a number of other formats.

STANDARDS, RECOMMENDED PRACTICES AND STRATEGIES

The Technical Committee of the International Association of Sound and Audiovisual Archives (IASA) has established general guidelines for safeguarding audiovisual heritage. One of these documents, known as IASA-TC 03, aims to identify problem areas and recommend the best practice for preservation while attempting to strike a balance between what is ideal and the realities faced in everyday situations (Schüller 2005). In discussing obsolescence of formats, this document explains that "with the exception of the audio CD, the DVD audio and the MiniDisc, all specific digital audio formats have become obsolete after a short period in the market leaving many carriers still in good condition but without the machines required to access the sounds" (Schüller 2005, section 4.b). The storage of content as data – that is, file formats in a computer environment – is here seen as "making the problem easier to manage than the digital audio formats driven by the consumer market" (2005). As most file formats, operating systems and storage media are threatened by obsolescence, this is presumably a less desirable scenario than working with short-lived formats and media such as the zip disk, which was popular in the late 1990s.

IASA-TC 03 also recommends attention is given to the preservation of the carrier – in this case, the CD itself – for as long as possible. This raises the question of ways to extend the lifespan of the carrier. However, with CDs it is evident that, because of the relatively short lifespan of the medium, it is better to plan for the subsequent copying of the information. There are other things to consider here, such as the fact that "removing the primary information from the original carrier raises the question of future authentication of the sound" (Schüller 2005). Because of this, "the importance of adequate secondary information increases" (2005). This means a systematic plan needs to be adopted to preserve secondary information contained in the original document. With the preservation of CDs, this would presumably refer to the writing or markings on the non-playing side of the CD, as well as the case, especially any cover art or sleeve notes packaged in the case (whether hard or soft) in which the CD was originally circulated. This potentially introduces the creation of digital imaging of the non-playing side of the CD, along with the preservation of the plastic object, as well as preservation of the plastic or paper case and the printed-paper materials containing cover art and other information such as track-listing details and song lyrics. In turn, this aspect of preservation around audio CDs raises a set of further issues related to standards and best practice on preserving paper-based works, as well as digitising them along with printed matter on the plastic discs. There is no urgent need to preserve these materials in a digital format. Static preservation of printed-paper and plastic objects requires little more than the scanning of flat surfaces to ensure these are readily accessible along with the data migrated from the original carrier.

These guidelines from IASA-TC 03 should also be read in the context of IASA-TC 04 (Bradley 2009), particularly Section Two on key digital principals. This is where things such as sampling rate (at a minimum of 48kHz, while IASA recommends 96kHz) and bit depth (the CD standard is 16-bit but 24-bit is recommended, particularly for preserving data from a damaged carrier) are discussed in detail. Importantly, this document recommends a *.wav format "because of the simplicity and ubiquity of linear Pulse Code Modulation (PCM)" (2009), which has been around since World War II through its use in telephony. To be more precise, it is the BWF *.wav file format that is recommended for archiving as this supports the use of metadata, which can be incorporated into the headers as part of the file. BWF stands for Broadcast Wave Format and is sometimes referred to as BWAV. The format was introduced in 1996 by the European Broadcasting Union (EBU 2011).

To put the IASA-TC 04 recommendations in perspective along with the physical evidence emerging from standard practice on audio CDs, we should not overlook the fact that the standard sampling rate for audio CDs is 44.1kHz at a 16-bit depth. Some audio CDs could have a higher sampling and bit depth than this, such as the SACD or DVD-A format, but more frequently the audio fidelity is lower, particularly when the audio files on the CD are in lossy formats such as MP3.

BEST PRACTICE

Adopters of the IASA recommendations include a number of institutions actively involved in the systematic preservation of audio CDs. For example, the National Archives of Australia (NAA 2013) has a very succinct outline of its compact disc preservation work in the audiovisual records section of its website. Whether within institutions or across DIY archiving projects, shared standards and best practice are ultimately useful for ensuring there is a clear understanding of key aspects in digital preservation across different regions around the world. It is crucial the digital data are not modified during migration from the original carrier. No subjective alterations or improvements should be made, and the preserved data must remain as true to the original source as possible.

Building on these fundamental assumptions, Casey and Gordon (2007) provide in-depth analysis of best practice for all types of audio preservation in relation to the Sound Directions Project at Indiana University's Archives of Traditional Music and Harvard's Archive of World Music. This study acknowledges that publications on standards or best practices for audio preservation are not plentiful. The recommendations for best practice from Casey and Gordon (2007) relating to the preservation of audio CDs are as follows:

1 Use audio engineers and technicians with solid technical skills and well-developed critical listening abilities at points in the preservation transfer workflow where their skill is required (2007, 14).
2 Perform preservation transfers in an appropriately designed, critical listening environment. If such a space is not available, choose a room that is quiet and is removed from other work areas and traffic, and be acutely aware of its sonic deficiencies (2007, 16).

These two recommendations, among several others they make relating to the broader field of digital audio, highlight the essential aspects of best practice with regard to quality control and quality assurance. There are also other things Casey and Gordon establish through the Sound Directions project. These are ensuring quality, providing an ethical foundation, encouraging sustainability, fostering interoperability and providing a migration path. To this end, the Casey and Gordon study provides a very useful resource, particularly because the project has produced digital tools that can be used by others involved in similar preservation projects.

ESTABLISHING A WORKFLOW MODEL FOR AUDIO CD PRESERVATION

The preservation of audio CDs is something that is slightly different from the preservation of CDs containing data other than audio. Data on audio CDs cannot easily be cloned for preservation. The music industry has lobbied the main operating system developers to curtail the duplication of CDs to crack down on the mass production of pirate copies (King 2002). While this is understandable from an intellectual property perspective, it is rather problematic from a preservation viewpoint. The published documents on this area of digital preservation, including those discussed earlier, contain no comprehensive examples of best practice related to data preservation from audio CDs. There are guidebooks on the preservation of the CDs themselves but next to nothing about the preservation of the data on the audio CDs. This area requires urgent attention because audio CDs may contain at-risk and decaying audio data on a fragile medium. Furthermore, certain types of audio CDs are nearing their end of life faster than others.

At the SPRUCE London Mashup[4] in July 2013, I proposed the creation of a workflow model for the preservation of audio CDs.[5] Working mainly with developers Peter May from the British Library and Carl Wilson from the Open Planets Foundation (OPF), and with casual input from other developers at the mashup, we established the main problem that needed to be resolved was the fact there was no open-source tool to easily create a disk image or clone of all the data on an audio CD. While this may seem like a straightforward technical project, it took no fewer than three experienced developers working on this problem for many hours before a practical solution was proposed, based on cdrdao,[6] which is free open-source utility software for authoring and ripping.[7] At least one off-the-shelf solution existed at this point, but for non-institutional projects it is likely open-source software is a better option in terms of sustainability as it is easier to acquire technical support for open-source software than for third-party proprietary software.

Having resolved the basic need to create a clone or disk image from an audio CD, the next step in this project was to explore how to catalogue the disk image and its contents, as well as normalise the audio files into the standard BWAV format. This was supported by a SPRUCE grant covering the period August–October 2013, involving the OPF's Carl Wilson with the participation of Darren Stephens from the University of Hull, who worked with me within MaMRI and in collaboration with the M3P Foundation. Through further consultation with digital forensics experts at the British Library and elsewhere, as well as systematic development, this project has addressed this issue directly and produced a cdrdao java wrapper called arcCD to facilitate the preservation of audio CD data as per the M3P's initiative.[8]

Once this fundamental open-source solution was in hand, our attention could be turned to the development of a four-step workflow model for the preservation of audio CDs. The four steps involved in this process are as follows:

1   disk imaging (stabilising the data)
2   cataloguing (by processing individual metadata files)
3   data ripping (normalising the data on the image)
4   open access to the catalogue (outputting the metadata).

Working with a specific initial dataset in the form of a small number of substantial individual CD collections mentioned earlier, a practical workflow model has been established. This utilises the solution proposed during the London SPRUCE mashup as a tool for steps 1 and 3 called arcCD. Through this work, an example of good practice has now been established in this under-explored area of preservation. Darren Stephens is also integrating further development on outputting the metadata into MediaWiki for easy access and editing of the catalogue, as part of his PhD research project entitled "A Framework for Optimised Interaction Between Mediated Memory Repositories and Social Media Networks."[9] Meanwhile, work on the preservation and cataloguing of Maltese music on CD continues, partly because the format is not obsolete yet and a substantial number of new CD releases continue to appear quite regularly. Eventually, this work has the potential to pave the way for other similar efforts in relation to music on vinyl records or tape. Thankfully, preservation standards and examples of best practice on such other formats are more readily available than for audio CDs.

CONCLUSION

There is much to be gained by making more than just a list of names of artists and recordings available outside closed circles. The M3P continues to pull together the voluntary resources of collaborative contributors while ensuring appropriate standards of digital curation and giving due attention to intellectual property rights matters.

In the context of the M3P's audio CD archiving project, it is useful to provide this overview of the salient issues related to the preservation of audio CDs with a particular emphasis on standards and best practice. As indicated earlier in more than one part of this chapter, there are various ramifications associated with preserving audio CDs and these have their own standards. Examples of best practice across the entire process of audio CD preservation – especially including long-term storage of the original carrier while migrating the data to another repository – are not common. However, some of the large-scale institutions involved in such practice continue to develop case studies of such work, and we can expect documentation from these will be widely available in the foreseeable future.

The M3P's CD catalogue will eventually be made publicly available through the wiki at www.m3p.com.mt, when further contributions to fill in the gaps will be invited as the core team proceeds to preserve and catalogue unique tape recordings in their collections and in those of others who choose to join them in the interim. In this spirit, the National Archives of Malta, the Malta Broadcasting Authority and other institutional entities are actively looking at the M3P as a collaborator in their own efforts to provide a national infrastructure for audio-visual archiving with proper plans for long-term preservation.

The intangible heritage preservation work described in this chapter involves the use of open-source software and new knowledge presented freely to other DIY music archives beyond the particular collections described here. The main issue in relation to any attempts to preserve such materials will be the appropriate handling of intellectual property rights. The software required to create an audio CD archive is license-free and available as an open source tool that can be refined and updated as needed by skilled software developers. The basic equipment required for the preservation of music and other data on audio CDs – a computer with a good-quality CD player – is fairly affordable and presently relatively easy to come by. CD players will soon become obsolete, so any DIY efforts in this area need to take place sooner rather than later.

ACKNOWLEDGEMENTS

The author is indebted to Mario Axiaq, Steve Borg, Michael Bugeja, Noel D'Anastas, Richard Hollinger, Jon Ippolito, Hannah Jones, Peter May, Andrew Pace, Darren Stephens and Carl Wilson for their input on the CD archiving project described in this chapter. Additional support from the Open Planets Foundation and the University of Hull's School of Arts and New Media have also helped make aspects of this work possible.

NOTES

1. See http://www.m3p.com.mt.
2. See http://www.hull.ac.uk/mamri.
3. For a discussion on lossy file compression see Butch Lazorchak's contribution to The Signal: DigitalPreservation, from the Library of Congress website at http://blogs.loc.gov/digitalpreservation/2013/05/hey-content-creator-make-mine-lossless.
4. The SPRUCE London Mashup was the final gathering under the Sustainable PReservation Using Community Engagement programme, which took place in the U.K. between May 2012 and November 2013. SPRUCE Mashups provided a productive environment for digital collection managers (including those from DIY archives) to work closely with digital preservation specialists to solve concrete digital preservation challenges. SPRUCE was a partnership between the University of Leeds, the British Library, the Digital Preservation Coalition, the London School of Economics and the Open Planets Foundation. It was co-funded by Jisc. For more see http://wiki.opf-labs.org/display/SPR/Home.
5. A brief summary of the intial proposal is available through the Open Planets Foundation at http://wiki.opf-labs.org/display/SPR/At+risk+and+decaying+audio+data+on+Cds.
6. Free download available from http://cdrdao.sourceforge.net for multiple platforms.
7. An outline of the initial solution is available through the Open Planets Foundation at http://wiki.opf-labs.org/display/SPR/Audio+CD+Preservation.
8. All materials produced for this project are available on GitHub at https://github.com/openplanets/arcCD.
9. For further information see http://www.m3p.com.mt/wiki/User:Stephensd.

REFERENCES

Baker, M., Shah, M., Rosenthal, D.S., Roussopoulos, M., Maniatis, P., Giuli, T.J. and Bungale, P. 2006. A fresh look at the reliability of long-term digital storage. *ACM SIGOPS Operating Systems Review* 40(4): 221–34.

Blau, J. 2006. 'Do burned CDs have a short life span?' *PCWorld*, January 10. Accessed September 26, 2014. http://www.pcworld.com/article/124312/article.html.

Bradley, K. (ed.). 2009. *IASA-TC04: Guidelines on the production and preservation of digital audio objects: standards, recommended practices, and strategies.* International Association of Sound and Audiovisual Archives. Accessed September 26, 2014. http://www.iasa-web.org/tc04/audio-preservation.

Byers, F.R. 2003. *Care and handling of CDs and DVDs.* Washington, DC: CLIR-NIST. Accessed September 26, 2014. http://www.clir.org/pubs/reports/pub121/reports/pub121/pub121.pdf.

Casey, M. and Gordon, B. 2007. *Sound directions: Best practices for audio preservation.* Bloomington, IN: Indiana University Press.

Chitode, J.S. 2007. *Consumer electronics.* Pune, India: Technical Publications.

Cohen, E. 2001. Preservation of audio. In *Folk heritage collections in crisis.* Washington DC: Council on Library and Information Resources. Accessed September 27, 2014. http://www.clir.org/pubs/reports/pub96/preservation.html.

European Broadcasting Union (EBU) 2011. *Specification of the Broadcast Wave Format (BWF): A format for audio data files in broadcasting* (EBU – TECH 3285). Geneva: EBU. Accessed September 27, 2014. https://tech.ebu.ch/docs/tech/tech3285.pdf.

King, B. 2002. Digital war of words: Now on CD. *Wired*, March 14. Accessed September 27, 2014. http://archive.wired.com/gadgets/portablemusic/news/2002/03/51070.

Knight, S. 2013. The CD turns 30: Time is ticking as the compact disc eyes obsolescence. *TechSpot*. October 9. Accessed September 27, 2014. http://www.techspot.com/news/50435-the-cd-turns-30-time-is-ticking-as-the-compact-disc-eyes-obsolescence.html.

National Archives of Australia (NAA) 2013. Compact disc preservation. Accessed September 27, 2014. http://www.naa.gov.au/collection/preserving/audio-visual-records/compact-disc.aspx.

Respers France, L. 2010. Is the death of the CD looming? CNN. 19 July. Accessed September 27, 2014. http://edition.cnn.com/2010/SHOWBIZ/Music/07/19/cd.digital.sales.

Sant, T. 2009. Addressing the need for a collaborative multimedia database of Maltese music. *Journal of Music, Technology and Education* 2+3: 89–96.

Schüller, D. (ed.). 2005. *IASA-TC 03: The safeguarding of the audio heritage – ethics, principles and preservation strategy.* IASA Technical Committee. Accessed September 27, 2014. http://www.iasa-web.org/tc03/ethics-principles-preservation-strategy.

10 "They're Not Pirates, They're Archivists"

The Role of Fans as Curators and Archivists of Popular Music Heritage

Jez Collins and Oliver Carter

This chapter explores the actions of activist archivists: fans who capture, preserve and share what Marion Leonard (2007, 148) terms "the material objects" of popular music. Responding to the political and economic limitations of rights-holders who prevent the commercial release of the marginal cultural texts of popular music, activist archivists are making materials available for distribution through online communities of practice. These communities are being formed to collectively make accessible popular cultural artefacts, with fans participating in what Andy Bennett (2009, 475) describes as "DIY preservationism."

We build on recent academic work into fans as archivists by De Kosnik (2012), Garner (2012) and Carter (2013) to examine how fans, specifically those of popular music, assume the role of activist archivist. To do this, we draw on virtual ethnographic research conducted in online fan communities relating to popular music, specifically the Bodega Pop, Electric Jive and Tanzania Radio Archives sites. We argue the practices demonstrated in these fan communities are an intended political response to the limitations of formal archives maintained by media institutions and traditional gatekeepers of cultural heritage, where specific content is often ignored or excluded for a variety of cultural and economic reasons. The resulting fan archives constructed by activist archivists therefore help to preserve the products of popular music and make them available to others. However, they also act as prompts for discussions that recall both individual and community histories, raising questions about the nature of the music archive, history and heritage. Our understanding of what constitutes heritage is derived from the recent European Union definition, which states: "Cultural heritage consists of the resources inherited from the past in all forms and aspects – tangible, intangible and digital (born digital and digitized)" (European Union, 2014).

First, we examine how past studies of fan archivists have tended to present the practice as a do-it-yourself activity, rather than as taking place within a community of practice. Second, we present our definition of the activist archivist, discussing how this idea emerges out of academic work on social history and community archives. We then illustrate this by using three examples of online activist archives relating to popular music, focusing on how they not only share artefacts but collectively construct cultural memory – that is, "the acts and products of remembering in which individuals engage to make sense of their lives in relation to the lives of others and to their surroundings, situating themselves in time and place" (van Dijck 2006, 358) – through the interactions between, exchanges of and insights into the production, distribution and consumption of the texts they share with other users of such sites. The chapter concludes with a consideration of the tensions that exist between activist archivists and the gatekeepers of popular culture, and how these threaten, and have even destroyed, extensive archives, thus highlighting the fragile and often temporary nature of activist archives.

FANS AS ARCHIVISTS

We present fan archivism – or, as we describe it, activist archivism – as a form of fan production. In his recent book on fandom, Mark Duffett (2013, 21) describes fans as "networkers, collectors, tourists, archivists, curators, producers and more," highlighting the multi-faceted nature of fandom. Typically, academic work has framed the fan as a collector rather than an archivist. It has only been recently that academics have begun to question the role fans occupy as archivists of media texts. For instance, Andy Bennett (2009, 475) presents fan archivism as "DIY preservationism," an activity where fans of rock music seek to construct their own discourses of this music by "remembering those artists overlooked and ignored in more conservative accounts [of rock history]." For Baker and Huber (2013, 513), the development of DIY institutions takes this practice further in the realisation of physical spaces staffed by "volunteers who are not expert in tasks associated with archiving, records management, preservation, or other elements involved in cultural heritage management [and who] learn skills along the way as they work to collect, preserve and make public artefacts related to popular music culture."

Similarly, Ken Garner's (2012) study of the late and much-lauded BBC Radio One DJ John Peel focuses on how fans of Peel's radio show had produced much more exhaustive archives of the broadcast than the BBC by using home recording technologies. These fan-made recordings were then later shared online for others to consume. Garner finds that the fans, through their archiving and sharing, share similar values to the professional archivists at the BBC but differ in that they choose to make the content available for consumption. Garner (2012, 92) discusses some of the political and economic limitations that face the BBC archive and prevent it from making available a wealth of audio and visual texts, as the Peel archive does. First, there are cost implications that render the digitising of an extensive archive financially unviable, due to the time and associated cost of labour it would take to digitise such a mass of material. Second, BBC policy meant that, before the 1990s, only "a small number of all programmes on all stations were 'selected' for the archive" (Garner 2012, 92). As a consequence, there are a number of texts to which the BBC no longer has access. The collections of fans can therefore fill in the gaps of those lost BBC archival holdings.

In the realm of film, Abigail De Kosnik (2012) uses a case study of "Joan," a female fan who uses file-sharing to extend her collection of film. De Kosnik presents Joan as an archivist of film, collecting and storing content that is often ignored by media institutions and remains commercially unavailable. Interestingly, Joan is described as a "personal archivist," downloading films and television shows to construct her own personal archive. This is a feature found in much of the literature on fans as archivists, presenting the practice as a private, do-it-yourself activity rather than a public activity – or, as we suggest, a do-it-together activity. In this chapter, we present the activist archivist as a community activity, one that relies on the collective efforts of a group of like-minded people who strive to make available the material objects of popular culture for consumption. It is this definition of the activist archivist that we now explore.

DEFINING THE ACTIVIST ARCHIVIST

Our definition of activist archivists differs from previous accounts of fans as archivists in that they construct archives for both private and public consumption. The completist desire of fans has been much discussed in academic literature (Geraghty 2014; Hills 2002; Klinger 2006; Shuker 2013). The activist archivist, though engaging in personal completist activities, strives to collaboratively construct archives of popular culture texts that might be ignored by those who curate formal archives or those that are commercially unavailable. Therefore, the activist archivist is responding to the political and economic factors that often render the material objects of popular culture unavailable for consumption. In addition to preserving texts and making these available, they are also involved in the wider practices of preserving memory and documenting history. For example, a wide range of related ephemera will be included as part of the preservation activity, as well as the archivists adding their own experiences and knowledge. In the context of popular music, this might include knowledge about the production of the artefact, distribution information, memories of gigs or discussion of its reception.

Our use of the term "activist archivist" originates in academic work within social history and archive disciplines. Historians Katherine Hodgkin and Susannah Radstone (2003) argue that to contest the past is not merely about the struggle of right versus wrong or truth versus untruth but rather who is entitled to speak of the past in the present. They state memory acts as an aid to the formation of history. Hodgkin and Radstone's work is influenced by, and develops, Raphael Samuel's (1994) theory of the complex relationship between history and memory. Samuel asserts that memory is active and dynamic, and is both dialectically related to, and shares a process of intellectual labour with, history. He goes on to argue memory is "historically conditioned, changing colour and shape," dependent on the moment and "far from being handed down in the timeless form of 'tradition' it is progressively altered from generation to generation" (Samuel 1994, x). Furthermore, Samuel, along with other social historians such as Hilda Kean and Paul Ashton (2009), and Roy Rosenzweig and David Thelen (1999), have called upon professionals to recognise the value of everyday lives and practices as areas of legitimate historical study and archival practice. Samuel (1994, 8), for instance, describes history as more than the preserve of the individual expert. Rather it is, he says, "a social form of knowledge, the work, in any given instance, of a thousand different hands."

Samuel highlights a number of amateur individuals, groups, associations and clubs that have been instrumental in our understanding of historical practices. Additionally, we might include activities of fans in this list. Samuel claims these amateurs and their work should cause us to rethink our approach to history-making – not, he says, as divided between "professionals" and "public" but rather if "history was thought of as an activity rather than a profession, then the number of practitioners would be legion" (1994, 17). For Samuel, this manifests itself in the uncovering of history in legends and myths, in folk ballads, in television and literature, and in other forms of popular cultural activity held within our individual and collective memories. For us, this is evident in the practices of curators of online popular cultural history and archive sites such as those we discuss later in this chapter.

Curators of online popular cultural history and archive sites might be identified as the latest manifestation of what Howard Zinn (1977) labels "activist archivists." In a presentation delivered in 1970, Zinn called upon the American archive profession to reconsider how archives are constructed and give more attention to objects that are often ignored. Instead of archives serving the needs of the powerful, Zinn urged archivists "to compile a whole new world of documentary material about the lives, desires and needs of the ordinary people" (Zinn, quoted in Johnson, 2001, 213). In this light, the creation of community archives, as recently described by Andrew Flinn and Mary Stevens (2009), constitutes a political act. While noting the wildly differing subject matter, approaches, aims and objectives of community archives, Flinn and Stevens identify two areas of commonality in such initiatives.

First, there is an underlying distrust of official fan archives and a desire by creators of community archives to maintain autonomy. De Kosnik (2012, 529) also suggests fans archive predominately out of a "mistrust of museums and rights holders," an observation that is further emphasised in Bennett's (2009) work on DIY preservationism. The implication here is that popular culture texts are often ignored for preservation, deemed culturally insignificant or unworthy of preservation by the formal gatekeepers of popular culture. When defining popular culture – of which popular music is, of course, a part – John Storey (2006) identifies it to be a "residual category." Therefore, for Storey, popular culture comes to be regarded as an "inferior culture" (2006, 6). We argue that this can lead to the construction of a discourse that seeks to undermine the products of popular culture – or, as Bennett (2009, 477) identifies, the existence of an "institutional bias" that removes the popular culture artefacts from a "heritage discourse." Because of this exclusion, there exists a wealth of texts that, for a variety of reasons, remain unavailable commercially, are only available in past home entertainment formats or exist as homemade, off-air recordings. The products discussed below can also be labelled as niche products, rendering them commercially unviable for release or ephemera that is deemed of little cultural significance such as promotional materials.

Second, for Flinn and Stevens (2009), community archives are motivated by the failure of mainstream heritage narratives and collections to reflect and actively represent their histories, stories and knowledge. As Flinn (2011) observes, the digital environment has had a major role to play in underwriting activism and the creation of community archives that allow new voices and new histories to be heard and that form around an unbounded plurality of tangible and intangible heritage objects. Also, formal archiving carries a considerable cost and can be heavily labour intensive. Not only is space required, either physically or virtually, to archive texts but professionals and costly equipment are needed to participate in the archiving process. As a consequence of these preventative issues, activist archivists are engaging in acts of preservation, taking it upon themselves to preserve the texts of popular culture before they become lost to time. They are investing in their own digital equipment and devoting a considerable amount of their leisure time to such a pursuit. As Garner (2012) recognises, the practices of fan archivists share many similarities with those of formal archivists in the ways they collect, record and preserve. However, our research shows the main difference here is that activist archivism is a collaborative process and one that intends to celebrate the products of popular culture by making them available for consumption for others. To do this, a variety of online platforms and digital tools, such as blogs and bulletin boards/Internet forums, are used to share material. These are platforms that encourage responses, insights and participation from others, again highlighting the community aspect of this practice. We include the fan archives we discuss shortly as extensions of the community archives Flinn and Stevens (2009) describe.

Using such a term as "activism" to label the collective practices of fans sharing popular culture artefacts might appear rather hyperbolic. For example, Baker and Huber (2013, 516) comment that Collins's (2012) past work on activist activism suggests an "explicit claim on activism or overt-politicality" from which they shy away in their study of everyday DIY music preservation. However, we share the view of Martha McCaughey and Michael Ayers (2013, 14), who recognise the difficulties of not only determining "what counts and does not count as legitimate online activism" but also seeing general activism as an activity that can take several forms that operate on varying scales of impact. We use the term "activism" in this context to describe the activities of fans seeking to address the institutional biases that govern the ways popular culture texts are preserved. It is their activities, which are often legally contentious, that are a form of activism, acknowledging the value of the forgotten and preserving them for others to access and enjoy.

To clarify, our extension of Zinn's (1977) concept of the activist archivist involves three significant practices. First, the activist archivist uses differing digital tools to preserve artefacts of popular culture in a digital form. This might include the capturing of audio from a vinyl record, the scanning of a promotional flyer for an event or the scanning of a fanzine. Second, the digital file is then uploaded and made available for sharing in a community of practice. File-sharing technologies such as cyberlockers and image hosts are the most commonly used methods of hosting uploaded artefacts, and are then shared on subject-specific blogs or forums that have a clear mission statement based on the making available of commercially unreleased artefacts. Third, the activist archivist encourages comments and feedback from fellow archivists that help to construct a historical narrative relating to the uploaded file. For instance, an uploaded promotional flyer of a music event may be supported by memories of the event or the sharing of other related artefacts that further help to bring attention to the significance of the event. Therefore this is not an act of a casual file-sharer. Rather, it is about the curation of popular cultural history, giving context and background to forgotten objects and untold histories that have been ignored or excluded.

As part of our research into activist archivism, we have been engaging in a virtual ethnographic study of a number of online communities of practice that share all manner of popular culture forms, such as film, television, magazines and photographs. For the remainder of this chapter, we focus on three examples of archives created and populated by activist archivists relating to popular music culture: Bodega Pop, Electric Jive and the Tanzania Heritage Project. According to Christine Hine (2000), virtual ethnography is a flexible methodology that can be adapted according to the virtual space being studied. Therefore the researcher can draw on a range of approaches that can enable them to better understand the online community they are studying. Over the course of two years, we have engaged with numerous pages of uploaded content but also participation through user comments. This has enabled us to observe how these communities of practice develop over an extended period of time, as well as enabling us to gain greater understanding of the practice of activist archivism on the sites we now discuss.

EXAMINING ACTIVIST ARCHIVES OF POPULAR MUSIC CULTURE

Popular music archives, heritage and histories are emerging online from a diverse set of fan practices, exhibiting a prodigious variety of reference points and modes of memory-making. Created, curated and populated by public history-makers and activist archivists, these sites are democratising our understanding of, and approach and access to, traditional history and archive collections, and can be seen as challenging the traditional gatekeepers of popular music heritage and dominant popular music historiography. Despite working across a range of genres and formats, and offering contrasting approaches, the three archives discussed below – Bodega Pop, Electric Jive and Tanzania Radio Archives – share a common purpose in preserving and making accessible aspects of popular music history.

Bodega Pop

Bodega Pop is a blog site dedicated to sharing music collected from small grocery stores in the United States called bodegas, which the founder Gary states "can almost never be found in the 'World Music' section of the few remaining places to buy CDs in the U.S., nor for that matter on iTunes or cheapo MP3 sites like Soundike" (Bodega Pop 2014). Gary digitises and streams albums as well as making them available to download alongside liner notes and images of the sleeves. Evidence of this practice can be found in the uploading of the Algerian musician Khaled's album *Yal Malblia*, which, according to Gary, was "reupped, due to the supreme awesomeness that is this album, here" and "found in Bay Ridge at one of the now-defunct Arabic music shops that used to dot Fifth Avenue below 70th Street" (Gary 2013). The sharing of this album elicits a number of user comments, thanking Gary for making it available and commenting on the quality of the music. This develops into a conversation about Khaled's other early work, similar Arabic musicians and the difficulties in being able to find or purchase it. One fan, using the handle "Hammer," then provides a number of hyperlinks to access other Arabic music, commenting: "It's one of those Russian multi-thread forums that hack into world cultures and post music by the truckload regardless of copyright and what-all. It's a good thing, though ..." (Hammer 2012).

In a separate blog post on the site titled "Guilty until proven innocent?" (Gary 2012), Gary underlines his rationale for running Bodega Pop. In this post, he protests against the Federal Bureau of Investigation-enforced closure of cyberlocker Megaupload. He is not explicit in his support of Megaupload but is more concerned with how its closure has led to "the loss of countless music blogs, the loss of the communities they fostered, the loss of the evidence of otherwise forgotten expressive culture(s) that they brought to the surface and shared." He refers to blogs such as Madrotter, Global Grooves, Mutant Sounds and The Vault: Japanese Music Junkies Unite as libraries, repositories of knowledge holding rare, obscure, out-of-print music. For Gary, these blogs share "expressive cultural artefacts." He adds that it is "not just the music, mind you, which is lovely. But artefacts that are now once again unavailable for, say, anyone studying the region and period." This post draws a range of passionate responses debating copyright law, discussing the implications of the enforcement of culture and the hypocrisy of both users and creators of sites such as Bodega Pop who download music that is commercially available. However, poster "GF," who mourns the loss of a similar music-sharing blog named Holy Warbles, expresses the overriding sentiments:

> I felt like I was part of something special, too, as someone else wrote. A thoughtful community with no rules or limits on what beautiful music is. This phenomenon can probably be attributed to Owl's presentation (and "personality") as much as any of the music (those mixtapes!), but I haven't really tried to analyze it that much. I just know I'll miss the hell out of the place and hope they Warble on somehow, somewhere, someday (GF 2012).

The actions of Gary and the Bodega Pop community, the members of which capture and share the obscure recorded materials they are seeking to preserve alongside their articulation of why they undertake such activities, are clearly politically motivated and expressed. In spite of the threat of prosecution and enforced closure, Gary continues to operate Bodega Pop, preserving and sharing obscure music that for him and many others has a cultural, rather than economic, value.

Electric Jive

Electric Jive is a collaborative blog site maintained by four fans of South African music who live in South Africa, America and the United Kingdom. Found on the front page of the website, the site's mission statement is to:

> collect vinyl and African sounds for the love of music – not profit. Africa is blessed with a heritage of music that must be passed on and appreciated again and again. We focus on out of print South African, and other African music that is very difficult to find. Requests for that long-lost recording are invited – who knows, someone may have it available (Electric Jive, n.d.).

The site gives access to rips of obscure and out-of-print South African music from across all genres. As well as providing a high-quality scan of the cover artwork, the authors write a detailed description of the artists and their music, and incorporate social and cultural history into their reviews. Electric Jive has recently incorporated the Ian Bruce Huntley Archive as part of the site. Huntley captured and preserved more than 1,500 South African jazz-related images and recorded over fifty-six hours of reel-to-reel audio of musicians in Cape Town during the apartheid era. As the site notes, this is a poorly documented and little-known era of music activity in South Africa, consisting of musicians who never had the chance to record and about whom very little formal archival material exists. Huntley has agreed to share his photos and recordings on the site for free, as well as providing a downloadable link to his recently published book, *Keeping Time: Photographs and Cape Town Jazz Recordings 1964–1974*.

Through its explicit non-profit approach to sharing rare music and related ephemera, Electric Jive positions itself as a guardian of South African music. For those involved, their cultural heritage needs to be protected, preserved and shared in order to provide a better understanding of South Africa's musical past. To achieve this, Electric Jive posts recorded music with and without the permission of rights-holders in order to "maintain memory through sharing pictures, sounds and stories that might otherwise become lost" (Albertyn 2014). While the rights-holders might disagree, lovers of the music shared on these sites, for whom it has a personal and collective meaning as a cultural rather than an economic object, claim it as their heritage through their actions in and around activist archive sites. Despite the risk of prosecution, there is a considerable amount of labour invested in the collections that populate such sites and the community that sustains them.

Tanzania Radio Archives

Another example of activist archiving and intervention relating to African music can be found at the Tanzania Radio Archives. In 1961, following independence from the United Kingdom, Julius K. Nyerere became Tanzania's first president. Focusing on culture as one of his key strategies in post-colonial Tanzania, Nyerere founded Radio Tanzania Dar-es-Salaam as the voice of the new, free people. Being the only radio station in the country, Radio Tanzania became the focal point for music and a hub for musicians to meet, play, record and broadcast their music. Recorded on reel-to-reel tapes, Radio Tanzania's archive grew over time to encompass over 15,000 tapes containing over 100,000 hours of unique Tanzanian music and political speeches. However, the tapes were not kept in an appropriate archive repository and have languished on shelves exposed to heat, humidity and natural decay.

In 2012, American Rebecca Corey and her friend Benson Rukantabula founded the Tanzania Heritage Project with the intention "to digitise and preserve the collection before it's too late" (Kickstarter 2011). Corey had learned about the precarious state of the Radio Tanzania Archive after a period spent studying in the country. Working with Bruno Nanguka, Chief Librarian of the Radio Tanzania Dar es Salaam Archives, the Tanzania Heritage Project has recruited other activists who are also keen to save the archive from being lost and who have drawn up a set of core values that provide context for their actions, intending to "preserve and promote endangered culture before it's lost" and "provide a platform to amplify the voices of the past, and of artists, communities, and cultures who want to keep their heritage alive" (Corey 2012). The project has also identified a set of five key goals, which are as follows:

1 Full assessment of the archive.
2 Pilot digitisation: 50 tapes, one digitisation station.
3 "Best of Radio Tanzania" CD remastered and released, including liner notes, photographs and historical background.
4 Scale digitisation: ten digital audio workstations, fifteen employees, digitisation and preservation of full collection (approximately 19,000 tapes).
5 Long-term online storage of digitised material, web platform to show-case the music and the development of an open-source model of participatory preservation.

To achieve some of these goals, the project launched *Radio Tanzania: Reviving the Forgotten Archives* using Kickstarter, a crowd-funding platform. A funding target of US$13,000 was set and a video was produced explaining the purpose of the project. A number of incentive rewards were offered to encourage donations. For example, those donating US$10 would receive three digital files of songs from the archives while a US$1,000 donation would allow the donor to come to Tanzania and participate in the digitisation project. The campaign was successfully backed by 235 people, pledging a total of US$17,040, which was US$4,000 more than the original target. The Tanzania Heritage Project is now underway, using the received funds to purchase specialist audio transfer equipment, and it has made contact with other similar archive projects and archive institutions across Europe.

The mission statements and actions of the activist archivists responsible for the Tanzania Heritage Project make their intentions and motivations clear. Without their intervention, an important part of Tanzania's post-colonial cultural heritage will disappear, leaving absences in the national history of the country. This direct action can be seen as an explicit response to the neglect of the archives and as an affirmation of Andrew Flinn's (2011) depiction of archival activism, whereby individuals and communities respond to the omission and under-representation of local histories in mainstream collections by collecting, documenting and preserving their own archives, heritage and histories themselves.

CONCLUSION

This chapter has considered how activist archivism might have value in showing how fans preserve, access and consume popular music in the digital age. We have sought to understand the practices we have presented in our three case studies as more than just acts of fandom. We argue the actions of fans in the capturing, preservation and sharing of the material objects of popular culture on the sites we have discussed here can be understood as a form of activist archivism, an extension of the concept introduced by Howard Zinn (1977). These examples demonstrate how fans are responding to what Bennett (2009, 477) refers to as the "institutional biases" of archival practices by collectively preserving texts that have particular significance for individuals and communities of practice that form online. The examples we have used also demonstrate a considerable investment of labour into the practice of activist archivism, with participants devoting time and money to an activity that has no obvious economic return. Instead, cultural heritage is the overarching goal.

All the examples referred to in this chapter demonstrate a discourse of preservation in the mission statements and the material they share. For instance, Bodega Pop digitally preserves music from the bodegas, much of which is hard to locate in a physical form. Electric Jive has a similar purpose, sharing South African music, but is also the home of a considerable archive of music, images and other ephemera. Our final example, the Tanzania Radio Archives, differs slightly in that it has sought donations using the crowdfunding website Kickstarter and its own website to be able to afford to digitally preserve the previously forgotten archives of Radio Tanzania. In addition to a discourse of preservation, as described in Bennett (2009), we have also identified a discourse of heritage in these three sites. All our examples demonstrate the role music, and its attendant heritage, play in the construction of a collective cultural memory, which (according to van Dijck 2006, 2007) involves uploaders and commenters adding unique insight into the production, distribution and consumption of artefacts that have been forgotten or ignored by the formal institutions that preserve the material objects of popular culture. This is the mission of the activist archivist.

However, we have merely scratched the surface of this complex and fast-evolving field. Tensions exist between rights-holders of material and those who seek to preserve, for little or no economic benefit, their cultural heritage. Therefore the existence of these archives can be very fragile, and thus sustainability becomes a concern for creators of these archives. The recent Stop Online Piracy Act and closure of file-sharing cyberlocker services such as Megaupload show how activist archives can quickly become obsolete, with the uploaded digital files and memories being removed from circulation and the effort and investment becoming redundant. As a response to this, sites are now circumventing such issues by using technologies that intend to preserve the archive. This involves using personal cloud storage services such as Dropbox or, in the case of the Radio Tanzania Archive, using crowdfunding to legitimately preserve material. Together, the practices we have explored raise questions about the nature of the archive, of history and heritage. Alongside the collection and sharing of music and other associated artefacts, the archive is manifest in the nature of the collective memory forged in online interactions. The presence of music as a motivating cultural force is apparent in generating so much preservation and memory work that attests to its historical importance in the lives of so many.

REFERENCES

Albertyn, C. 2014. Electric Jive: The Huntley archive. Accessed November 29, 2014. http://electricjive.blogspot.com.au.

Baker, S. and Huber, A. 2013. Notes towards a typology of the DIY institution: Identifying do-it-yourself places of popular music preservation. *European Journal of Cultural Studies* 16(5): 513–30.

Bennett, A. 2009. Heritage rock: Rock music, representation and heritage discourse. *Poetics* 37(5–6): 474–89.

Bodega Pop 2014. Blog. Accessed November 29, 2014. http://bodegapop.blogspot.com.au.

Carter, O. 2013. Sharing All'Italiana. Riproduzione e distribuzione del genere I sui siti Torrent (Sharing al'Italiana. Reproduction and distribution on Torrent file-sharing websites). In R. Braga and G. Caruso (eds.), *The Piracy Effect*. Milan: Mimesis Cinergie, 147–57.

Collins, J. 2012. Multiple voices, multiple memories: Public history-making and activist archivism in online popular music archives. Unpublished MA thesis, Birmingham City University.

Corey, R. 2012. About the Radio Tanzania Project, Tanzania Heritage Project. Accessed November 29, 2014. http://www.scribd.com/doc/111888749/About-the-Radio-Tanzania-Project.

Council of the European Union 2014. Conclusions on cultural heritage as a strategic resource for a sustainable Europe. Education, Youth Culture and Sport Council meeting, Brussels, May 20.

De Kosnik, A. 2012. The collector is the pirate. *International Journal of Communication*, 6. Accessed November 29, 2014. http://ijoc.org/ojs/index.php/ijoc/article/view/1222/718.

Duffet, M. 2013. *Understanding fandom*. London: Bloomsbury.

Electric Jive 2014. Heita! [blog]. Accessed November 29, 2014. http://electricjive.blogspot.co.uk.

Flinn, A. 2011. Archival activism: Independent and community-led archives, radical public history and the heritage professions. *InterActions* 7(2): 1–21.

Flinn, A. and Stevens, S. 2009. "It is noh mistri, wi mekin histri." Telling our own story: Independent and community archives in the U.K., challenging and subverting the mainstream. In J.A. Bastian and B. Alexander (eds.), *Community archives: The shaping of memory*. London: Facet.

Garner, K. 2012. Ripping the pith from the peel: Institutional and internet cultures of archiving pop music radio. *The Radio Journal—International Studies in Broadcast & Audio Media* 10(2): 89–111.

Gary 2012. Guilty until proven innocent. Blog, January 27. http://bodegapop.blogspot.co.uk/2012/01/guilty-until-proven-innocent.html.

Gary 2013. Khaled | Yal Malblia. Bodega Pop. Blog, September 15. http://bodegapop.blogspot.co.uk/2012/04/khaled-yal-malblia.html.

Geraghty, L. 2014. *Cult collectors*. London: Routledge.

GF 2012. Guilty until proven innocent. Blog, January 29. http://bodegapop.blogspot.co.uk/2012/01/guilty-until-proven-innocent.html.

Hammer 2012. Khaled | Yal Malblia. Bodega Pop. Blog, May 2. http://bodegapop.blogspot.co.uk/2012/04/khaled-yal-malblia.html.

Hine, C. 2000. *Virtual ethnography*. London: Sage.

Hills, M. 2002. *Fan cultures*. London: Routledge.

Hodgkin, K. and Radstone, S. 2003. *Contested pasts: The politics of memory*. London: Routledge.

Huntley, I.B. *Keeping time: Photographs and Cape Town jazz recordings – 1964–1974*. Accessed November 29, 2014. http://electricjive.blogspot.com.au/2013/09/keeping-time-1964-1974-photographs-and.html.

Johnson, L. 2001. Whose history is it anyway? *Journal of the Society of Archivists* 22(2): 213–29.

Kean, H. and Ashton, P. 2009. Introduction: People and their pasts and public history today. In P. Ashton and H. Kean (eds.), *People and their pasts: Public history today*. Basingstoke: Palgrave Macmillan, 1–20.

Kickstarter 2011. Radio Tanzania: Reviving the forgotten archives. Accessed November 29, 2014. https://www.kickstarter.com/projects/radiotanzania/radio-tanzania-reviving-the-forgotten-archives.

Klinger, B. 2006. *Beyond the multiplex: Cinema, new technologies, and the home*. Berkeley, CA: University of California Press.

Leonard, M. 2007. Constructing histories through material culture: Popular music, museums and collecting. *Popular Music History* 2(2): 147–67.

McCaughey, M. and Ayers, M. 2013. *Cyberactivism: Online activism in theory and practice*. London: Routledge.

Rosenzweig, R. and Thelen, D. 1998. *The presence of the past: Popular uses of history in American life*. New York: Columbia University Press.

Samuel, R. 1994. *Theatres of memory: Past and present in contemporary culture*, Vol. 1. London: Verso.

Shuker, R. 2013. *Wax trash and vinyl treasures: Record collecting as a social practice*. Aldershot: Ashgate.

Storey, J. 2006. *An introduction to cultural theory and popular culture*. London: Pearson.

Tanzania Heritage Project 2014. Website. Accessed November 29, 2014. http://tanzaniaheritageproject.org.

van Dijck, J. 2006. Record and hold: Popular music between personal and collective memory. *Critical Studies in Media Communications* 23(5): 357–74.

van Dijck, J. 2007. *Mediated memories in the digital age*. Stanford, CA: Stanford University Press.

Zinn, H. 1977 [1970]. Secrecy, archives and the public interest. *Midwestern Archivist*, 2(2): 14–27.

11 Coming Together
DIY Heritage and The Beatles

Stephanie Fremaux

DIY heritage might initially be considered an oxymoron. This is because the practice of heritage has largely been institutionalised over increasing concerns related to the protection and conservation of important historical sites. For example, Smith (2006, 21–2) chronicles the establishment of the National Trust in England in 1907 and the adoption of the English model by the United States and Australia in the 1940s. Smith (2006, 23–8) also notes the important charters of the 1970s led by the International Council on Museums and Sites (ICOMOS) and the United Nations Educational, Scientific, and Cultural Organization (UNESCO), which created guidance on heritage and preservation practices worldwide. Do-it-Yourself (DIY) culture, on the other hand, is suggestive of a rejection of institutionalisation. As Spencer (2005, 12) notes, DIY practices emerged as early as the 1930s in an attempt to "create a new cultural form and transmit it to others on your own terms." It is also a practice that uses "the resources available ... to cross the boundary between who consumes and who creates" (2005, 11). Using the 1960s pop group The Beatles as a case study, this chapter argues DIY practices are increasingly being recognised as valuable heritage practices that provide an alternative to institutionalised, museum-based heritage. In some instances, as the case studies illustrate, DIY heritage gives the community a voice and an identity when local and national authorities are unable or unwilling to invest in certain projects.

At a time when museums are under threat of closure due to lack of government and public funding (Steel 2012; Gov. UK 2012), DIY heritage provides a low-cost alternative that not only promises the potential of a global audience but also allows for both a personalised and community experience. Gauntlett (2011, 6) uses the analogy of a communal allotment – a large plot of land divided into smaller, individual plots to grow produce – to describe the changes in the post-millennium world when community shifted from a culture of "sit back and be told" to one of "making and doing" (2011, 8–11). Arguably, this paradigm shift has been influenced by the rise of online social networking platforms such as YouTube, Facebook and Twitter, which encourage users to collaborate and to document any aspect of their lives. This signalled a shift from user as audience to content creator/collaborator. Furthermore, these developments in the ways ordinary people engage with

DIY practices have led to an inclusive definition of fan and fandom that no longer just denotes the more extreme activities that have come to characterise fan behaviour. This is partly due to how the "changing communication technologies ... reflect the increasing entrenchment of fan consumption in the structure of our everyday life" (Gray, Sandvoss and Harrington 2007, 8). These fan creations, which can include fan club and appreciation societies, fan-produced magazines, public art and graffiti, and specialised walking tours, can in turn be used as a new kind of currency where value is added through labour rather than fans being solely restricted to investing in their interests "via cash transactions in the marketplace" (Frith 2007, 94). Beatles fans have been one of many fan groups to take advantage of this new fandom discourse and as a result have become participants in a wider DIY heritage community.

Although these fan creations can lead to a problematic and uncertain tension between complex copyright and intellectual property laws and fans' desires to be content creators, there is no documented evidence of The Beatles' company, Apple Corps Ltd, bringing legal action to prohibit fan creations that clearly infringe on the trademarked Beatles logo and band likeness. Arguably this is because Apple Corps, created in 1968 to manage the business affairs of The Beatles with greater autonomy, knows how important the band's audience has been in promoting The Beatles' brand and how those fan creations have brought The Beatles to a younger market. Speaking to BBC Radio 5 Live in 2010, The Beatles' former PR officer Geoff Baker noted that if the band had stayed with its original audience rather than seeking a new, younger audience, it would have been very difficult for the band's legacy to remain commercially sustainable (BBC 2010). Since The Beatles' breakup in April 1970, the popularity of the band has rarely waned. In recent years, there have been a number of notable events including the fiftieth anniversary celebrations of the band's first single, "Love Me Do" (October 2012), and The Beatles' first United States appearance on *The Ed Sullivan Show* (February 2014). These anniversary events have not only signalled a renewed interest in the band's output but have also helped The Beatles to remain relevant in a highly mediatised age where a multitude of products compete for consumers' attention. For a long-disbanded group whose story has been officially told for fifty years, the emerging DIY creations discussed in this chapter demonstrate the DIY ethos is flourishing in localised physical projects created by ordinary members of the fan community. By analysing key contemporary examples such as the John Lennon mural in Liverpool, England and Rutherford Chang's exhibition *We Buy White Albums*, this chapter seeks to highlight how the intrigue of The Beatles' lasting legacy is no longer as focused on understanding the magic of the Fab Four but rather on understanding the desire for fans to insert themselves into The Beatles' story. In their work on heritage and identity, Graham and Howard (2008, 2) argue that value is not placed on heritage itself but rather on "artefact and activities", which have imprinted on them meanings that provide insight into culture and society. Using this idea as an impetus for this chapter, the investigation of these examples show that, despite the problematic relationship between copyright protection and fandom, there are still innovative ways in which Beatles fandom perseveres fifty years on.

THE DIY ORIGINS OF BEATLES TOURISM

Before examining contemporary examples of Beatles-related DIY heritage initiatives, it is first necessary to establish a context by outlining how Beatles tourism in key heritage sites like Liverpool in the United Kingdom and Hamburg in Germany was initially born out of DIY initiatives led by entrepreneurs. Later these initiatives became part of a larger institutionalised tourism strategy through the creation of museums, the renovation of old performance sites, statues, guided tours and other authorised activities. For Liverpool, The Beatles' legacy is the main drawing card used to attract visitors to discover all the city has to offer but for Hamburg, the city's role in The Beatles' story is becoming increasingly distant as it projects a new image of culture, commerce and financial stability. Although some of the physical landmarks used to attract visitors, such as the Cavern Club in Liverpool and the Star Club in Hamburg, rely on "staged authenticity" (MacConnell 1976, cited in Roberts and Cohen 2013, 5), both cities hold legitimate and direct claims to being important influences in the development of The Beatles' sound and image.

While this section will focus on the rise of Beatles heritage in Liverpool, it is worth noting briefly Hamburg's significance in The Beatles' legacy. Geographically and infrastructurally, Hamburg shares many similarities with Liverpool, although the roles The Beatles play in the tourism and heritage strategies of the two cities differ greatly (see Fremaux and Fremaux 2013). The Beatles undertook a series of residencies, performing in four clubs along Große Freiheit and the Reeperbahn in the St Pauli district of Hamburg between August 1960 and December 1962. Most significantly, these residencies were crucial in refining The Beatles' skills as musicians and performers while also crafting a distinctive style that would contribute to what was later termed the Liverpool sound or Merseybeat (see Inglis 2010, 2011; Lewisohn 2013). In Hamburg, 2008 saw the dedication of Beatles-Platz (Square), a DIY initiative prompted by a local radio station and supported through donations by the public. A year later, the Beatlemania Museum replaced the Erotic Art Museum, another initiative by entrepreneurs looking to recognise the city's contribution to The Beatles' legacy as the surrounding infrastructure slowly crumbled away from neglect. The museum closed in 2012 due to financial problems. Its failure as a DIY institution was arguably the result of a lack of support from Hamburg City Council to promote and invest in the museum as part of the wider tourism agenda (Fremaux and Fremaux 2013, 317). In both Hamburg and Liverpool, the public-sector tourism offices have been slow to capitalise on The Beatles' connection to each city and in working with the established entrepreneurial ventures in any meaningful way.

Considering the lasting popularity of The Beatles and each member's success as a solo artist, it can be tempting to assume Beatles heritage tourism was a given for either city. For Hamburg, The Beatles are linked to a seedy and outdated past that no longer represents the city's gentrified image (Fremaux and Fremaux 2013). For Liverpool, the problem seemed to be how to rectify a problematic image that had not been celebrated positively before. For example, Strachan (2010, 45) writes about the periods of economic decline Liverpool faced in the twentieth century, citing first a decline in the shipping industry and then a period in the 1970s and 1980s when the city experienced high levels of unemployment, a lack of investment in maintaining infrastructure, due partly to outward migration, and an increase in social and racial tensions. Leigh (2010, 33) adds that 1960s Liverpool was not a tourist destination. Arguably, this was in part due to an established London-centric focus and an "it's grim up North" attitude with which many industrialised, working-class cities were stigmatised. Both Cohen (2007, 171–2) and Leigh (2010, 32) note that many in Liverpool felt The Beatles "deserted the city" after relocating to London in 1963, at a time when the North would have benefited from the positive publicity the band's success represented with regard to social mobility and the emerging meritocracy. In addition, Bill Heckle, co-director of the Cavern Club in Liverpool, speaking at the Business of the Beatles symposium at Liverpool Hope University on 26 June 2014, argued that in the wake of John Lennon's assassination in December 1980, the city was unprepared and unable to cope with the increased demands from growing numbers of visitors making pilgrimages to Liverpool. For example, there were no memorials, statues or plaques dedicated at the time, and there were very few hotels and restaurants to accommodate visitors.

As a result of these factors, early examples of Beatles-related heritage arose from DIY initiatives led by private-sector entrepreneurs. Cohen (2007, 164) charts the development of two key enterprises: the Beatles Shop, located on Mathew Street and opened in 1982, and Cavern City Tours, established in 1983, which quickly became "the main dominant player in local Beatles tourism." Cavern City Tours offerings include the Magical Mystery Tour, where fans ride around on a replica of the coach from the *Magical Mystery Tour* (BBC 1967) television special, walking tours and a number of private tours that cater to the individual's or group's requirements. Though these commercial ventures would later form part of Liverpool's Big H heritage (see Roberts and Cohen 2013), initially these two examples began as "'bottom-up' activities of … community-based enterprises" that took the initiative "in asserting ownership over and expertise in [a specific aspect of] popular music's cultural history" (Baker and Huber 2013, 515, 514). It is also important to establish that both endeavours were, and remain, largely independent of the ambivalent Liverpool City Council (LCC), which did not even begin to consider Beatles-related heritage as a tourism venture until the mid-1990s. As Cohen (2007, 165) writes, it was not until 1995 that the city council began to be involved in Beatles-related initiatives such as the Mathew Street Music Festival, an initiative driven by Cavern City Tours. The city council did contribute to the £20-million renovation of the Liverpool Institute of Performing Arts (LIPA) in 1996 after Paul McCartney led the campaign to save it from further dereliction. However, the continued ambivalence of LCC led to the creation of the Beatles Group, founded in 2005. This group includes the main entrepreneurs leading the Beatles Story Experience (Martin King), Cavern City Tours (Bill Heckle and Dave Jones), A Hard Day's Night Hotel (Mike Dewey) and Market Liverpool (Duncan Frazer). It is a non-public facing group but its members do stay in conversation with LCC. While it may appear that Beatles heritage has become institutionalised and is firmly entrenched in Liverpool's wider tourism industry, this is not in fact the case. A number of delegates attending the Business of the Beatles symposium as part of 2014's International Business Festival noted a distinct lack of anything relating to The Beatles on their arrival at Lime Street rail station, a main entry point into the city for visitors.

Recently published reports co-published by Visit Britain and UK Music in 2013 and 2014 provide LCC with justification for spending public money towards developing a more visible Beatles heritage industry. These reports investigated the impact of music-related tourism by focusing on festival attendance (the *Wish You Were Here* report: see Visit Britain and UK Music 2013) and on music tourism in general, in which Liverpool was ranked as the primary exemplar of good practice (the *Imagine* report: see Visit Britain and UK Music 2014). The first report noted that 44 percent of those surveyed considered music to be "an integral part of Britain's culture and heritage," with many participants making specific reference to The Beatles tour in Liverpool (Visit Britain and UK Music 2013, 9). The report also argues that "other towns in Britain can replicate Liverpool's ambition and push their own music heritage" (2013, 12). The *Imagine* report (Visit Britain and UK Music 2014, 8) found Beatles attractions alone bring in £70-million to Liverpool annually. According to the *Imagine* report, there were 23 million visitors to Liverpool in 2013 and nearly one million of those visitors came primarily for Beatles-related attractions. To put these figures into perspective, The Beatles Story Museum attracted 254,000 visitors in 2013 alone, 70 percent of whom were international (Visit Britain and UK Music 2014, 10), whereas the Beatlemania Museum in Hamburg only received a total of 150,000 visitors between 2009 and 2012.

CURRENT BEATLES DIY HERITAGE PRACTICES

Roberts and Cohen (2013, 4), drawing on the work of Smith (2006), argue authorised heritage discourse "represents a 'canon' in that it produces and reproduces ideas about what is worth being classified and promoted as heritage where its value lies." Liverpool's tourism strategies clearly adhered to this discourse once the city council became involved in the early DIY initiatives. While Liverpool's institutionalised approach helps to coordinate such large-scale efforts, it also reinforces an official version of The Beatles' story, an account that has already been greatly mythologised as part of the clean, mop-top image promoted during the early days of Beatlemania. In considering the subjective practice of identifying worth against formalised criteria, it could be argued fan participation within that canon becomes limited to one of tourist and/or consumer. There may be an opportunity to recall or share a personal story or connection associated with the Beatles through common experiences in these authorised heritage practices, but rarely is there an opportunity within the authorised space to create a lasting artefact that allows the fan to contribute to The Beatles' story as a whole.

Despite rapid developments within an increasingly digital landscape, there is evidence physical artefacts still hold significant importance to fans. This section explores two examples of Beatles DIY heritage that embrace the physical artefact as a conduit for fandom and identity, practices that are as much a part of The Beatles' story today as Beatlemania was in 1964. The examples of the John Lennon mural and *We Buy White Albums* exhibition discussed below represent a wider trend whereby fans increasingly are becoming prosumers, "simultaneously cultural consumer and producer" (Miller 2014). This notion of the prosumer has "enabled DIY culture to become more accessible and less elitist, but, remarkably, it hasn't diminished the enduring appeal" (Spencer 2005, 13) of creating physical objects. Reynolds (2012, 30) also argues that archiving rock music artefacts is a sign heritage no longer has to be a "posh activity." Through these physical objects, DIY artefacts announce to a global audience how heritage practices are changing from authorised practices (Frost 2008; Howard 2003; Timothy and Boyd 2003) to allow DIY initiatives to be recognised as valuable and legitimate contributions to the heritage landscape.

John Lennon Mural

Completed in May 2008, the John Lennon mural is situated at the end of a row of terraced houses on Croxteth avenue in the Litherland area of Liverpool, which runs along the dock roads north of the city centre. It features a 14-foot-high (4.26 metre) painting of Lennon standing in a doorway from a photograph taken in Hamburg and used for the cover of his *Rock 'n' Roll* album (1975) (Figure 11.1). Also part of the mural are four large mop-top Beatles recreated from the *With the Beatles* (1963) album cover (Figure 11.2). Smaller paintings of original members Pete Best and Stuart Sutcliffe are also included. The image of Lennon is flanked by worn tour posters promoting some of the local Litherland gigs the band would have played, including Lathom Hall situated across the street from the mural.

Figure 11.1 The John Lennon mural represents an emerging DIY ethos in Beatles heritage. Photo by Mark Fremaux.

Figure 11.2 Mop-top-era Beatles represented in the John Lennon mural. Photo by Mark Fremaux.

The John Lennon mural was originally the idea of two Liverpool artists, Greg Brennan and Peter Morrison, who travelled to Belfast, Northern Ireland in 2005 to tour that city's murals. Belfast's murals are often very politically and socially charged, depicting the history of the sectarian troubles between the Republicans and the Loyalists. Inspired by the power of the Belfast artwork, Brennan and Morrison created The Liverpool Mural Project (TLMP) and enlisted the talents of two Belfast artists, Republican and former prisoner Danny Devenny and Loyalist Mark Ervine (Campbell 2007). TLMP submitted a proposal to the Liverpool Culture Company, the Capital of Culture organisers, for a series of murals depicting Beatles album covers all over the city. The proposal was rejected, but with support from the literary community and a commission from Hugh Owen of the Riverside Group, a housing and regeneration organisation established in 1928, the project for what became the John Lennon mural eventually gained the Culture Company's backing (LMP 2008). Owen sought "a non-political iconic image" that would "encourage communities to work together," believing the political differences of the main artists working side by side would perfectly symbolise that ethos (LMP 2008).

It is tempting to read the initial rejection of TLMP's heritage initiative as another example of authorised, Big H Heritage being overprotective of the established Beatles heritage in the city. However, the group's perseverance and partnership with the Riverside Group represent the essence of "the DIY principle that you should create your own cultural experience" (Spencer 2005, 16). Rather than being an inauthentic recreation of an authorised heritage site, much like the recreated Mathew Street and Cavern Club inside The Beatles Story Museum, the mural helps to reclaim the area's symbolic value, "serving as a physical, earthly focus for something greater and intangible" (Brooker 2007, 163). In this way, The Beatles help transcend divisions because of the meaning created through the choice of location and in the artists' conflicting ideologies. Of the legacy these murals will create, Morrison commented: "The murals represent public art that is accessible to all. We hope to represent the communities in which we work in future mural projects, so that people can take ownership of their murals as local works of art" (*Housing News* 2008). The mural and subsequent projects by TLMP are archived in a series of blog posts that show members of the community getting involved in the creation of the murals as well as the artists passing on their skills to a younger generation of aspiring artists.

We Buy White Albums Exhibition

Another example of DIY Beatles heritage is Rutherford Chang's exhibition *We Buy White Albums*, chronicled in the online publication *Dust & Grooves* (February 13, 2013). The exhibition consists of Chang's (to date) 1,018 original copies of numbered White Albums (official title *The Beatles*, released in 1968) on display in a small shop-front gallery in the Soho area of New York City. Chang also brought the exhibition to the Liverpool new-media arts centre FACT, where he was in residence in 2014. The collection of these albums is interesting in and of itself, as each copy holds clues to the previous owner's connection to the physical object. While the majority of the albums are in good to poor condition, many feature artwork, notes, doodles and poetry on the blank, white covers. Chang views these pieces as "cultural artefacts" through which visitors to the exhibition are able to create "an imagined history based on the condition of the albums" (Paz 2013). In collecting these artefacts, Chang has compiled individual stories of Beatles fandom contained deep within each piece. By documenting each piece as well as recording 100 album copies in order to compile a layered recording of Side One, Chang has imprinted his own fandom in the project. For example, the exhibition's website consists of nothing more than an image of 100 unique White Album covers, four links to reviews of the exhibition and a SoundCloud file of the layered recording he created. The website digitally archives the project's existence and represents Chang's authorship as a prosumer.

Lidchi (2003, 160) notes physical artefacts are not merely *objects* but rather *ideas* (original emphasis). Arguably, the ideas behind those objects might represent authorised or official versions of meaning when they appear in museums, as monuments or as institutional sites of heritage. In Big H Heritage, this would involve a strict set of agreed criteria. However, DIY practices allow an exhibition space to accept alternative meanings, and are often valued through a different set of criteria. In the case of *We Buy White Albums*, since an official record of meaning behind each album is not available, visitors are invited to project their own meanings onto each piece as they thumb through the collection physically in the gallery. Visitors are also invited to select a copy of the album to be digitised for Chang's layered compilation. At the exhibition in Liverpool, Chang made his version of the White Album available for purchase, further reinforcing the notion of fan as producer and consumer. By allowing others to participate in this exhibition, fans are sharing what they believe the White Album represents in Beatles fandom and adding to that story with their own memories.

CONCLUSION

While the above case studies only scratch the surface of the ways in which Beatles fans around the world are engaging in DIY heritage practices, these two examples do highlight how the physical object is still very integral to the relationship between heritage and identity. Smith (2006, 276) argues that such objects can be "focal points" for understanding and "preserving identity," not only with regard to groups of people but in relation to individuals as well. While cities like Liverpool and Hamburg have grappled with how much of The Beatles' legacy should feature in regeneration plans and tourism branding strategies, DIY practitioners have demonstrated through initiatives like the John Lennon mural and *We Buy White Albums* the extent to which The Beatles continue to resonate in people's lives. For instance, both case studies demonstrate a coming together of community spirit similar to that represented in The Beatles' music and their role as cultural icons. Writing about Beatlemania in the 1960s, Bennett and Peterson (2004, 9) note Beatles fans geographically removed from the localised scenes in Liverpool and London, where most of the band's activity was based, "reinterpreted the Beatles to fit the image and music of the band into their own cultural experience." Fifty years on from the first *Ed Sullivan Show* performance that would herald the beginning of Beatlemania, people are still engaged in precisely that same activity of inserting their own meaning through these cultural experiences. DIY heritage practices enable participants to create lasting experiences for communities and individuals despite changes to agendas and policies within an authorised heritage. Therefore these DIY artefacts enable The Beatles' story to be re-presented through the fans' and the communities' own personal perspectives.

Smith's (2006, 297) work emphasises control as a key factor in authorised heritage practices, citing the potentially damaging effect on communities and individuals if "ideas about who they are or should be" are reinforced. Arguably, both of the case studies presented in this chapter can be read as a reaction to the control over The Beatles' story by authorised heritage practices endorsed by Apple Corps and Liverpool City Council's continued ambivalence about investing in Beatles heritage – as seen, for example, in the council's stance on demolishing Ringo Starr's birth home at 9 Madryn Street. Instead, DIY campaigners rallied to preserve the original structure until a public inquiry could be held to evaluate the site's heritage potential. In addition, authorised heritage is limited to and controlled by what story (and whose story?) can be represented. Notably, Graham and Howard (2008, 2) argue that, with regard to heritage, the emphasis is not on the material artefact but rather on "the meanings placed upon them and the representations which are created from them." Despite the physical landscape becoming increasingly commercialised, the control over local landscapes that DIY initiatives are taking affords a chance for even the most casual Beatles fans to create an artefact recording The Beatles' importance in their lives – often the very thing that authorised sites of heritage are unable to provide.

REFERENCES

Baker, S. and Huber, A. 2013. Notes towards a typology of the DIY institution: Identifying do-it-yourself places of popular music preservation. *European Journal of Cultural Studies* 16(5): 513–30.

BBC 2010. Beatles brand "advances with technology." *BBC News*, 17 November. Accessed December 3, 2014. http://www.bbc.co.uk/news/entertainment-arts-11774269.

Bennett, A. and Peterson, R. 2004. Introducing music scenes. In A. Bennett and R. Peterson (eds.), *Music scenes: Local, translocal, and virtual*. Nashville, TN: Vanderbilt University Press, 1–16.

Brooker, W. 2007. A sort of homecoming: Fan viewing and symbolic pilgrimage. In J. Gray, C. Sandvoss and C.L. Harrington (eds.), *Fandom: Identities and communities in a mediated world*. New York: New York University Press, 149–64.

Campbell, D. 2007. Mural painters of the troubles join forces to put the Fab Four on Liverpool's walls. *The Guardian*, 31 August. Accessed December 3, 2014. http://www.theguardian.com/uk/2007/aug/31/northernireland.artnews.

Cohen, S. 2007. *Decline, renewal, and the city in popular music culture: Beyond The Beatles*. Aldershot: Ashgate.

Fremaux, S. and Fremaux, M. 2013. Remembering The Beatles' legacy in Hamburg's problematic tourism strategy. *Journal of Heritage Tourism* 8(4): 303–19.

Frith, S. 2007. *Taking popular music seriously: Selected essays*. Aldershot: Ashgate.

Frost, W. 2008. Popular culture as a different type of heritage: The making of AC/DC Lane. *Journal of Heritage Tourism* 3(3): 176–84.

Gauntlett, D. 2011. *Making is connecting*. London: Polity Press.

Gov. UK 2012. Arts Council England makes future funding decisions. Accessed December 4, 2014. https://www.gov.uk/government/news/arts-council-england-makes-future-funding-decisions.

Graham, B. and Howard, P. (eds.). 2008. *The Ashgate research companion to heritage and identity*. Aldershot: Ashgate.

Gray, J., Sandvoss, C. and Harrington, C.L. (eds.). 2007. *Fandom: identities and communities in a mediated world*. New York: New York University Press.

Heckle, B. 2014. Cavern City Tours: Past, present, and future. Paper presented to Business of the Beatles Symposium, Liverpool Hope University, June 26–27.

Housing News n.d. Riverside celebrates the Beatles Mural. *Housing News*. Accessed December 4, 2014. http://www.housingnews.co.uk/enews/displayArticle.asp?ArticleID=174772.

Howard, P. 2003. *Heritage: Management, interpretation, identity*. London: Continuum.

Inglis, I. 2010. Historical approaches to Merseybeat: delivery, affinity, and diversity. In M. Leonard and R. Strachan (eds.), *The beat goes on: Liverpool, popular music, and the changing city*. Liverpool: Liverpool University Press, 11–27.

Inglis, I. 2011. *The Beatles in Hamburg*. London: Reaktion Press.

Leigh, S. 2010. Growing up with The Beatles. In M. Leonard and R. Strachan (eds.), *The beat goes on: Liverpool, popular music, and the changing city*. Liverpool: Liverpool University Press, 28–42.

Lewisohn, M. 2013. *The Beatles: All these years, volume one – Tune in*. London: Little, Brown.

Lidchi, H. 2003. The poetics and politics of exhibiting other cultures. In S. Hall (ed.), *Representation: Cultural representations and signifying practices*. London: Sage, 151–222.

Liverpool Mural Project 2008. Liverpool Mural Project. Accessed December 1, 2014. http://theliverpoolmuralproject.blogspot.co.uk.

MacCannell, D. 1976. *The tourist: A new theory of the leisure class*. London: Macmillan.

Miller, T. 2014. Who invented the prosumer? CSTOnline. Accessed December 1, 2014. http://cstonline.tv/who-invented-the-prosumer.

Paz, E. 2013. Rutherford Chang – We Buy White Albums. *Dust & Grooves*, February 13. Accessed December 1, 2014. http://www.dustandgrooves.com/rutherford-chang-we-buy-white-albums.

Reynolds, S. 2012. *Retromania: Pop culture's addition to its own past*. London: Faber and Faber.

Roberts, L. and Cohen, S. 2013. Unauthorising popular music heritage: Outline of a critical framework. *International Journal of Heritage Studies*, 20(3): 241–61.

Smith, L. 2006. *Uses of heritage*. London: Routledge.

Spencer, A. 2005. *DIY: the rise of lo-fi culture*. London: Merion Boyars.

Steel, P. 2012. Closures hit museums across U.K. Museums Association. Accessed December 1, 2014. http://www.museumsassociation.org/museums-journal/news/01112012-closures-hit-museums-across-uk.

Strachan, R. 2010. From sea shanties to cosmic scousers: The city, memory, and representation in Liverpool's popular music. In M. Leonard and R. Strachan (eds.), *The beat goes on: Liverpool, popular music, and the changing city*. Liverpool: Liverpool University Press, 43–64.

Timothy, D.J. and Boyd, S.W. 2003. *Heritage tourism*. Harlow: Prentice Hall.

Visit Britain and UK Music 2013. *Wish you were here: Music tourism's contribution to the UK economy*. Accessed December 1, 2014. http://www.ukmusic.org/research/wish-you-were-here-2013.

Visit Britain and UK Music 2014. *Imagine: The value of music heritage tourism in the UK*. Accessed December 1, 2014. http://www.musicheritageuk.org/about-us/imagine.html.

12 Trading Offstage Photos

Take That Fan Culture and the Collaborative Preservation of Popular Music Heritage

Mark Duffett and Anja Löbert

My memories live in a shoebox in the back of my wardrobe. Age yellowed paper getting more fragile as the years go by but no less vibrant for the era they evoke. Symbols in biro, scene-setting in code, written in a dialect not of the author's own. Each a little window into a part of my past.

These are the letters, the photos, the ephemera from the first time round being a Take That fan. A box of crap. Or a box of little bits of love. Pre-digital ways of talking to other fans, analogue ways of building and sharing a world revolving around our boys.

I'm not alone in having such a collection. There are probably hundreds of us with these half-forgotten gateways to our teenage selves. The Thatter Exhibition at the lovely Kraak Gallery brings some of those memories out of hiding and transports you back to that world (The Memory Girl 2011).

In the first half of the 1990s, Take That fans took thousands of photos of the band offstage and traded them with each other by letter. This practice was by no means exclusive to Take That fan circles, and surrounded other 1990s boy bands and Brit Pop groups as well. The fans who loved Take That during their first incarnation (1990–96) formed a living social network of music enthusiasts invigorated through their engagement with a glossy yet academically glossed over end-of-teen pop culture. To what extent can we describe the photos and their social use as forms of self-produced music heritage? In recent years, a culture of nostalgia and the preservation of associated texts and artefacts has become increasingly pervasive (Fisher 2013; Reynolds 2011). A number of researchers have begun to think through the issue of heritage culture in terms of a more or less clearly defined distinction between official and DIY forms. Using a study of Take That pop fandom, this chapter suggests the distinction is sometimes not quite so clear. We begin by reviewing some recent contributions to the debate on popular music heritage, and consider the place of a specific example of a music heritage phenomenon. We then discuss the results of Anja Löbert's empirical study among 438 Take That fans from around the world (Löbert 2014) and consider her 2011 photo exhibition in Manchester as a way of assessing the usefulness of the concept of DIY popular music heritage.

POPULAR MUSIC HERITAGE FRAMEWORKS

Andy Bennett's (2009) discussion of "heritage rock" provides some general pointers for framing our study because he discusses the connections between popular music and heritage. Bennett argues that "consecrating institutions" (Bourdieu 1991) associated with media industries have increasingly turned their attention to popular culture. Where heritage was once associated with the folk traditions that shaped geographic identities, it has now become linked to commercial products and the marketplace. Bennett uses this frame to examine an emergent discourse of heritage rock that alternately draws on the genre's critical canons and celebrates alternative versions of it. The first strategy is epitomised by the Classic Albums Live phenomenon, which stages the entire live performance of rock LPs endorsed by magazines such as *Mojo* as milestone recordings. Classic Albums Live borrows its rhetoric from classical-music recitals and prioritises replication of the musical text over the spontaneity of its makers. The second strategy is pursued by those who contest mainstream canonical discourse and use "DIY definitions" (Bennett 2009, 475) and approaches to preserve the legacy of bands whose music has informed those more widely celebrated than themselves. Bennett (2009) examines this in relation to the Canterbury Sound website and Songworks record label. He notes that heritage rock discourse can prioritise shared generational memory instead of nostalgia for specific historical moments or places. Bennett sees heritage phenomena as manifestations shaped by a discourse that emerged from a number of institutions of "retrospective cultural consecration" (Allen and Lincoln 2004). These include retro music magazines, film and television, prestige-granting bodies, the music industry and tribute bands. All of these have helped to reclassify rock as a heritage phenomenon in late modernity. They provide a context within which DIY preservationists can operate.

Collins and Carter (Chapter 10, this volume) extend the line of discussion by drawing on Howard Zinn's (1977) notion of "activist archivists." They contrast private collectors with activist fans who "collaboratively construct archives of popular culture texts that might be ignored by those who curate formal archives or that are commercially unavailable." Collins and Carter note that such archivists act "politically" because they emphasise what they are doing is not a frivolous pursuit. In archiving texts they are also involved in the wider practice of preserving shared memories. In relation to this, Baker and Huber (2012, 2013) discuss the idea of "DIY institutions" in more detail. They describe these as places of popular music preservation, archiving and display that exist outside the bounds of official or national projects of collection and heritage management. For Baker and Huber, such parallel institutions are staffed by volunteers and operate on donations or grants but often aim towards the organisational structures and professional standards of their official counterparts. They do not simply pool existing collections but are social, institutional structures that preserve items for public display or benefit. Baker and Huber see such community-based projects – such as the Victorian Jazz Archive in Melbourne, Australia (see Chapter 17, this volume) – as lying on a continuum between individual private collecting and official archiving, noting that such institutions may sometimes champion specific community histories or forms of activism but are just as likely to aim simply at creating a more complete picture of past popular music culture as it was lived. Such institutions are understood as repositories of culture guided by fannish values such as community self-representation, the development of social networks and doing things for the love of music. Baker and Huber (2013) explain that in DIY institutions, social interaction happens in ways that are rooted in a DIY ethos and sense of "collective collecting" at the community level (see Chapter 4, this volume).

Roberts and Cohen (2014) also attempt to outline a critical framework of popular music heritage, this time in relation to questions of authorship. They argue that heritage constitutes a complex set of phenomena that operate within the context of other discourses. They also divide popular music heritage activity into officially authorised, self-authorised and unauthorised categories, the last of these being "heritage-as-praxis – that works in dialectical opposition to authorized heritage, or what we've more loosely termed 'Big-H' heritage" (2014, 244). Whereas Bennett (2009, 476) notes that, in the case of rock musicians, "the music itself comes to be regarded as the primary focus legacy," Roberts and Cohen (2014, 242) suggest "music heritage increasingly encompasses a range of practices that are not reducible to 'the music itself' but linked to the wider social, cultural, and economic processes surrounding the production and consumption of popular music histories and music heritage canons." Cautioning against the "rigid binarism" of top-down and bottom-up forms of heritage, they nevertheless suggest that the point of devising categories of heritage authorisation is really to explore their interplay (Roberts and Cohen, 2014, 243). In particular, an exploration of questions of authority and authorisation raises issues about the ownership of heritage, as if asking whose heritage is being preserved for whose sake.

In Roberts and Cohen's schema, heritage represents an arena in which legacies are actively forged and contested. To examine this, they look at the placement of plaques as markers of heritage. The first example they offer is the controversy over whether English Heritage would commemorate The Who's drummer Keith Moon with a blue heritage plaque (Roberts and Cohen 2014, 247). English Heritage's recognised institutional status and narrow criteria for plaque selection place it as a contested endorser of official heritage. Like Bennett (2009), Roberts and Cohen (2014, 248) offer a series of music and media institutions that they say shape heritage along official lines, including canonical lists, magazines, box sets, documentaries, promotional agencies (musicians, audiences, entrepreneurs, organisations) and tourism industries. They contrast the official authorship of heritage created by English Heritage with the less staid processes of plaque development offered by the charity the Heritage Foundation. What makes such bodies different is that they often have to consider the importance of fan love for artists. Roberts and Cohen carefully note the pitfalls of such populism:

> However, looked upon as another criteria, the extent to which a musician was loved by his or her fans is an extraordinarily difficult factor to measure. By definition a popular musician or artist who commands a devoted and loyal fan base is inevitably held with some degree of affection, hence popular culture, by dint of its popularity, automatically becomes popular heritage. Taken to its logical extremes, it is possible to envision a scenario whereby this more "democratized" or free-for-all model of heritage eclipses the very culture to which it seeks to pay tribute: heritage culture (or cultural heritage) as a self-sustaining industry: pop indeed eating itself. The material analogue of this future vision of mass heritage pandemic is the spectacle of commemorative plaques breaking out like pustules on the façade of every other building (2014, 250).

The discussion here is reminiscent of Simon Reynolds' book *Retromania* (2011), which describes popular music culture as "repeating itself" in a recent avalanche of nostalgic documentaries, reunions, museum exhibits and re-enactments. What is interesting, however, is that, first, commercial populist processes still have a selection mechanism built in, whether sales figures or commercial charts, and as a social phenomenon heritage is not simply a reflection of fan love but of sociocultural stasis (see Fisher 2013). After all, fans of popular cultural forms were vocal about their passions in the 1950s, 1960s and 1970s, the high modern era where heritage concerns were not as pervasive as they are now under neoliberalism. Nevertheless, the elitist assumptions embedded in some of the language Roberts and Cohen use ("pandemic," "pustules") come not from them but rather from official heritage itself as a selective process. The authors contrast this by examining the case of graffiti found in a Soho flat that was once occupied by The Sex Pistols' John Lydon. The case of audience-made markings raises issues for Roberts and Cohen (2014, 256) of "anti-plaques" and even punk "anti-heritage": the notion that a revolutionary or even simply present-focused music genre should not fall into the trap of celebrating the past. The authors conclude by suggesting different formations of heritage may indicate that there is an issue over "just how meaningful authorized popular music heritage discourses are in terms of how individuals celebrate and curate their own musical memories" (Roberts and Cohen 2014, 258).

The range of scholarship discussed here positions music heritage in part as a set of DIY activities, institutions, oppositional politics or cultural forms. What these various pieces have in common is that they both explore a terrain in which official and DIY or grassroots heritage activities are to some extent contrasted, and in which they also tend to reflect conventional structures of cultural capital, either by celebrating cultural forms more widely recognised as worthy of remembering (heritage rock, punk, jazz) or by finding associated antecedents. Where other cultures are archived or displayed, they are preserved under a framework of historical completism or actively contesting attributions of triviality. Viewed from the perspectives associated with cultural studies and fan studies, there may be theoretical reasons to consider other heritage activity as less contrasting than the emerging discussion suggests. Specifically, pop fandom exists in relation to a context that includes the production and consumption of commercial culture. While it cannot be reduced to those concerns, nor is it entirely a folk or oppositional form. Aligning it with resistance – in this case, resisting the official narratives of the heritage industry or the ways in which commerce can itself enshrine memory – misses the acts of collusion and mutual support that can also occur.

TAKE THAT "OFFSTAGE PHOTOS"

In 2010 and 2011, Anja Löbert conducted an empirical survey of 438 participants from the early to mid-1990s Take That fan pen-pal scene, a virtually all-female scene that exchanged letters and swapped Take That-related material through the post. The fan community was distinctly international in scope: 72 percent reported to have had pen friends in the United Kingdom, 64 percent in Germany, 35 percent in Italy, 29 percent in the Netherlands and around 20 percent in each of Spain, France and Belgium. Other countries further afield also featured prominently, such as Australia, the United States, Japan, Chile and Thailand. Löbert's study of Take That fans suggested the pursuit of fannish intimacy with famous people demanded investigation, as it became the premise of further interactions between fans. Fans were eager to have a contact person in places where Take That was famous and went on tour so they could be sent posters, newspaper clippings and offstage photos from those countries in exchange for duplicate items from their own collection. On average, each member of the scene had twenty-five pen friends and received nine letters per week. Nine out of ten members of the scene said they collected photos of Take That. Featuring most prominently among those were so-called offstage photos.

"Offstage photos" is the term members of the scene used to refer to self-taken pictures of the members of Take That. They were candid pictures taken of the band outside or inside hotels, outside venues and radio or TV stations, or even outside their private homes.

Figure 12.1 Example of offstage photo circulated by Take That fans: 17 October 1997, Mark outside *TFI Friday Show*, UK (Karen Skilling). Photo courtesy of Manchester Music City Tours Ltd.

Figure 12.2 Example of offstage photo circulated by Take That fans: 24 February 1994, Howard outside *5 O'Clock Show*, Holland (Corrie Wouters). Photo courtesy of Manchester Music City Tours Ltd.

Back in the 1990s, trading Take That offstage photos began as a form of offline participatory culture, a means of social networking that mediated between fan competition and friendship by facilitating shared pleasures. Some 76 percent of the respondents exchanged offstage photos. Traded primarily in glossy 4" x 6" format, these informal photos were chosen by 46 percent of respondents as the "thing they most liked to receive from their penpals," making these photos the most popular exchange item, followed at a remote second by videos (15 percent). The average member of the scene owned 295 offstage photos. The unwritten rule within the community was anyone sending something rare and valuable deserved an equally valuable item in return. For example, one respondent wrote: "I only sent photos to people who sent good photos back."

There was a profound disparity between supply and demand of these rare real-life pictures. While over three-quarters of the girls surveyed said they swapped offstage photos of Take That, only 18 percent actually owned original photos they had taken themselves when meeting Take That. In other words, only about every fifth member of the scene owned the all-important negatives. This comparatively low percentage makes sense if we consider that being able to follow and get close to Take That required that a teenager could afford to do so, that she had her parents' permission, was located in a particular country, and possessed the inside knowledge and connections to even trace the boys. Only a minority of fans were able to do so.

In order to conjure up offstage photos to swap – despite the owner never having met the band – many fans made copies of the authentic pictures they received from others. This practice was frowned on by the owners of original photos, who invariably tried to protect their copyright by writing "No copies, please" on the backs of the photos they sent to their pen pals.

In different contexts, the trade in these photos could involve giving, swapping or buying, a fact that did not make it simply a gift economy. One fan explained:

> Another thing we used to do in Spain was buying pictures from fans. Sometimes, we met on the weekends with a group of fans from our own city and spent evenings looking through each other's albums, we picked our favorite member pictures and bought them.
>
> (Eve M., Spain)

The female Take That fans were dedicated collectors of a certain kind. What is interesting is that discussions in popular music studies about collecting as a practice frequently relate it to male-dominated cultures and vinyl record collecting (see Shuker 2011; Straw 1997). Some of the original female fans who had taken and traded the much-prized photographs of their heroes still had them among their possessions well over a decade later, and could contribute them to Anja's study and the Manchester exhibition. Indeed, as part of her survey, Anja found 81 percent of the members of the scene still had the photos they bartered in the 1990s in their possession and 38 percent of those who had taken photos had kept the negatives. They had not relinquished these self-taken images or thrown them away. Instead, they continued to value these items, even if they were rarely, if at all, circulated between fans or displayed in the public sphere. As the blogger in the epigraph beginning this articles put it: "My memories live in a shoebox in the back of my wardrobe."

OFFSTAGE PHOTO TRADE AS HERITAGE PRACTICE

The trading of offstage photographs formed a living culture in the 1990s, and its material trace had an interesting relationship to music heritage. On one hand, taking a photograph is a voluntary and automatic act of preservation. Writers such as Susan Sontag (2002) and Roland Barthes (2000) have explored the nature of photography as a ubiquitous practice and noted various contrasting facets of the medium. The photograph acts to frame its subjects, highlighting and making them important. It allows what is unique to be reproduced. If the medium itself offers opportunity for expression, it seems to do this through capturing rather than copying reality. Photographs "are a way of imprisoning reality" (Sontag 2002, 163). They therefore allow a very particular kind of spectatorial knowing. Photography invites us to visually experience lives, events, times and spaces that would otherwise necessarily exclude us. The images it creates "now provide most of the knowledge people have about the look of the past and the reach of the present" (Sontag 2002, 6). Photographed subjects, in their looks, can evoke certain propriety or interiority, keeping emotions within themselves or giving them away (Barthes 2000, 114). Captured images "do not seem to be statements about the world so much as pieces of it, miniatures of reality that anyone can make or acquire" (Sontag 2002, 4). Photography is therefore a form of surrogate possession, enabling us to keep a slice of time and space as our own. However, it is also a form of quotation, in that photographs encourage us to empathise with the perspective of those who take them. Their images make us feel closer not only to the pictured subjects but also to the takers. Photography also shows that the photographer was there. It is an active process, transforming the subjects who do it (photographers) from passive spectators to active recorders, a point that is particularly important given female pop fans have often been mistaken for passive consumers of music. Taking pictures is thus an event in itself, one that refuses to fully intervene in present activity but that subordinates the present to its future representation (Sontag 2002, 11). It is therefore also associated with dissociation, nostalgia and loss.

On the other hand, pop music has traditionally been understood as indicative of the ephemeral blooming of each new post-war generation. Young pop fans have often understood themselves to be participating in a social process that unfolds in the present moment and shapes public opinion about their artist. Take That fans responding to the questionnaire emphasised the photos as reflections of a present moment:

> I have to say that I really loooooooooooved to swap offstage photos because it allowed me to see a part of the boys that you couldn't see on stage or in interviews. For me it was the "real life." I always had that feeling. You could see them getting in touch with fans, how they reacted in front of them, or just to see them being spontaneous with fans.
>
> (Eve M., Spain)

> In principle, the idea was to take nice offstage photos yourself and then swap these with other people for their offstage pictures. I think that, behind all this, there was the desire to take a peek into the boys' "real" lives. Through these pictures you had the feeling, at least for a short moment, that you were looking into their "private life." It was nicest when the photos were taken by your pen pal herself, and there was a "story" behind them. Pictures that had been copied and recopied a thousand times over were practically worthless.
>
> (Kathrin H., Germany)

What these responses highlight is that offstage photographs of Take That were not taken by fans with an eye to them becoming historical artefacts. In fact, these images, and the practices surrounding them, have only become heritage when claimed, or rather reclaimed, in recent times for a new purpose that now positions them as such.

When fans circulated the photos between themselves in the early 1990s, Take That was still actively releasing records and touring. By 2002, Tara Brabazon observed the organised faction of Take That's fan culture had almost slipped into non-existence:

> Take That split in early 1996. The fan allegiance evaporated very quickly. While a Take That Appreciation Page survives on the web, the bulletin board shows highly intermittent messages. There are very few regular members – so few that an event scheduled to commemorate the group's dissolution became embarrassing in its unpopularity:
> "It is with much sadness that we have to announce that the 2001 Thatters Reunion has been cancelled due to lack of response. We are very surprised that so few Thatters wanted to get together to remember the guys on the 5th anniversary of their split, but we guess a lot of fans have moved on. We have received a total of 25 payments so far but unfortunately because we have to pay the hotel by the end of February, we cannot wait any longer to see if more fans will be coming."

Melancholy punctuates this message. There is a tragedy in establishing a relic of youth that no one visits. It is a virtual ghost town. This vacant fandom is odd, not only when considering the place of Take That in recent memory, but also the current fame of Robbie Williams. His present fans practice textual amnesia about his boy band past. "Thatmania" has disappeared even faster than the Duranmania, Rollermania and Beatlemania.

(Brabazon 2002, 8)

This suggests Take That fandom operated as a living culture. Although each photo represented a moment or memory that was later shared, its trading was still part of a fan practice based on a fascination with present-time celebrity intimacy. The domestic mass adoption of the Internet had little effect in maintaining an organised fan community following the band's split, while the existence of some other fan bases – Beatles fandom, for example (see Chapter 11, this volume) – has appeared to be more continuous. Take That's breakup did not quickly translate into developing heritage practices around the band. Nor did the coming of online archives or a more pervasive nostalgia culture. Indeed, the example from Brabazon indicates early memory sites and activities were unsustainable. It was not until Take That's reunion as a five-piece act in 2010–11 that heritage practices around the band began to come to full fruition.

In the context of fans pursuing heritage practices, it is relevant here to consider Baker and Huber's (2013, 528, n. 7) comment on the work of Leadbeater and Miller (2004):

Leadbeater and Miller's report on the "Pro-Am Revolution" (2004) noted the increasing cultural importance of amateurs who acquire skills that approach those of professionals. However, we connect these DIY institutions to this broad trend with the caveat that many of the people involved in running the institutions we investigate did not necessarily begin with the intention of becoming professional amateurs.

The issue of intent is interesting, because it brings into focus why people pursue heritage projects in the first place. It could be argued that while there are various reasons for music heritage preservation, in some instances one of the primary motivations is a fannish one: to keep alive the memory of particular performers, to celebrate their talents and help more people reflect on their connection with them. Crucial to this is that people did not begin their heritage practice with the intent of developing capacities as pro-am curators or archivists. Rather, they started as fans and their fandom became a motivation for developing these other roles. There may even be a sense in which heritage preservation is not a predisposition primarily chosen by pop fans in relation to their object but is something forced on them with the passage of time.

FANS, ACA/FEN AND THE COMPLEXITIES OF POPULAR MUSIC HERITAGE

Anja Löbert's research led to the creation of an exhibition curated in affiliation with the University of Salford. It was advertised on a website, http://www.fan-networks-exhibition.org, which received 509 Facebook likes from fans and was titled *Fan Networks in the Predigital Age: Take That Fans Between 1990 and 1996*. This installation was staged from June 2–28, 2011 at the Kraak Gallery in Manchester and attracted a stream of visitors, many of whom were in the city to witness the reunited band play live at Manchester City's Etihad Stadium.

The exhibition was based on fan-created materials – among them, offstage photographs – that were both designed for preservation and yet previously transient in their social circulation. It was a form of "collective collecting" at the community level (Baker and Huber 2013; see also Chapter 4 this volume) that allowed fans to curate and celebrate their previous experiences by collaboratively constructing an archive of popular culture materials that had previously been "ignored by those who curate formal archives or that are commercially unavailable" (Collins and Carter, Chapter 10 this volume). Thus comments left in the exhibition guest book included: "Thanks for all the memories. What a wonderful celebration of something that was much, much more than 'just' being a fan!" On the other hand, Löbert had augmented her earlier interest in Take That with academic qualifications and publications as a fandom scholar. She wished to consider the generational memories of the fan base in which she had participated. Was this therefore an example of DIY heritage preservation? In order to answer that question, it is relevant to consider the relationship between fandom and the academy.

Researchers who self-consciously serve and speak for fan communities by using their own identities as fans are, in effect, academic fans or aca/fen, as they are known (the second part of this hybrid term denoting a plural of fans). Henry Jenkins (2006, 251) summarises this position when he states: "I come to both *Star Trek* and fan fiction as a fan first and a scholar second. My participation as a fan long precedes my academic interest in it." Similarly, Will Brooker (2002, 19) declares his own fandom and its role in his study: "This entire book is an example of a childhood passion channeled into an academic career." Scholars like Jenkins and Brooker are, in effect, people who synergise two roles. They are ethical and articulate popular culture enthusiasts who are schooled and tooled, ready to use the space of academia to their advantage as fans. Since the rise of fields of study based on popular culture, including popular music studies, such researchers have used their fandom productively to both contribute to their disciplines and increase wider understandings of their fan communities. One might even posit that most popular music researchers are fans in some sense.

Our analysis of Take That heritage culture provides one example of a wider process of collusion between fans and legitimating agencies of the kind that can sometimes be ignored when music researchers contrast official and fan-created heritage. The University of Salford-affiliated 2011 Kraak Gallery exhibition capitalised on a commercial moment in which discussions about Take That were revived in the public sphere when the band staged a reunion. In turn, a consideration of generational memories was sparked within Take That's resurgent fan base. The exhibition was pursued by Löbert as an aca/fan, collectively sourced and authorised by the academy. It was therefore a curation of popular music's material past that simultaneously fitted the categories of both DIY heritage and authorised culture. To use Roberts and Cohen's (2014) terms, heritage-as-praxis and Big-H heritage may not always be separate, far apart on a continuum or even in a process of interplay. In some circumstances, such as the Take That exhibition, they might instead be barely distinguishable as constituent parts of the same process. This is not to say there is no worth in exploring the term DIY preservation in this context but rather that more work needs to be done in exploring the ways in which popular music archivists, fans, aca/fen and other scholars evoke it as a kind of discursive strategy or resource to support specific music heritage projects (e.g. see Baker and Huber 2012).

Popular music heritage is evidently a complex and empirically variable phenomenon. Rather than seeing academia as a bastion of elitism assaulted by fans, or as a means by which official heritage could move into the cultural territory of fandom, the idea of the aca/fan suggests universities can be used as a vehicle for the concerns of fans levering consecrating or prestige-granting institutions to include their interests in official or authorised heritage phenomena. In the realm of history, this has meant that such bodies have become conduits that can help to redefine the material ephemera of fan communities as part of legitimate fields of historic inquiry and heritage production, a process that is actively created and pursued by scholars who are also dedicated fans. In light of this we would suggest pop fans do not usually set out to be DIY preservationists any more than they set out to be amateur professionals. Indeed, there is a danger of oversimplifying the production of music heritage, and perhaps also patronising its fan participants by the use of such terms. Any portrayal of fans as marginalised, different and resistant forgets the ways in which they can collude with and mutually support both commercial culture and prestige-granting institutions in their bids to assert the legitimacy of shared cultural interests and generational memories.

Since the exhibition ended, the displayed materials gathered from a total of twenty-six fan donors have been in the possession of Anja Löbert. Some fans only donated their materials under the condition their originals would be returned to them safely, itself an indicator of the sentimental value of these items. In these cases, photos were digitised in order to preserve them for the purposes of the archive, as the long-term aim is to set up a publicly accessible digital archive of these offstage photos, as well as other constituent artefacts of this female fan scene, at the University of Salford.

REFERENCES

Allen, M.P. and Lincoln, A.E. 2004. Critical discourse and the cultural consecration of American films. *Social Forces* 82: 871–94.

Baker, S. and Huber, A. 2012. Masters of our own destiny: Cultures of preservation at the Victorian jazz archive in Melbourne, Australia. *Popular Music History* 7(3): 263–82.

Baker, S. and Huber, A. 2013. Notes towards a typology of the DIY institution: Identifying do-it-yourself places of popular music preservation. *European Journal of Cultural Studies* 16(5): 513–30.

Barthes, R. 2002 (1980). *Camera ludica: Reflections on photography*. London: Vintage.

Bennett, A. 2009. Heritage rock: Rock music, representation and heritage discourse. *Poetics* 37: 474–89.

Bourdieu, P. 1991. *Language and symbolic power*. Cambridge, MA: Harvard University Press.

Brabazon, T. 2002. We're one short for the Cross: Abbey Road and popular memory. *Transformations* 3: 1–16.

Brooker, W. 2002. *Using the force: Creativity, community and Star Wars fans*. New York: Continuum.

Fisher, M. 2013. *Ghosts of my life: Writings on depression, hauntology and lost futures*. Winchester: Zero Books.

Jenkins, H. 2006. *Fans, bloggers, gamers*. New York: New York University Press.

Leadbeater, C. and Miller, P. 2004. *The pro-am revolution: How enthusiasts are changing our economy and society*. London: Demos.

Löbert, A. 2014. Penfriendships, exchange economics and FBs: Take That fans networking before the digital revolution. *Popular Music and Society* 37: 5.

Reynolds, S. 2011. *Retromania: Pop culture's addiction to its own past*. London: Faber and Faber.

Roberts, L. and Cohen, S. 2014. Unauthorising popular music heritage: Outline of a critical framework. *International Journal of Heritage Studies* 20(3): 241–61.

Shuker, R. 2010. *Wax trash and vinyl treasures: Record collecting as social practice*. Farnham: Ashgate.

Sontag, S. 2002. *On photography*. London: Penguin.

Straw, W. 1997. Sizing up record collections: Gender and connoisseurship in rock music culture. In S. Whiteley (ed.), *Sexing the groove: Popular music and gender*. London: Routledge.

The Memory Girl 2011. Thatter Exhibition, Kraak Gallery, Manchester. Mirror of the Graces. Blog, June 14. Accessed November 13, 2014. http://mirrorofthegraces.blogspot.co.uk/2011/06/thatter-exhibition-kraak-gallery.html.

Zinn, H. 1977 (1970). Secrecy, archives and the public interest. *Midwestern Archivist*, 2(2): 14–27.

Part II
Case Studies

13 Pompey Pop

Documenting Portsmouth's Popular Music Scenes

Dave Allen

In the second volume of his study of the British 1960s, historian Dominic Sandbrook suggests "DIY was one of the great success stories ... and probably tells us more about ordinary life than a thousand psychedelic records" (2006, 191). This claim supports one of his main objectives: to challenge received wisdoms about the Swinging Sixties. Sandbrook offers extensive archival evidence, questioning whether young people's "views and values clashed with those of their parents, or that they were always the first to embrace change," and he describes "ordinary people, actively holding on to their familiar habits" (2006, 190–1). Sandbrook offers a reasonable corrective to some of the excessive claims and myths about the period, but he goes further in arguing the Swinging Sixties was restricted to a small area of London. By 2012, on BBC television, he suggested "the Swinging Sixties only happened to about fourteen people in a few privileged enclaves" (*The Seventies*, 2012). While clearly an exaggeration, it confirmed his view that the provinces were for the most part stuck in the 1950s.

Sandbrook's view was entirely at odds with my lived experiences as a teenager in the 1960s. His misrepresentation was one of the motives for the Pompey Pop project, which seeks to tell the story of popular music and culture in and around the city of Portsmouth, the United Kingdom's only island city, on the coast of central southern England. Pompey Pop's initial focus was the 1950s and 1960s, hence the particular interest in Sandbrook, although it has since extended to cover a longer period before and after. It began in a piecemeal fashion around twenty years ago but has been more coherent since a well-attended public lecture in October 2009. This was followed by a City Museum exhibition early in 2010 and then the establishment of a website and a blog.[1] There have been three publications, and recently the establishment of a permanent exhibition in the city's Guildhall, which is now run by a Community Trust.

While Sandbrook's views stimulated our response, there were equally positive reasons to create a permanent record of our lives, articulated by my local contemporary Trevor Lovett, who described the years 1960–69 as "the most wonderful times of my life. ... If I had the chance to do it any differently, no I wouldn't" (cited in Anderson 2014, 5). In that spirit, Pompey Pop has generated a great deal of pleasure as well as a growing archive of memories, contemporary accounts, images and artefacts.

LOCAL HISTORIES

Pompey Pop also responded to a number of recent local histories of the city, which covered entertainment and/or lifestyle but ignored almost entirely the experiences of my generation around popular culture. A couple of publications, notably by Sadden (2009) and Balogh (2002), make brief references to a few of the city's venues and visiting acts, but while most other recent histories of the city address arts and leisure topics, including festivals, theatres, cinemas, variety shows and dancing, they say little or nothing about popular music and associated fashions over the past sixty years. A City Museum publication offers "The complete photographic history of Portsmouth, 1900–1999" organised by decade, yet for 1960–69, its thirty-one photographs include just one of a "social evening for members of Young Labour" in 1960 with an accompanying text identifying the "fashion revolution" that "has not yet begun" (Portsmouth Museum & Records Service 1999, 108). Otherwise, entertainment in that decade is represented by a single photograph of the crowd in deckchairs on South Parade Pier watching one of the regular bathing beauty contests. Pompey Pop responded with a book of about 450 images from the period (Allen and Cooper 2011), while there are many more photographs available on the websites and blog. In terms of local histories, we did it ourselves because it seemed no one else would, and the book's print run sold out within two years.

We wondered whether the local, largely professional, often academic historians were dismissive of recent popular culture. Staff at the City Museum suggested informally that it was more probably explained by the fact these local historians worked mainly from archival research in the city's main institutions. Until Pompey Pop, there was very little information available in these archives, whereas there was more evidence of the more formal entertainment run by the City Council, entrepreneurs and major companies such as Mecca Ballrooms.

Initially, our most extensive source of evidence beyond personal memories was the archives of the local newspaper, in particular the classified advertisements, occasional news stories about music, fashion and young people's behaviour, and two regular columns written under pseudonyms: the "Jazzmen," covering jazz, blues and sometimes folk music, and a pop column by "Spinner." My colleague Mick Cooper and I have spent hundreds of hours working our way through these pages to establish a factual foundation for the project's inquiries, and versions have been published in a free document, *Here Come the Sixties* (Allen 2009) and on our two websites.

There is another point to be made about Pompey Pop that might be considered fortuitous (although not unproblematic) and it is the only element that, in research terms, is not easily replicated in any other local project. I have been one of the key figures in the project, and at times the central figure. I am now a retired academic from the local university where I worked in the arts, cultural studies and popular music, so I was familiar with most of the relevant research questions and methodological issues. But, unusually, I was based in the university of my home city, where I grew up as a fan and then a musician, briefly professional and for forty-plus years semi-professional. As a consequence, I knew many local people outside the university well enough to share memories and artefacts and, as the project began, the network grew rapidly. This is not unproblematic because there are questions of distance and balance in my involvement. However, it seems to me to bring distinct advantages, since I am a part of the city's culture outside the academy while also able to utilise the resources and procedures available to me as an academic. Ultimately, the significance of this unusual position is for others to evaluate. Clearly it requires of me a constant reflexivity.

POMPEY POP AND THE WIDER WORLD

Those of us involved in Pompey Pop have begun to establish a fairly significant archive, real and virtual, the latest manifestation of which is a literal archive in the local history section of the city's main library. But the final missing element is the documentation of Portsmouth in broader popular music histories. This is not entirely a problem, since anyone in our position seeking to pursue a project called, for example, Liverpool, London or Manchester Pop would need to negotiate a vast amount of existing ideas and material, and it may even be there is little to add. Portsmouth, on the other hand, rarely features in the broader pop music histories. For example, David Roberts's (2011) *Rock Atlas* lists 650 United Kingdom locations but for Portsmouth offers only a few lines about Mike Oldfield's record *Portsmouth* and a list of musicians born in Portsmouth. There is, for example, no mention of the appearance of Tony Crombie & His Rockets at the Theatre Royal in September 1956, despite it being almost certainly the first live appearance by a professional, recording British rock 'n' roll group. Nor does he mention the somewhat fortuitous live premiere of Pink Floyd's *Dark Side of the Moon* at Portsmouth Guildhall in 1974.

For these reasons and perhaps because all the principal participants are in their sixties and seventies and inclined towards nostalgia and reflection, we developed Pompey Pop. Initially, we had no clear plan beyond the next event. Sometimes we initiated things and sometimes we responded to overtures from public institutions like the City Museum, Guildhall Community Trust and library. The 2009 public lecture that really launched the project was enabled by money from a national Teaching Award with the support of the university. The websites and publications are all self-funded and maintained individually, and more recently we have begun to work with younger people who were involved with and/or know about the later decades up to the present.

PROCESSES AND PROCEDURES

Why Pompey Pop? "Pop" here is an abbreviation for popular in its broadest sense, an umbrella term reflecting discussions about nomenclature in the
academic community. In Pompey Pop, it embraces most major genres and
styles including the dance bands, pop, rock, jazz and folk. Over the past five
years, there is no question that most interest has been shown in the guitar-
based music that grew from rock 'n' roll in the late 1950s. Mick Cooper has
been particularly keen to pursue the preceding and parallel histories of the
dance bands and mainstream entertainers, while I have sought stories about
the folk and jazz scenes. However, these have been largely fringe elements to
a dominant interest in rock 'n' roll, the beat groups, rhythm 'n' blues (R&B),
soul and psychedelia. The subcultural tribes have occupied some attention,
notably on the blog. In particular the 1960s Mods and their clubs, especially the Birdcage, have attracted sufficient interest to be featured in other
national publications (e.g. Hebditch and Shepherd 2012; Anderson 2014).

Figure 13.1 Screenshot from the Pompey Pop blog.

Mick Cooper and I began our searches of the local newspaper coincidentally and independently, but we knew each other as fellow musicians in the late 1960s and found pooling our resources and efforts productive. Nonetheless, research is one thing; making it available is something rather different. With regard to that, by 2009 two pieces of good fortune made the next stage easier.

The first was I had surplus funds from a teaching award and the university agreed I might present the public lecture and free booklet as a part of my work in popular music studies but very clearly for a public audience. In the event, around 700 people attended the two lectures (afternoon and evening) and very few were from the university. In the audience were members of the City Museum, and they decided to extend a *Birth of British Rock* touring show to include a local element, which I was invited to organise. Then, in 2010, I was offered an early retirement deal (at the age of 61). I was pleased to take it, and used part of the enhanced lump sum to fund the photographic book, which we self-published in November 2011. When it sold out, the small profit enabled us to fund further initiatives, including the website hosting and some contributions to the permanent Guildhall exhibition. It is not unreasonable to suggest that without the teaching award surplus and retirement package, a great deal less would have been achieved, and after many years of funded institutional academic research, the almost total freedom to do it ourselves was a delight.

NEW SONGS, OLD SONGS

As an academic, I worked for many years in the visual arts and cultural studies, often with a focus on pedagogical issues. Methodologically, I had a broad interest in ethnographic procedures and developed a specific interest in the case study work of Stake (1995) and others. I derived perhaps three key aspects from that, which were relevant to the development of Pompey Pop. The first was the importance of the serendipitous moment or event, which happens with remarkable regularity. The second was the value of presenting accounts to other informed readers without the need to impose or spell out every theoretical implication of the inquiry results. The third was a reflexive approach: positioning myself quite clearly and explicitly in all the work but seeking to understand how and when that positioning impacts on the project.

For example, during the 2010 Museum Show, we set up all kinds of devices to obtain further information and artefacts, including a comments book and Post-it wall, and I went there every Monday morning to meet visitors and hear their stories. This worked sufficiently well that it led almost immediately to the setting up of the blog. On one occasion, I was at the exhibition when a younger friend from the university who taught in my faculty visited the show. As we chatted, she mentioned that her aunt had been in a film about Portsmouth in the 1960s, and I realised that this was a thirty-minute documentary called *Citizen 63* made by a young John Boorman for the BBC, which had been broadcast in September 1963. I was astonished, as I knew it only by reputation and had failed to obtain a copy in any approaches to the BBC. A meeting was arranged with the subject, Marion Knight, now in her mid-sixties, a copy was obtained and I began working on various public events and publications using the film, not least because it provided considerable documentary evidence about the music, fashion and leisure activities of Portsmouth teenagers in 1963, just as The Beatles were enjoying their first hit records and had recently visited Portsmouth twice. From mid-2010 until early 2013, when Marion and I (separately) attended a screening at the South Bank, I was able to gather a great deal of information about the film and the various participants. Then, very suddenly in April 2013, Marion died. At the wake, I met one of her daughters and discussed the work I had done on the film. I shared the feeling that Marion had never quite trusted my motives and that feeling was confirmed. A few months later, a man living in France contacted me, having found a reference to the film on the blog, and explained he was the clarinetist in the beach scene. He provided information about his band at the time and more broadly the Trad jazz scene in Portsmouth in the early 1960s.

That is just one example of a case study, chance encounters and the need for reflexivity, but there are many more to be seen in the publications and on the Pompey Pop blog and associated websites. I have mentioned the first impact of The Beatles contemporaneously with the filming of *Citizen 63*, and elements of their influence can be seen in at least one hairstyle and some of the clothes. Musically, Marion Knight's peer group is seen stomping to records of British Trad jazz in the youth club and at the beach to the live group that played regularly in the local pubs. They also appear singing an anti-war folk song by Ian Campbell, accompanied by one acoustic guitar. In the summer of 1963, the Portsmouth folk scene was growing rapidly, as it was across the country in what is generally known as the folk revival (e.g. Brocken 2003), whereas Trad jazz had shifted from early 1950s cult status to a compromised and rather tired pop form. In the week the film was broadcast in mid-September 1963, The Beatles led the charts with "She Loves You," followed by Billy J Kramer & the Dakotas, with fellow Liverpudlians The Searchers in the Top Ten and the first Rolling Stones single "Come On" just outside the Top Twenty. "Merseybeat" and British R&B were the new popular sounds.

This was part of a significant shift in popular tastes and behaviours in the United Kingdom, but what it did not signal was the end of anything. Just as the dance bands adapted to the popularity of rock 'n' roll and the beat groups, the British Trad jazz bands continued to perform and record through the following decades. The development of popular music has not been a case of one style replacing another but rather of the various styles fanning out and shifting only in terms of prominence and popularity. In this particular sense, Sandbrook's key point holds good. While certain styles and fashions dominate commercially at any given moment, in popular culture this is not a matter of one ousting the other but of accommodation and expansion.

In *Citizen 63*, Marion Knight holds a Ray Charles album while she dismisses the banality of much pop music and the pressures to conform that come with the industries of popular culture. Later she discusses the group's fashion preferences, contrasting them with the local rockers at the funfair. The members of her group are wearing many black items, including polo-necked jumpers and PVC macs, and Marion sports a cap while her pal "Honk" brushes his hair forward. Honk was Dave Arney, a dockyard apprentice who would leave his trade to manage a local boutique and spend his life in the fashion industry. By early 1964, he and Marion (at least) of the *Citizen 63* group were leading figures in the growing Mod scene in Portsmouth, which would eventually centre on the Birdcage Club. Once again, we have here a (brief) indication of the shifts that occurred in popular culture. Cultural histories and the media often seek to fix group identities – if you're a Mod you're not a Rocker – whereas young people often shifted styles, resisted being pinned down and responded creatively to a range of opportunities that presented themselves: they often did it themselves.

A retrospective account that denies these subtle shifts occurs in a book about Syd Barrett, in which Chapman (2010, 142) describes how, in early 1967, Pink Floyd "left the sanctuary of the counter-culture and ventured out into Top Rank territory where their live set was often met with indifference or downright hostility." He cites Portsmouth's Birdcage Club, which he says "was a mod stronghold and the audience greeted 'Interstellar Overdrive' accordingly" (2010, 142). But Chapman, too young to have been there, offers no evidence and misses entirely the flexibility and creativity of mid-1960s Mods, who were always seeking new experiences. The Birdcage was an independent club, and those of us who attended it remember being somewhat surprised by aspects of Floyd's show, but there is no recollection of hostility. By the time the band arrived (January 1967), we had seen The Who and Small Faces regularly, Cream just the month before and other live acts outside mainstream soul (a residency by The Move, surfers The Summer Set and others). The Beatles had released *Revolver* months before, Jimi Hendrix was in the charts and we were open to the new possibilities. Hair and fashions were shifting, as were the drugs, which were increasingly psychedelic. Chapman's claim has no substance. It is merely another misrepresentation of provincial life. Pompey Pop seeks to address each one and build a more accurate, multilayered account of the times.

FINAL THOUGHTS

Despite the significance of *Citizen 63* and the local press's reaction to it, it is in one respect atypical of much of the Pompey Pop project in that it focuses on a teenage girl. Our publication *Pompey Pop Pix* is full of the boys in the bands, and our attempts to persuade women to provide images of themselves as fans and audience members largely failed. The same thing occurs with the blog, where the majority of correspondents, especially the regular ones, are boys from the 1960s.

The blog is the best example of the inestimable importance of the Internet in developing Pompey Pop. In the first four years, there were around 3,000 posts and 8,000 comments. Most of the comments are generally amicable, sometimes humorous and tend to be dominated by facts (sometimes disputed) and opinions, although there is less interest in ideas. It is, of course, difficult to know exactly what people are engaged by, and it may be misleading to judge that solely on the basis of responses. There are other chance encounters around the city where people discuss the project and some use my email address to send things directly to me.

There is no pretense that Pompey Pop has told the whole story, since it is, like all documentaries, a construction based on evidence and available footage. But it is an increasingly full documentary with many layers and diversions and as yet no end in sight. And it is most certainly DIY!

NOTE

1. The online presence of the Pompey Pop project includes a blog (http://pompey-pop.wordpress.com), the Pompey Pop! website (http://www.pompeypop.co.uk/Pompey_Pop) and another website called "The Popular Portsmouth Music Scene – 1944 to 1969 And BEYOND!" (http://www.michaelcooper.org.uk/C/pmsindex.htm).

REFERENCES

Allen, D. 2009. *Here come the sixties*. Portsmouth: Author.
Allen, D. and Cooper, M. 2011. *Dave & Mick's Pompey Pix*. Basingstoke: Moyhill.
Anderson, P. 2014. *Mods: The new religion*. London: Omnibus Press.
Balogh, E. 2002. Leisure, pleasure & entertainment. In J. Stedman (ed.), *People of Portsmouth: The 20th century in their own words*. Frome: Breedon Books, 123–45.
Citizen '63. 1963. BBC Television. September 11.
Brocken, M. 2003. *The British folk revival 1944–2002*. Aldershot: Ashgate.
Chapman, R. 2010. *Syd Barrett: A very irregular head*. London: Da Capo Press.
Hebditch, I. and Shepherd, J. 2012. *The action: In the lap of the Mod*. Bristol: The Action.
Portsmouth Museum & Records Service 1999. *Portsmouth in the twentieth century: A photographic history*. Somerset: Halsgrove.
Roberts, D. 2011. *Rock atlas: 700 great music locations and the stories behind them*. London: Clarksdale Books.
Sadden, J. 2009. *Portsmouth: A century of change*. Stroud: The History Press.
The Seventies 2012. BBC2, April 23.
Sandbrook, D. 2006. *White heat: A history of Britain in the Swinging Sixties*. London: Little, Brown.
Stake, R.E. 1995. *The art of case study research*. Thousand Oaks, CA: Sage.

14 Ketebul Music

Retracing and Archiving Kenya's Popular Music

William "Tabu" Osusa and Bill Odidi

For many decades, a debate has been ongoing in Kenya – a country blessed with a diversity of cultures across more than forty communities – about the development of its musical identity. Musicians have lacked a point of reference from earlier generations and the unavailability of a consistent and reliable music archive has made it impossible for emerging artists to retrace the rhythmic path and innovate with the rich sounds available.

In June 2007, a group of stakeholders in the Kenyan music industry embarked on an ambitious mission to carry out research, archive, develop and promote the diverse music traditions of East Africa. Ketebul Music was born. The name Ketebul means "drumsticks" in the language of the Luo people of Western Kenya, and so was a natural choice for an organisation with a vision of an African society that celebrates its cultural identity and recognises the special role artists play every day in people's lives. The idea was the brainchild of William "Tabu" Osusa, who has worked in the music industry in East and Central Africa for about forty years as a singer, producer and manager.

Ketebul Music was set up by people concerned that cultural actors have been unable to get their due space in the history of independent Kenya. The musical traditions and innovators that once sprang up in terms of the personalities, sound, music and lyrics, and that should be a connection between different generations of musicians, have not been enabled and as a result there are very few resources from which musicians can borrow today.

What we observed is that there has been an absence of the cultural memory that is essential to make connections between the past and the contemporary – the key to inspiring a new era of music-making. Given the changing world in which we are living, it is no longer tenable to rely on oral practices, as is culturally the norm across much of Africa. Further, the dearth of performance venues due to social, cultural, political and economic erasure and transformation needs to be addressed and reconstructed as part of documentation and archiving.

Those arms of the Kenyan government mandated to deal with the preservation of art and culture have failed to provide the foundation required for the sector to thrive. These institutions have not enacted clear guiding cultural policies, thereby leaving musicians and other artists at the mercy of the media and multinational corporate organisations, and their agenda, through the ubiquitous TV talent shows, is purely commercial.

As a consequence, the country does not have a national repository of music specifically or the arts in general. The audiovisual library at the Kenya Broadcasting Cooperation, which is the country's national radio and television station, has suffered severe neglect. A visit to the institution several years ago showed a total lack of professionalism in the manner in which important artistic materials of national interest have been stored. The library is housed in an old, dusty room, with most of the material scattered on the floor. Reel-to-reel film and audio tapes languish in a heap in one corner, and vinyl records and compact discs are piled in another corner. Attempts to digitise the catalogue floundered years ago, so the entire record of material held in the library since 1960 remains on yellowing cards.

The situation is no better at the Kenya National Archives, where the bulk of material preserved, with a few exceptions, comprises a record of official government events with scant attention paid to the country's cultural heritage. The country's National Museum houses some basic musical instruments from parts of Kenya but lacks cataloguing and detailed information that could stimulate any interest in young minds.

It was the realisation that future generations of Kenyans would have little or no musical antecedents that prompted the team at Ketebul Music to initiate its own efforts towards archiving the musical legacy of Kenya. Achieving this goal was always going to be a challenge because of the enormous resources required, and also because the personnel at Ketebul Music had little or no training or experience in archiving. There was also the complication of searching for recordings, photographs, and even the musicians and other crucial personalities who would provide the missing pieces of the puzzle. As it turns out, a lot of this information is scattered over many different parts of the world.

LEARNING FROM OTHERS: THE KENYA AUDIO VISUAL STUDY GROUP

Through a grant from the Ford Foundation Eastern Africa in 2008, Bill Odidi and Tabu Osusa of Ketebul Music were part of a group that came to be known informally as the Kenya Audio Visual Study Group. This group of professionals, which comprised members drawn from key institutions like the Kenya National Museum and the Kenya National Archives, set out to learn from best practices around the world.

The group's first trip was to the Gramophone Records Museum and Research Centre (GRMRC), founded in 1994 by Kwame Sarpong, a retired Ghanian military officer, and located in the premises of the Centre for National Culture in the Cape Coast. It holds a unique collection of 78 rpm shellac discs, vinyl records, cassettes and reel-to-reel tapes consisting mainly of Ghana's highlife music from the 1920s. GRMRC was an eye-opener with regard to the role private individuals can play in supporting the development of arts and culture through the collection and preservation of archival recordings.

It was a very different experience at the British Library in London, a massive institution with sound recordings going back to the nineteenth century, which provided important lessons on building a heritage of archives. Our group was quite amazed to hear cylinder recordings made in East Africa in the 1940s, which would be of immense interest today, not just in the communities where the recordings were made but also to the wider public. Dr Janet Topp Fargion, the curator of the library's World and Traditional Music Sound Archive, travelled to Kenya a year later to conduct a training workshop with archivists from various organisations, including Ketebul Music, as part of the British Library World Collections Program.

The study tours also involved a trip to Germany to meet ethnomusicologist Dr Wolfgang Bender at the University of Bayreuth and view an immense collection of music, mainly from West Africa and dating back to the 1940s. Dr Bender told us how he was able to help replace the music of Sierra Leone from the material he had earlier collected for his personal archive. This was after the entire music library at the country's state broadcaster burnt down following a *coup d'état* in that country. It was a crucial lesson on creating back-up files of any archives we hoped to set up at Ketebul.

Finally, the team headed to the International Library of African Music (ILAM) at Rhodes University in Grahamstown, South Africa. The centre, founded by the twentieth-century English musicologist Hugh Tracey, boasts one of the largest archives of African music in Sub-Saharan Africa. Tracey, who dedicated his life to recording music from Central, Eastern and Southern Africa, travelled across Kenya in his large recording truck recording various musicians from 1948.

These study tours, spread over most of 2008, only served to reaffirm the importance of conservation, preservation and restoration, particularly of sound recordings, to establish a legacy for future generations. Although most DIY organisations lack the expertise and resources the official institutions can access, both public and private entities have a role to play in complementing each other's work by sharing some of the digital documentation and information in their databases. We also realised a lot of Kenya's musical heritage was held in archives around the world, mostly because no institution has taken up the initiative to collect, document and preserve such recordings.

RETRACING KENYAN MUSIC

Over the last six years, Ketebul Music has spearheaded projects that retrace the people, places and styles of performance from a broad representation of the country's cultures. We have achieved this through reprofiling past and present generations of musicians, their experiences and influences, and sensitisation and exposure of the public to the history of Kenyan music genres through rereleases of recordings and different publications.

The research not only dwells on the different music genres in the region, largely inspired by the guitar rhythms of Benga, but also involves the recollections of the musicians themselves, their families, industry players such as producers, promoters and media personalities, and the general market audience. Ketebul has established itself as a leading content-provider with the ultimate responsibility to research and locate artists, audiences and influences on East Africa's musical icons and their performance spaces.

Ketebul Music now possesses skilled personnel with a strong passion to preserve the region's diverse music culture and heritage through their proper documentation for both local and international audiences. Every study on a genre of music undertaken by Ketebul has produced in-depth authoritative research in a market-friendly multimedia package. Each package comprises a shorter, succinct popular version of the academic report and is contained in an attractively designed booklet, supplemented by an audio CD featuring rereleases of influential recordings along with a video documentary carrying extensive interviews, analyses, stage performances and archival footage.

In a series titled Retracing East African Rhythms, Ketebul Music has successfully produced four well-researched packages titled *Retracing the Benga Rhythm*, *Retracing Kikuyu Popular Music*, *Retracing Kenya's Funky Hits* and *Retracing Kenya's Songs of Protest*, officially launched in 2014. The text and illustrated narratives capture the various subjects, accompanied by professional analysis, along with audio discs of carefully selected past recordings and video documentaries that visually capture the players in the industry. The productions are of unparalleled quality and depth on the subjects covered.

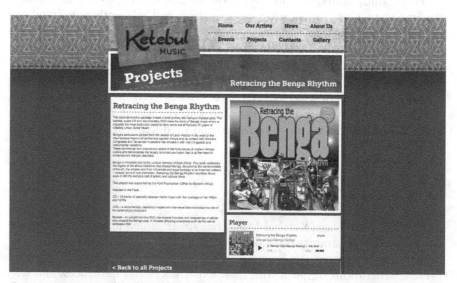

Figure 14.1 Screenshot from the Ketebul Music website promoting *Retracing Benga Rhythms*.

In addition, Ketebul Music has partnered with Abubilla Music, a not-for-profit institution based in the United Kingdom, on a project titled Singing Wells to make field recordings of traditional music in various communities in East Africa. The recordings have taken place in Kenya (Coast, Western and Rift Valley regions). Further recordings have also been undertaken in Eastern and Northern Uganda and Tanzania. The recordings are then packaged in digital media, and this access has breathed new life into the hitherto fast-disappearing traditional music styles of the respective communities.

The work of Ketebul Music in retracing genres and makers of Kenyan popular music from the past makes an important contribution to several areas. The first is the informative content this work provides to print media, radio and television broadcasting. The second contribution enhances the debates on Kenyan identity, since this work examines the moments and practices that have shaped Kenya's increasingly cosmopolitan cultural heritage. These Retracing projects demonstrate the extent to which Kenyan culture is the constantly shifting sum of many layers borrowed over time from local ethnic traditions and diverse global influences that include American country, Christian hymns and Congolese rumba, among many others (e.g. see the foreword to *Retracing Kenya's Funky Hits*, Ketebul Music 2011).

Throughout the projects, Ketebul Music consolidates the scattered knowledge that currently exists in different places about the relationship between the Kenyan music of the 1960s, 1970s, 1980s, 1990s and today. Documentaries produced for TV broadcast include detailed narratives of Kenyan singers, their lives and the inspiration behind their creative output. We track the contribution of traditional media, radio, television and newspapers, and the emergence of the Internet and new media in shaping popular cultural trends in Kenya and the greater East Africa region over the last fifty years.

The Retracing series provides an accessible compilation of the songs and musicians that have captured Kenya's imagination over the fifty-year period and is truly representative of the nation's identity. The series has documented the achievements of influential personalities in music and related fields through audiovisual interviews and photographs.

We have broken down the tasks in each project into the following areas:

- *Research work to locate artists, audiences and influences:* Interviews with musicians (both past and present), promoters, music producers, radio and TV journalists, and audiences form an integral part of each project. Identifying useful respondents comes after archival research and the few studies of Kenyan popular music that currently exist, including past successful projects by Ketebul Music and related organisations. Ketebul relies on its strong team of researchers, music producers and journalists, guided by several academic advisers who are hired on consultancy basis.

- *Cataloguing:* Text and scriptwriting, as well as editorial meetings, give shape to the eventual documentary and print publication. Retrieving audiovisual recordings from personal collections, old recording studios and broadcast stations forms the background work in the preparation of the audio CD.
- *Training:* The project involves painstaking studio work to restore old vinyl records, reel-to-reel tapes and videotapes, and migrating analogue content to digital formats. As with the preparation of the documentary, this studio work also provides an opportunity for Ketebul to offer on-the-job training for the team of technicians, studio engineers, researchers and editors.
- *Publication and dissemination:* The documentary, audio CD and print booklet are packaged in a single multimedia unit. This material is useful as a reference for researchers and the general public on music trends in Kenya and socio-cultural influences since independence.

Using physical and online distribution, Ketebul Music always makes its material accessible to a wide range of local and foreign researchers who have an interest in Kenyan music. We also work with broadcasters, like the Kenya Broadcasting Corporation, to make our content available to as wide an audience as possible.

Ketebul Music believes proper documentation and recording are essential for archiving the past and making it available to new generations of economic, social and political actors. This kind of documentation also fills critical gaps in Kenya's print, broadcast and emergent media, which are all seeking informative local content presented in a creative and imaginative format.

We are also responding to the opportunities available during this transition from analogue to digital broadcasting in Kenya. The convergence of radio, TV and the Internet offers great opportunities for independent content-producers like Ketebul Music.

When Ketebul Music released the documentary *Retracing the Benga Rhythm* in December 2008, the country's leading TV stations were quick to embrace it as value-adding and well-produced content for their stations. The fact that these stations aired this documentary several times without demanding broadcast fees is indicative of the rich relationship that can be cultivated between both state-run and commercial broadcasters and independent producers embracing the values of informed reportage, public-interest issues and quality production. This partnership has been extended to subsequent projects in the series, which have been widely transmitted on national TV and received glowing reviews in the country's press.

SPOTLIGHT ON KENYAN MUSIC

The archival work at Ketebul Music is tightly related to production projects with the current generation of musicians. The organisation runs an in-house functional audiovisual music production studio, built with the objective of identifying, supporting, promoting and offering musicians from all walks of life an opportunity to realise their musical dreams through a mentorship program and subsidised recording deals.

Many of the existing recording studios in Nairobi peg their rates to commercial tariffs that are far beyond the reach of young musicians, who generally hail from humble economic backgrounds. There has been a strong preference from producers and the popular radio stations for the hip-hop-flavoured sound that is often a carbon copy of the hits playing in the United States. As a consequence, artists who play an alternative sound that urban producers don't "understand" have been marginalised, making most recordings a preserve of individual musicians based in the urban centres of the country.

Ketebul Music has the goal of building a bridge between the country's musical heritage and global influences through the program Spotlight on Kenyan Music. The enhanced profile of Ketebul has given birth to partnerships with organisations like Alliance Française in Nairobi for the Spotlight series, which identifies talents spread throughout different regions of the country and exposes it through recordings, live performances and other forms of skills development.

Tabu Osusa co-chairs the steering committee for Spotlight on Kenyan Music and since 2005 the project has introduced rhythms, melodies and arrangements that embrace the present, capture the past and propel the rich musical traditions into the future. Household names in Kenyan music today, like Sauti Sol, Makadem and an all-female singing group from the Somali Gargar, have built successful careers from the foundation of Spotlight on Kenyan Music. What these musicians have in common is the production of a contemporary sound with roots firmly planted in a distinct Kenyan traditional genre.

THE SINGING WELLS PROJECT

After two years of planning, the Singing Wells Project was officially launched in 2011 when Ketebul Music entered into partnership with Abubilla Music, a record label in the United Kingdom, on a project aimed at recording and archiving traditional music from Eastern Africa with the intention of keeping these rhythms alive for current and future generations.

To achieve our goals, we work in and with communities whose music has never been documented, travelling to remote villages of greater East Africa with a mobile recording studio. This ensures the music of these communities is recorded in an environment with which the singers and dancers are completely familiar.

In every village we visit, large audiences – from the youngest child to the village elder – all congregate and create the ideal atmosphere for the performances and recordings. We work with musicians to ensure their traditions continue to be practised and can be shared with the widest audiences. This provides tangible and enduring benefits to the musicians and communities that Singing Wells visits.

Figure 14.2 Singing Wells engineers from Abubilla Music and Ketebul Music
listening back to a recording. Seated (L–R): Willie Gachuche, Andy
Patterson and Jesse Bukindu. Standing (L–R): Steve 64 Kivutia and
Mwamuye Deche. Photo courtesy of Ketebul Music/Singing Wells.

The pilot project was implemented in March 2011 when the team travelled
from Nairobi, the Kenyan capital, to the Coastal region. Jimmy Allen of
Abubilla Music notes:

> In the first village we visited we confirmed the mission of Singing
> Wells. It is necessary but not sufficient to just archive the performances
> of these amazing groups. We must work to make the songs, the heri-
> tage, the culture relevant to today's artists. Part of that mission then is
> to help create an East African music identity to rival the successes in
> South and Western Africa.

Since that first trip to record the Coastal communities of Kenya, the Singing
Wells team has travelled to record the music of the following communities
across East Africa: Luo, Marakwet, Pokot, Sabaot, the Tugen, the Batwa
of Southern Uganda, and the Acholi, Alur, Langi and Iteso of Northern
Uganda. Some of these groups have also travelled to the Ketebul Studios in
Nairobi for additional recording sessions to supplement what was captured
in the field. The Batwa singers, for instance, made the forty-eight-hour road
trip from their home in Kisoro, Southern Uganda to Nairobi in November
2011 to record. This is a community widely believed to have been the first
human residents of the forests that stretch across Uganda, Rwanda, Burundi

and the Democratic Republic of Congo but who find themselves pushed out of their ancestral home to make way for a national park near the town of Kisoro. The Singing Wells team was able to capture the extraordinary music that reflects the heritage and culture of the forest people.

One of the key objectives of the Singing Wells project is to introduce traditional music to a new generation of musicians and listeners who may not be familiar with it. Our Influences series consists of original music compositions that are a fusion of traditional and contemporary styles: new songs created from the influence of traditional harmonies and instruments. The Influences series is led by musicians from the Ketebul stable like Winyo who, together with other singers and writers who record both in the field and at the Ketebul Studio in Nairobi, produces unique, new songs.

REPATRIATION OF RECORDINGS FROM THE INTERNATIONAL LIBRARY OF AFRICAN MUSIC (ILAM)

The project between Ketebul Music and the International Library of African Music in South Africa seeks to re-study field recordings in the communities where the legendary Hugh Tracey made recordings in the 1950s. The project will involve returning copies of Tracey's field recordings to the communities where he made them to stimulate interest among the members of the community, especially the younger generation.

Director of Ketebul Music Tabu Osusa has been using field recordings made by Tracey to locate and document musicians in Kenya and Uganda who continue to perform on instruments first recorded by Tracey in 1950 and 1952. Together with Professor Diane Thram of ILAM, with whom we first made contact during a study visit to ILAM in 2008, Osusa has located communities and musicians to which to return the many hundreds of Kenyan and Ugandan recordings Tracey recorded. The plan is to rerecord present-day musicians in these communities using the Singing Wells format of capturing the music in their own villages. The Singing Wells Project has provided videographers to document the repatriation process with the footage used to produce a documentary video to be promoted through ILAM, Ketebul Music and Singing Wells internationally as evidence of ILAM's intention to repatriate its field collections in ways that revitalise interest in the community's music heritage and work to benefit community musicians and keep the heritage alive.

In the long term, there will be similar extensive repatriation of Hugh Tracey's recordings in the remaining regions of Kenya, Rwanda and Uganda in 2015 and beyond. Tracey recorded throughout Sub-Saharan Africa to create a famous legacy of field recordings that are archived at ILAM. Other countries where repatriation of these recordings remains to be done are Tanzania, Zanzibar, Mozambique, Malawi, Zimbabwe, Zambia, Botswana, South Africa and Namibia.

KETEBUL MUSIC IN THE FUTURE

The various projects undertaken by Ketebul Music have contributed to the work of various cultural actors, including scholars, researchers and even artists working on the history of Kenyan popular music. The Kenya Broadcasting Corporation has also run the Retracing documentary series on national television, creating a renewed interest in the rich music heritage of the country. Expanding our local and international network with partners like the Ford Foundation, the Permanent Presidential Commission of Music (Kenya), UNESCO, ILAM, Abubilla Music and others has drawn attention to the task of preserving Kenya's diverse cultural expressions, especially through music, at different levels. Ketebul Music curated the music program at the 2014 Smithsonian Folklife Festival in Washington, DC, the biggest-ever international showcase of Kenyan music, past and present. Projects like the Singing Wells and the Repatriation of Kenyan music in collaboration with ILAM are highlights of our mission to introduce the recording and performing history of Kenya to a whole new generation, who can use this as a platform to create music for today and the future. The work is not made any easier by a culture that has never fully embraced the value of archiving, especially in the cultural field. Items of immense historical value like audiovisual recordings and photographs have been destroyed or are stored away in libraries in Europe, as we discovered in the course of researching the Retracing series. Our mission now, and in the years to come, is to showcase the value of cultural archiving and to influence official policy towards supporting both public and private efforts that contribute to the success of this mission.

REFERENCE

Ketebul Music 2014. Accessed October 27, 2014. http://www.ketebulmusic.org.

15 Bokoor African Popular Music Archives Foundation

Ghana's Highlife Music Institute and the Need for Popular Music Archiving

John Collins

Whereas it seems quite sensible for African countries to preserve their traditional art, it is not so obvious that popular music needs the same attention, as it is current and ongoing. Nevertheless, popular music in Africa is now quite old itself, tracing its roots back to the nineteenth century. During the ensuing years, there has been a succession of changing styles, with the old giving way to the new. Moreover, wars, coups and socioeconomic crises have negatively affected the growth of popular music and the livelihoods of its practitioners and audiences. Thus there is a need for archives that preserve African popular music. This chapter looks at one such archive, the Bokoor African Popular Music Archives Foundation (BAPMAF), which I established in Ghana in 1990. In fact, this non-government organisation (NGO) was the country's very first popular music archive, set up after almost twenty years of military rule that had resulted in the collapse of the local music industry, the demise of highlife music and a brain-drain of talented performers abroad. This chapter provides a chronological history of the development of BAPMAF.

THE BEGINNING OF BAPMAF, 1990–2007

BAPMAF is a Ghanaian NGO that I put together in 1990, encouraged and assisted by some leading Ghanaian highlife musicians such as King Bruce of the Black Beats band, E.T. Mensah of the Tempos band, the guitarists Koo Nimo and Kwaa Mensah, and the media man (and grandson of a famous Pan Africanist) Beattie Casely-Hayford, who sadly passed away shortly before BAPMAF was formally launched. We were all concerned with the lack of research and information on local Ghanaian highlife music, and particularly disturbed by the demise of the classical dance band and guitar band styles of highlife that occurred during the various military regimes of the 1970s and 1980s, when the country's commercial highlife music scene collapsed.

The core of the BAPMAF holdings is my own extensive music archives, which I began collecting from the late 1960s with further important contributions from the five core supporters mentioned above. Other contributions were made by Mr Y.B. "Opia" Bampoe of the Jaguar Jokers bands, the highlife composer Oscarmore Ofori, the veteran guitarists T.O. "Jazz" Ampoumah and Edinam Ansah, the drummer Kofi Ghanaba (a.k.a. Guy Warren) and actor Ben Ahorlu Adjokpa. Special mention must also be made of Ghana's first Minister of Information, Jimmy Moxon, and some of the staff of the University of Ghana at Legon: Professor Atta Annan Mensah and Professor Mawere Opoku of the School of Performing Arts, Robert Sprigge of the History Department (and pianist for the Red Spots band) and my own late father, Edmund Collins, of the Philosophy Department, who was a keen follower of the guitar band music of Onyina, Yamoah, E.K. Nyame and Love Nortey. Some later BAPMAF affiliates were the Afro-jazz reed player Jimmy Beckley, the "gyil" xylophone player Aaron Bebe Sukura, recording engineer Panji Anoff, the late American jazz percussionist Juma Santos (Jim Riley), and the university lecturers Peter Arthur and the late Dr Zabana Kongo.

In its early years, BAPMAF donated materials to the W.E.B. Dubois Centre, the Padmore Library, the University of Ghana's Institute of African Studies, Professor J.H.K. Nketia's university-based International Centre for Music and Dance, Achimota and Saint John's schools, the British Council, the American USIS Library, the Ghana Broadcasting Corporation and the Ghana Folklore Board.

In February 1996, BAPMAF and the German Goethe Institute in Accra (under Director Sabine Hentzch) organised a Highlife Month that included the *Golden Years of Highlife Music* photographic exhibition, seminars and films on highlife, and performances by the Ankobra and Grassroots highlife bands, Nii Noi Nortey's Mau Mau Musiki and the Afro-jazz drummer Kofi Ghanaba (who also runs the African Heritage Library). Many organisations attended this month-long event, including the Dubois Centre (Director Ebo Hawkson), the National Theatre (Director Dr Komla Amuoko), the Musicians Union of Ghana MUSIGA (President Joe Mensah), King Bruce (B.B. bands), the University of Ghana (Professors Kofi Agovi and Kwesi Yankah), the Ghana Copyright Administration (Director Betty Mould-Iddrisu), the Ghana National Folklore Board (Chairman Colonel Amuzu), the Ghana Concert Party Union (Executives Mr S.K. Oppong and Mr Mensah) and the Ghana Record Producers Union (Executives Dick Essilfie-Bondzie and Kojo Donkoh).

After the 1996 BAPMAF/Goethe Highlife Month, the *Golden Years of Highlife Music* photographic exhibition was moved to a temporary space in my Bokoor House premises at South Ofankor, Accra. This was open to the general public until 2001. It hosted many local and foreign visitors, and was televised twice: for Ghana Broadcasting in 1996 (Producer Cynthia Jikpani) and in 2000 by the London Shai Shai company (Producer Martine Stone). Then, in mid-2001, with the help of Harmattan Productions and the French Embassy, the BAPMAF Highlife Photo Exhibition was remounted and displayed in Accra at the Alliance Française (Director Didier Martin) as part of the Story of Highlife event.

The following January, BAPMAF and the Swiss Embassy organised the launch at the DuBois Centre of the Basel Mission/UTC compilation CD *Ghana Popular Music 1931–57*, put together by the scholars Veit Arlt and Serena Danquah. From February to March 2002, BAPMAF arranged a series of seven lectures/performances at the National Theatre for the United States Embassy Public Affairs Section for Black History Month. Then, in 2004, BAPMAF was involved in local work with the Presence musical youth talent-scout organisation, Seth Adam's Pan African Arts NGO, which involved a highlife photo exhibition at the British Council in October and a workshop on "Researching Ghanaian Theatre" held at the University of Ghana's Institute of African Studies, Legon in 2005. It was also in February 2005 that BAPMAF again helped the United States Embassy Public Affairs Section organise African American Heritage/History Month.

In September 2005, BAPMAF was involved with the opening of Kofi Ghanaba's revamped African Heritage Library at Medie, and in March the following year, BAPMAF provided photos for the Rocky Dawuni/Africa Live Independence Splash: Ghana Music Revival Explosion at the Accra International Conference Centre. Then, in 2007 as part of Ghana's 50th independence celebrations, BAPMAF curated the Ghana Music Exhibition held in October at the Greenwich Heritage Centre in London and organised by the African Image Alliance.

ESTABLISHMENT OF THE BAPMAF HIGHLIFE INSTITUTE, 2007–11

As part of extensive rebuilding of Bokoor House in the mid-2000s, after receiving my university pension I included proper accommodation for BAPMAF. This consisted of 2,400 square feet of premises, comprising a photo and memorabilia exhibition room, seminar room, audio-video and digital documentation lab, and a library for photos, video, printed matter and recorded music. The new BAPMAF premises was opened in 2007 as the BAPMAF Highlife Institute. It was also in 2007 that BAPMAF supplied seventy highlife songs and other materials related to gender issues for the Changing Representation of Women in Popular Culture project of the University of Ghana's Institute of African Studies Centre for Gender Studies & Advocacy.

Numerous local and foreign musicians, researchers and media people continued to come to BAPMAF. This included groups of foreign students coming for lectures and workshops, such as from the University of Arlington in Texas (led by Dr. Michael Varner and Sierra Leonian Professor Alusine Jallo), the United States SIT summer school students (led by Gavin Webb and Olayemi Tinuoye) and students from Simon Fraser University (led by Dr. Albert Smith). Drummers in the United States also brought groups to BAPMAF such as the Ghanaian Obo Addy, who brought musicians from

Portland and Vida, and Big Joe Galeota, who came with a group from Arlington. During 2007–08, a team of New York students (including Seth Paris, Mikey Hart and Richie Levinson) began cataloguing on spreadsheets the audio component of the BAPMAF archives. In December 2008, my longtime friend and fellow archivist Kofi Ghanaba passed away, and I drew on the BAPMAF archives to help his family prepare a funeral booklet.

In 2009, the German Goethe Institute in Accra (Director Mrs Eleonore Sylla) provided a grant to BAPMAF for technical equipment, the creation of a website and assistance with the public display side of the BAPMAF Highlife Institute. With the new equipment, a substantial component of the BAPMAF music, photographic and video holdings were digitised. Also digitised were some works brought to BAPMAF by artists like the singer Pat Thomas, multi-instrumentalist Amartey Hedzoleh, Anum Telfer and drummer Glen Warren. The BAPMAF website[1] was created by my son, Thomas Kojo, and Raymond Gyemeki.

This German assistance was celebrated by an event at the BAPMAF Highlife Institute that attracted 120 visitors, including students, journalists, researchers and diplomatic staff. Some of the many Ghanaian musicians who came were the Ramblers dance-band trumpeter Peter Marfo, the trumpeter Edmund Mensah (son of E.T. Mensah), the leader of Hewale Sounds Dela Botri, the hiplifer Wunlov the Kobolor, Stan Plange and Kpakpo Addo of the old Uhuru band, the Afro-jazzist Nii Noi Nortey, the percussionist Johnson Kemeh, Daniel "J.B." Koranteng Crentsil (Fela Kuti's conga player) and the atratoa/televi instrument player Kay Opare.

The same year, there was also an exchange of materials between BAPMAF and the Nigerian Legacy Museum and Hall of Fame. This had been set up in Benin City in the mid-1990s by Nigeria's highlife maestro Victor Uwaifo, who at the time was the Commissioner of Arts and Culture for Edo State and with whom I had recorded in the 1970s. Towards the end of 2009, BAPMAF supplied historical photos for the High Vibes Festival at Ghana's National Theatre, sponsored by the French Embassy, UNESCO and the Ministry of Chieftaincy and Culture. In early 2010, BAPMAF digitised seven records for T.D.B. Adjekum of the Happy Stars guitar band. In September 2010, I was involved with a musical and written tribute to the late Mac Tontoh, who had been one of the founders of the Osibisa Afro-rock group and had donated photographic materials to the BAPMAF archives.

By September 2011, the BAPMAF holdings consisted of 1,200 photographs, 700 publications and many rare documents, speeches, brochures, posters, record sleeves, eighty videos and 1,600 hours of recorded music, including 780 old highlife songs on shellac 78 rpm records and master-tapes of Ghanaian artists recorded by John Collins Bokoor Recording Studio in the 1980s. The materials of the *Golden Years of Highlife Music* photo exhibition were organised chronologically on fifteen separate boards in the BAPMAF exhibitions room in Bokoor House, where there was also a display of numerous documents, posters, album covers, musical instruments, artefacts and memorabilia. Streams of visitors came to call at the BAPMAF premises between 1996 and 2011 to access materials in the collection and to view the curated exhibition. These included African music scholars and researchers from Nigeria, Ghana, Botswana and Zimbabwe; African musicians from Ghana, Nigeria, Togo and Cameroon; composers from Ghana, Holland and Germany; journalists from Ghana, Germany, Holland, France, Nigeria, Jamaica and South Africa; Western scholars of African music; Ghanaian music producers and promoters; World Music producers and promoters; documentary-makers; radio broadcasters; and diplomatic staff from the embassies of France, Germany and Spain.

FLOODS HIT BAPMAF IN OCTOBER 2011

Figure 15.1 Flood damage to downstairs library and documentation room at BAPMAF. Photo by John Collins.

Disaster struck the BAPMAF premises on October 26, 2011. At this time, flooding occurred over many parts of Accra due to an unseasonal and massive rainfall compounded by people building in or blocking waterways so rivers could no longer easily run into the sea. In our particular Taifa-Ofankor area, this was compounded by the construction of a section of the Kumasi highway without adequate storm gutters – and the fact that some of the saw-millers in the immediate neighbourhood had been dumping sawdust in rivers and wetlands over the years. The resulting flood was unprecedented, with almost 6 feet (1.8 metres) of water smashing walls around the BAPMAF land and 4.5 feet (nearly 1.4 metres) entering the downstairs house and premises where some of the BAPMAF archival holdings were kept. About 10 percent of the material in the BAPMAF archives was damaged or lost, along with thousands of dollars' worth of technical equipment.

Figure 15.2 Post-flood, BAPMAF member Ben Ahorlu Adjokpa camps in the upstairs exhibition room to help sort out the damaged archives. Photo by John Collins.

After the flood, numerous friends, family members, well-wishers and organisations donated monies to help rebuild the grounds, make them secure against future floods, replace some of the technical equipment and relocate all valuable BAPMAF holdings upstairs where the BAPMAF Highlife Institute exhibition was located. Although it is impossible to mention all those who helped financially or in kind, I would like to mention four in particular. First, the School of Performing Arts at the University of Ghana, where I had been working for the last eighteen years, instantly helped me financially. In Canada, Batuki Music quickly organised a benefit for BAPMAF called Highlife Help at the Lula Lounge in Toronto in December 2011,[2] which featured a Toronto-based Ghanaian Afrafranto highlife band that includes a number of musicians I know personally, like vocalist Theo Yaw Boakye, guitarist Paa Joe, drummer Kofi Ackah (Jewel Ackah's son) and bassist Marshall Nketiah. Another fundraising show was organised in London in June 2012, put together by Rita Ray and Max Reinhardt of The Shrine dance club. This featured Ghanaian acts by Kari Bannerman, Konkoma, Pax Nicholas, Wunlov the Kubolor and Mensah. As Mensah stated: "We're sleeping on a hero. This man is not only preserving our music but our history and more importantly our culture and unique identity. It's rather unfortunate that he's not getting the support he deserves but here is a good place to start."[3] Also in June, BAPMAF received a substantial grant from the Dutch Prince Claus Cultural Emergency Response Program, which was to replace lost technical equipment, repair the BAPMAF physical infrastructure and strengthen its perimeter walls with embankments and dykes to stop future flooding.[4]

POST-FLOOD BAPMAF ACTIVITIES, 2012–14

With all this assistance, BAPMAF was able to begin operating again, although the public exhibition component of BAPMAF was temporarily closed down. Nevertheless, all the other research, preservation and promotional work of BAPMAF continued. As early as January 2012, I was interviewed on the origins of highlife by Susan Lamptey of Radio Gold 90.5FM for its weekly Saturday *Solid Gold Countdown* show, and provided some music samples from the BAPMAF archives. In March 2012, the sad death of the veteran guitar band leader F. Kenya occurred, and BAPMAF was able to supply some biographical information to his family for the funeral booklet. Some of the BAPMAF archives are now being used for the new PhD courses on African popular music that I am helping set up for the Music Department at the University of Ghana.

The BAPMAF archives were also consulted for the Musicians Union of Ghana (MUSIGA) research project entitled Revitalizing the Creative Art Industry: The Contribution of the Music Sector to the Socio–Economic Development of Ghana. This MUSIGA project was publicly launched in January 2013, and we hope our figures will convince the government to create ways to restructure the industry, reduce regulatory burdens, deal with music piracy and upgrade the teaching of music in Ghanaian schools.

In March 2013, I used BAPMAF photos and music samples for a presentation on The Concert Party in Ghana for the International World Theatre Day Celebration held at the National Theatre, Accra. Around this time, I was also awarded a Ghana Music Honor by MUSIGA at the National Theatre and later in the month the ex Fela-Kuti Ghanaian percussionist Daniel J.B. Koranteng donated 175 highlife records to BAPMAF.

The BAPMAF public display and seminar space were reopened in mid-2013. Visitors started coming again, including the American historian Douglas Sofer and calypso researcher Alison Okuda, the German music photographer Bugs Steffan, Dan Walter of the Sigauque Recording Studio in Maputo, Mozambique, the Ghanaian musicologist Nat Damptey, the American music lawyer Laurence Singer, the Holland-based Ghanaian musician Sloopy Mike Gyamfi, the musicians Ekow Micah and Akosua Agyempong of the Ghana Music Council, the Ghanaian-New Zealand musician Leila Adu-Gilmore, Ashesi College students, Titus Arko of the Ghana Fire Service dance-band and Hayford Siaw, Director of Volunteer Partnerships for West Africa (VPWA) NGO.

In September 2013, BAPMAF began collaborating with the MUSIGA for its planned Music Academy, and in December, BAPMAF supplied materials for two films. One, on Ghanaian masquerades, was for Ernest Abbeyquaye's Trumpet African Production and the other, on South African popular music, was for a Ghana TV news film on the death of Nelson Mandela. In mid-2014, BAPMAF became involved with the first annual Bands Competition of the Ghana Security Agencies (BACOSA) organised by the Ministry of the

Interior and held at the National Theatre in Accra on October 3. At the time of writing, October 2014, BAPMAF is currently collaborating with Dinah Reindorf of the Dwanesie Cultural Institute in Accra for its planned score book, *Ghanaian Folksongs and Highlife for Schools and Colleges.*

FINAL THOUGHTS

In Ghana, there are various government-financed or supported bodies that deal in the preservation and dissemination of traditional musical instruments and performance. These include the National Museum, the Arts Council, the nine Centres for National Culture, the National Commission on Culture and the various universities. However, there are just a few local archives dedicated to Ghanaian popular music, and these are all operated by private persons or their estates. These are Kwame Sarpong's Gramophone Museum in Cape Coast, the African Heritage Library at Medie near Accra, put together by the late Ghanaian Afro-jazz musician Kofi Ghanaba, and the BAPMAF Highlife Institute. There has been very little or no state support for these archives, and these organisations have only been able to survive through assistance from outside organisations like the German Goethe Institute, the Alliance Française, New York University in Ghana, the Canadian Daniel Langlois Foundation for Art, Science and Technology, and the Dutch Prince Claus Fund. This Ghanaian governmental blind-spot for local popular music stems from the music being contemporary and therefore deemed not to warrant the state support afforded to older, more traditional forms of music. This should be rectified, as today's popular will be tomorrow's tradition.

NOTES

1. The website can be found at www.bapmaf.com.
2. See http://batukimusic.com/index.php?option=com_content&view=article&id=76.
3. See http://www.richmix.org.uk/whats-on/event/the-2-jonz-benefit.
4. See http://www.princeclausfund.org/en/activities/bapmaf.html.

16 Proyecto Caracas Memorabilia

Reconstructing Pop Music History in Venezuela

Coromoto Jaraba

Proyecto Caracas Memorabilia is a collaborative non-commercial initiative that aims to offer a reconstruction of the history of pop music in Caracas, Venezuela. It is important to highlight that we use the term "pop" instead of "popular" to avoid confusion with Venezuelan popular traditional music and particular rhythms (see Ramón y Rivera 1976). The term "pop" is used in a broad sense to cover the genres of music that originated in or have been developed in the United States since the 1950s.

The project's main source of information is the Internet. As this is a very new endeavour, we have not yet started producing oral interviews with the people involved in its history. The project draws together blogs, video logs and specialist web pages on this history, and importantly brings fans, musicians and producers together in a Facebook forum called Proyecto Memorabilia Caracas. Contributors come from across Venezuela, including other important cities such as Barquisimeto and Valencia, where heavy metal surfaced. Yet Caracas has always been somehow pivotal to the popular music scene in Venezuela. Caracas is a city very close to the Caribbean Ocean, although separated from it by the National Park Waraira Repano (formerly called El Avila), part of a big mountain range on the northern coast of Venezuela. The weather and the vibe are pretty much Caribbean, so the music mostly heard in Caracas is salsa, merengue, reggeton, different kinds of Latin rhythms and Afro Caribbean music. For rock lovers, this is no paradise. Nevertheless, there has always been a rock scene, a pop music scene, a punk and ska scene, and a heavy metal scene, and all of these scenes had a particular momentum during the 1980s and 1990s.

Before the spread of the Internet, it was harder to find out about bands from the regions but between 1983 and 1999, Caracas bands were widely known across Venezuela. Radio programs on brand-new FM stations at the beginning of the 1990s were crucial for the promotion of bands, but very few bands were long-lived and knowledge of them soon dissipated. Venezuela has only a handful of successful bands with careers spanning more than twenty years. They include Desorden Público, Zapato 3 and Caramelos de Cianuro. Our Facebook forum provides a space where music enthusiasts can interact and relate their own experiences of concerts and venues. Like the short-lived bands, venues also keep disappearing in Caracas, so the forum is a site that works to preserve memories of Venezuelan popular music culture.

Proyecto Caracas Memorabilia specifically aims to document the history of pop music in Caracas between 1980 and 1999. Following the Un-Convention[1] that was held in Caracas in 2012, and inspired by Un-Convention attendee Jez Collins's online Birmingham Music Archive (see Chapter 6, this volume), I decided to more formally organise my own memorabilia, scanning and archiving popular music culture artefacts I found while browsing through the pieces of history that were gathering dust from my own adolescence.

I established a blog under the name Proyecto Caracas Memorabilia but my own artefacts were not enough, and I wanted other people to share their own memorabilia and stories. That is how the Facebook group came about. Friends started inviting their own contacts and at the time of writing, more than 300 people have shared their favourite music and memories of Caracas on this virtual heritage site. The use of Facebook has been of great importance in this project. It is where people meet and find friends from their youth. Any morning, you can wake up and find you have been tagged in a picture from twenty years ago or more, and I guess that is part of the magic of Facebook and what makes it a valuable tool in DIY popular music heritage activities. People with a variety of interests and ages, some of them living outside Venezuela, and even some musicians have also been part of this collaboration.

Rules have been established for the Facebook group to ensure a heritage focus is maintained. Contributors are asked to only post about music and memorabilia and to not publicise new bands or events. Users are also requested to keep politics out of discussions, since politics is such a controversial topic in Venezuela. Contributors are encouraged to promote events related to bands that were founded more than ten years ago and to share photographs of friends taken in the period of interest to the project. These images need not have been taken in a particular Caracas venue. Rather, the aim is to catch a glimpse of what the fashion of the time was. Some people also share items of nostalgia from different blogs and that is also allowed.

At the time of writing, Proyecto Caracas Memorabilia has a blog, a Facebook group, a Facebook community page and a Twitter account. The Facebook community page is linked directly to the Twitter account, @ccsmemorabilia, which is used to publicise upcoming events in Caracas and other towns and cities. In these ways, we maintain our music profile to encompass all rock and pop styles, including punk, metal, ska and reggae.

Through the existence of the social network sites devoted to this project, and also via some additional research, I was fortunate to make contact with Eddio Piña Rojas, an editor and researcher who has recently published the first of several books on the history of rock in Venezuela. This particular encounter has been important because it has opened up access to other, more difficult to find memorabilia. Because most of the project's members are aged only in their late thirties, in the 1980s we were still children, meaning most of us saw our first gigs in the early 1990s. For this reason, there is a part of the story of the Caracas scene that is encompassed by the project but of which we have only heard secondhand. The memorabilia I have been able to access by way of the connection with Eddio Piña Rojas helps the project to form a more comprehensive picture of the city, the gigs and the venues.

The project draws on information from a range of different sites devoted to the sharing of memories and to paying homage to certain important characters in the story of the Caracas pop rock scene. Of particular importance are Hoy en la Historia del Pop Rock Venezolano, La Historia del Rock en Venezuela, Ska en Venezuela, Punk en Venezuela, Punks en Venezuela, Movimiento Metal, Punk, Rock Venezuela and Minitequeros.com.ve. Some of these sites started as blogs more than ten years ago, but they mostly are dedicated to circulating news about gigs played by bands in the current pop-rock scene. These sites act as content-issuers in the sense they provide information to feed our different social network spaces. If it is memorabilia, it is posted to the discussion group, and when it is related to forthcoming gigs, the information is uploaded to the community page.

Through the Facebook forum, we have been able to interact with a range of music enthusiasts who share their own experiences in concerts and venues. Since venues keep disappearing in Caracas, the project provides an important way for us to preserve memories of these venues, and in doing so hopefully contribute to our current and future local music industry.

The aim is for the project to serve as a meeting point for musicians, producers and fans, and for the public and private sectors. The project is expecting to deliver a foundation in the coming years.

NOTE

1. Un-Convention is a development agency and music network based in the United Kingdom, with events and projects held globally. See http://unconventionhub.org/about-us.

REFERENCE

Ramón y Rivera, Luis Felipe (1976). *La música popular de Venezuela.* Caracas: Author.

17 The Australian Jazz Museum – All That Aussie Jazz

A Potted History of the Victorian Jazz Archive, 1996–2014

Ray Sutton

For many years, the Australian jazz fraternity was very concerned about the fate of its combined collections of recordings, publications, photos, instruments, banners, posters and other memorabilia. The ad hoc conservation work and the ongoing practical and departmental policy restrictions imposed on the National Film and Sound Archive (NFSA) in Canberra exacerbated this concern.

Moreover, Melbourne was recognised as the major Australian inspirational and actual centre for the post-World War II revival of jazz. Bands led by Graeme Bell OBE, AM and his brother Roger Bell, Adrian Monsbourgh AO, Frank Johnson, Len Barnard AM and his brother Bob Barnard AM, Frank Traynor, Bruce Clarke OAM, Don Banks AM and others all contributed to a uniquely Australian style of this music – it is alleged "Lazy" Ade Monsbourgh said, "You can even smell the gum leaves" – a style continued to this day by bands, composers, musicians and singers, many of them household names. The international reputations of these people attest to their force in the development and performance of jazz in Europe and indeed the United States.

The final impetus for the creation of the Victorian Jazz Archive Inc (VJA) came with the strongly voiced desire to preserve Victoria's jazz heritage within Victoria, and for it to be readily accessible to musicians, collectors, donors and others, both here and interstate.

FROM THE VICTORIAN JAZZ ARCHIVE INC. TO THE AUSTRALIAN JAZZ MUSEUM

Victorians in particular were reluctant to see their collections evaporate in Canberra, so the foundation of a state archive was mooted. Approximately sixty people attended the inaugural meeting in August 1996, and the VJA was born. Incorporation followed in October of the same year. The Archive, as it is colloquially known, initially started life in the garage of a private home. However, after six months or so, the lady of the house insisted the car be moved back into the garage. A small room was obtained at the Melbourne Museum for a short while until it too was required for other needs of the museum.

While a number of people were actively involved in the formation of the archive, John Kennedy OAM and Dr Ray Marginson AM were the real driving forces in its creation and successful operation during the first nine years. Both were very insistent that the VJA, and in particular its collection, were to be maintained according to standard museum practices, using appropriate procedures, protocols and archival materials to adequately archive the jazz artefacts.

Because of his network of contacts in art and philanthropy circles, during these formative years Dr Marginson was very instrumental in obtaining seed funding for the organisation through grant applications to state and federal government departments and other sources. Great support for the initiative was received from Museums Australia (Victoria), the University of Melbourne, the Performing Arts Museum, philanthropic trusts and individuals. Major funding from the Myer Foundation, Dame Elisabeth Murdoch OBE AC and the Potter Foundation, and a grant from the Victorian state government through its Community Support Fund – an extraordinary benefactor to many charities – facilitated our initial building works and basic equipment. Security of tenure is very important when seeking funding from government or philanthropic organisations. Our current twenty-one-year lease of the premises from Parks Victoria, negotiated in 2013, will take us to 2034.

After much exploration and frustration, we began negotiating a lease with Parks Victoria in May 1997 for the use of a disused motor-vehicle repair workshop in Wantirna, our present home. This building was a completely empty steel shell that had not been used for several years. Many hundreds of volunteer hours were spent cleaning and preparing the premises for what it has become today.

Figure 17.1 Founding members of the Victorian Jazz Archive, Dr Ray Bradley AM and Dr Ray Marginson AM, making a door at the Wantirna premises. Photo courtesy of the Australian Jazz Museum.

During 1997, three six-metre insulated shipping containers were purchased and moved into the Wantirna building to act as repository vaults for what we thought would be sufficient storage for many years to come. How wrong we were! We have since had to purchase and install another container located outside the main building, converted waste space to repository areas and lease a room at Millers Homestead in Boronia, a historic building owned by the Knox City Council. Commencing in 2007, all vaults and repository areas were installed with pre-loved steel compactus units and shelving, providing us with in excess of 600 lineal metres of storage capacity. Wall partitions, floor covering and air-conditioning as well as other amenities were added over time as funding became available. In excess of A$300,000 of capital expenditure has been outlaid to date.

Exemption from income tax and charity status was granted in July 2000, and after three years' hard work, full accreditation with Museums Australia (Victoria) was granted in April 2003. The latter was only possible due to the foresight of our founders, who insisted on working with museum standards from day one, no matter how slow this made progress seem at times.

Reaccreditation came in 2007 and again in 2012, taking us to 2017. Anyone who has been involved with accreditation will realise just how much work is involved to ensure everything is properly and correctly documented and protocols are adhered to, and the VJA is no exception. During 2008, we underwent a significance assessment and a preservation audit. Our policies, procedures and protocols, including collections, acquisitions, deposit contract, disaster recovery and office administration, together with all related forms, were re-evaluated for relevance in relation to current museum practices. An extract from the MAP Reaccreditation Report of 2012 reads:

> Accredited in 2003, the Victorian Jazz Archive (VJA) provides a unique insight into the development of Jazz in Australia from the 1920s up to the present day and is regarded, both nationally and internationally, as the largest archive in Australia. The Museum continues going from strength to strength, and since being Re-Accredited in 2007 has successfully acquired funding from various avenues to upgrade and improve its collection stores. ... The Victorian Jazz Archive is one of the leading volunteer run museums in Victoria. The museum standards attained in previous Accreditations are exemplary and the VJA has demonstrated its commitment to continuous improvement. A number of model documents from the VJA are currently used as resources for other museums in the MAP program.
>
> (Museums Australia (Victoria) 2012)

For a number of years now, the Victorian Jazz Archive Inc. has been considered the de facto Australian Jazz Archive/Museum by many jazz musicians, aficionados, collectors and enthusiasts in Australia, principally because of the successful operation we conduct at our Wantirna premises. We currently receive material donations from interstate, the most recent being 200 different 78 rpm and 300 LP records through the State Library of Western Australia.

In recognising this fact, and to better reflect our current operating environment, early in 2014 our Committee of Management approved a change of name. We now trade as the Australian Jazz Museum (AJM), while still retaining the legal entity of the Victorian Jazz Archive Inc. The new name was officially launched by the Hon. Heidi Victoria, Minister for the Arts, who was guest of honour at a jazz concert at the Knox Community Arts Centre in Bayswater, to celebrate International Jazz Day on April 30, 2014.

THE MISSION OF THE AUSTRALIAN JAZZ MUSEUM

Through its primary and secondary collections, the AJM provides a unique insight into the development and influence of jazz in Australia from its earliest introduction and inception in the 1920s, through the dance band era of the 1930s and 1940s, to the emergence of trad and be-bop and to the present time, when jazz is taught in tertiary institutions and enjoyed in clubs and concert halls around the country. The provenance of all material held within the collection is well documented, with many collections having been donated by notable members of the jazz community throughout Australia.

Although some jazz archives exist in other states, few have dedicated premises. Instead, they tend to be small ad hoc organisations. AJM is being regarded by many Australian and overseas musicians and archivists as the largest museum in Australia housing jazz items. Consequently, our collection will continue to grow, with donations of artefacts, records, books, cassettes, CDs, DVDs, videos, photographs, posters, instruments and ephemera regularly being received.

As space is at such a premium and our collection is ever expanding, we are exploring with our landlord ways and means by which we can gain additional space for our collection, administration and entertainment activities at the Wantirna premises. The first-stage plan includes additional storage for the collection and a larger and more suitable display and entertainment area.

We have extended our lease of a room at Millers Homestead in Boronia for another two years, with an option for a third year. Jazz sheet-music arrangements are stored in acid-free polypropylene zip-lock sleeves in fifty-five archive boxes stored on metal shelving at Millers, and this will be expanded as the never-ending task of sorting through masses of material continues. An avid collector in New South Wales has offered the AJM a very large collection of sheet music, some 13,000 songs, 2,000 orchestrations and 200 rags, and we have provisionally accepted this collection.

Time is one of our enemies. Many of the early recordings are on acetate discs or old reel-to-reel tapes. These – indeed all records, audio tapes, photos, films, historical musical instruments, posters, programs and other ephemera – are subject to deterioration and accidental damage, but acetates particularly as they peel off their glass or aluminum base.

Collections that have been gifted or bequeathed to us are not usually catalogued or even sorted by the donor. Copyright details may be obscure or in need of negotiation. Each of these challenges needs to be met by an ever-expanding team of volunteers.

Music is painstakingly transferred to CDs and stored as both archival and accessible. The AJM now has in excess of 2,000 CDs preserving important Australian jazz performances from the 1940s onwards. This has been done to high professional standards, a quality recognised by awards for conservation and preservation from both Museums Australia and the National Bank of Australia Nationwide Conservation Program.

Preservation copies of the CDs are held on site but copies are also lodged with the NFSA. We have catalogued in excess of 150,000 individual tracks and/or records and personnel details into a searchable database that currently is available through our website. We are digitising posters and photographs and identifying the people and places wherever possible, a job that at times taxes even our rather catholic range of volunteers. Oral histories initially recorded on cassettes and radio programs are being transferred onto CDs. We have embarked on the process of cataloguing posters and programs and registering them in the database. Digitised images of posters and record covers (front and back) are also being uploaded to the database.

In order to make the recorded material the AJM has rescued and preserved available for enjoyment and research, and to provide an understanding of the history of jazz in Australia, we have a program of issuing CDs for sale to our members and visitors. Detailed notes, personnel listings, and the results of our investigation and research accompany these rare, collectable jazz from the archive CDs, of which there are now thirty. Our work in this area has given rise to a steady development of research inquiries, with several investigators currently preparing material for books, articles and other publications. We have also published several works ourselves, including the third volume of Jack Mitchell's *Australia Jazz Discography*.

And that only deals with the local jazz. A considerable proportion of all gifts and bequests, as might be expected, is of international material: 78 rpm records, LPs, EPs, cassettes and tapes of jazz, blues, swing and gospel artists from around the world. These are clerically catalogued but, due to workload constraints, cannot yet be fully databased. They are, however, available for reference along with our library and our unique collection of discographies. In a third vault, the AJM holds the Archives of the Australian Jazz Convention, the longest running (since 1946) annual jazz convention in the world, which began, not coincidentally, in Melbourne.

The AJM has mounted exhibitions, both at our own premises and in places such as public libraries. We have arranged Senior Citizens' open days and twice-weekly public open days. We contribute to community radio programs and make our premises available for music workshops and teaching programs for both junior and senior groups, utilising experienced jazz musicians. And, of course, more gifts, bequests and extensive collections are regularly received from new and current donors.

THE NEXT STEPS

The AJM is not limited to the heritage of old music, as jazz is ever-evolving. Our experience to date has been that young musicians of today are unfortunately not yet conscious of the heritage nature of their art. However, we are slowly making headway in seeking copies of their CDs for our collection. Our policy has always been to welcome jazz musicians from all generations and include their music (from classic to contemporary) in the museum. Meanwhile, much work remains to be done. The AJM web page is constantly evolving and, through an alliance with the Eastern Regional Library Corporation, details of our Australian Collection are available for international research at any time. We are also playing a role in keeping jazz music alive by contributing to local community FM radio stations.

All of this requires money. Basic everyday operations of the museum include leasing the property, security, power and electricity, telephone, insurances (building, contents, volunteers), equipment, general maintenance, rubbish removal, kitchen, office and toilet consumables, stationery, auditing of our financial records, general archival materials and production of our *VJAZZ* magazine, with an annual operating cost of around A$40,000. While we try to contain these costs as much as possible, many are constantly increasing – for example, energy, security, rubbish collection.

We can usually cover such costs with three income streams: AJM membership (currently in excess of 600), museum shop sales (principally CDs) to members and visitors, and regular group tours, which bring in about a quarter of the annual costs associated with keeping the museum open. This is a very positive way for the AJM to continue its aim of spreading the word about Australian jazz and keeping it alive. These group tours also assist us to maintain and increase membership and improve sales of jazz-related material through our museum shop. Additional income comes from donations, fundraising activities (including external concerts) and grants for specific projects.

Currently, our annual membership subscription is A$40 per family and includes a free *VJAZZ* CD (one of the thirty rare collectible jazz from the Archive series, which are usually sold to members for A$22.50). Benefits of membership include receiving the sixteen-page quarterly *VJAZZ* magazine, packed with interesting jazz-related articles, a discount on most items in the extensive AJM merchandise shop, borrowing books and other items from the members-only borrowing department, and access to an extensive reference library.

Thanks to a successful application to the Australian federal government's Volunteer Grant Program, in 2013 we created a paved and shaded area outside the building to enable better use of a disused space for lunch breaks and some meetings during clement weather.

All the AJM's office administration, database entry and web access are handled via a computer network with twenty personal computers throughout the building attached to a file server. We purchase and use refurbished all-in-one computers where possible, and are fortunate in having a small IT network consultancy to help us with professional advice and technical assistance at very reasonable rates (some pro bono). We've standardised on a Microsoft computer network and application software (Business Server 2013, Windows 7 operating system and Office 2013) where possible. Some proprietary software such as Sony's SoundForge, for transferring sound from original source media, is also used.

The museum is run entirely by volunteer labour. In 2013, for example, some 17,000 hours were contributed by more than sixty people, aged from thirty to ninety years, with many individual contributions in excess of twenty-four hours per week. Since 2007, we have developed position descriptions to assist with recruitment and training. During the early days, people with a common interest in jazz came from the ranks of musicians, aficionados and enthusiasts to volunteer their services (several musicians are still with us). However, in more recent years, as the numbers of serious jazzophiles have dwindled, volunteers have come from those who need to maintain support from the federal government's Newstart Allowance job-seeking program or who wish to return something back to society by volunteering in their local community.

Since 2006, our Collections Manager, Mel Blachford, has been the mainstay in acquiring, archiving and disseminating material and artefacts for the overall collection. Through support from Museums Australia (Victoria), the National Library in Canberra and the NFSA (Canberra), together with appropriate training from professional conservators, Mel has moulded his team to the high standard required for archiving and preserving our Australian jazz heritage. A jazz enthusiast and lateral thinker, Mel has brought a high degree of jazz knowledge and professionalism to the AJM.

Our staff recruitment has mainly been through local council volunteer recruitment agencies, as they conduct initial interviews (with the local council covering the cost of police checks and so on), with appropriate referral to the AJM. Our executive conducts a final interview before offering an invitation to join us, and a comprehensive *AJM Volunteer Handbook* is provided to each new recruit. Turnover is modest, as our general policy is to encourage volunteers to learn about other activities at the centre so that time spent is as interesting and enjoyable as possible. Multiskilling can assist greatly when there is a need to cover unscheduled absences of other volunteers. Over the years, the AJM has become an ideal social outlet for retirees, singles and senior citizens with an interest in jazz.

RECOGNITION OF OUR WORK

In 2005, the Archive was the recipient of the Knox City Council's Knox Pride Award for Outstanding Archive of Everything Jazz. In 2007, founder John Kennedy was presented with an award from the Australian Sound Recording Association (Inc) for outstanding achievement and leadership in the Jazz Archiving community. The same year, the AJM won the prestigious Victorian Community History Award for an eight-panel display depicting Jazz Spans the Decades. In 2009, the AJM was the recipient of a Community Heritage Award and Grant for Archival storage materials for its Australian poster and photographic collection and conservation training workshop, while in 2010 we won a Special Commendation in Knox City Council's Environment Awards. The AJM was the successful recipient of a Victorian Museum Award in 2012 for volunteer-run museum organisations "aiming for the highest standard in all areas of documentation."

During 2014, the Public Records Office Victoria (PROV) appointed the AJM as a Place of Deposit (PoD) for holding and preserving public records of local significance or interest. We have now joined a network of more than 150 community organisations across the state making up PROV's PoD program, all of which are committed to caring for and providing access to our state's history and heritage. As such, we successfully applied for the Sir Rupert Hamer Records Management Award, which recognises the efforts of community archives and government agencies or authorities in preserving and making accessible records of significance to their local communities. Such an appointment also emphasises the need for the AJM to continue its important work in archiving and preserving our material collection according to museum standards.

ADDRESSING CHALLENGES

In 2011, we organised a series of two-hour think-tank workshops facilitated by our President, Terry Norman. About thirty-five volunteers at different levels in the organisation participated. This led to the adoption of a new mission statement: Proactively Collecting, Archiving and Disseminating Australian Jazz. Following a SWOT analysis, we looked at our business, products, customers and competitors. Positive feedback from all sessions demonstrated that this exercise was worthwhile, and it has changed the way we think about our collection and how we go about enhancing/expanding the heritage of Australian jazz.

We look at our current and future challenges in the following way:

1 *Respect the past.* It is important for us to remember and respect the contribution made by our foundation members and the volunteers who have developed our museum.

2 *Enjoy the present.* It is critical for us to involve everyone and to enjoy each day we work together as a jazz community.

3 *Plan for the future.* We need to plan and take action for the future to ensure the long-term viability of our museum.

To make these goals happen, we developed and implemented a strategy to look ahead and identify the changes needed to ensure the museum will survive and prosper, and a business plan to focus on important projects and take actions to achieve our strategy:

> Our thinking is not to be restricted by being unable to afford it. Decide what we need, then find a way to fund the project.

During the past twelve months, our president, in conjunction with the Committee of Management, has further developed our three-year business plan to include a number of projects designed to enhance the organisation and keep alive our wonderful heritage of Australian jazz, while moving towards a more modern electronic museum environment. Apart from the name change, some of these projects include the following:

Digital Museum Management System

The AJM is currently looking into a suitable centralised system to better cater to our overall needs and requirements into 2015 and beyond. Systems being investigated are DSpace and eMu (used by the Smithsonian Institute in America and many other museums around the world). While both systems appear to be suitable, the former is very complex to configure and set up, and would need specialist IT support, while the latter is very expensive. We are continuing to investigate further options.

Digitising Heritage Materials

This is probably the largest, most complex and longest project we need to address. A suitable plan is currently being developed to encompass much of the latest digitisation protocol in order to meet Museum Australia (Victoria) accreditation standards and requirements. This project includes digitising all sound recordings, images, text documents and periodicals, sheet music, posters and books, so is very extensive. The project will be ongoing over many years, perhaps with some of the more intricate activities needing to be outsourced to professionals, for which we will seek appropriate funding.

Our first official foray into this project will be the digitisation of nine scrapbooks (some 1,850 pages) from Graeme Bell, which he donated to the State Library of New South Wales many years ago. After protracted negotiations, our Collections Manager has now entered into a limited on-loan agreement with the State Library to undertake this project. The first three on-loan scrapbooks were received at the AJM in August 2014, and we are, at the time of writing, determining the equipment required to digitise each page according to the protocol issued by the State Library.

New Website

We are developing a new and modern-looking AJM website, which includes a shopping cart for worldwide viewers to purchase our CDs and other items, with payment being made via PayPal. The new website was revealed in late 2014.

Reading the above, one could be excused for thinking all was beer and skittles in relation to funding the organisation. However, this is far from the truth! In the early days, every cent had to be scraped together, and even now funding is a major concern for the AJM's Committee of Management.

We have been fortunate to receive several monetary bequests over the years, which have assisted the AJM with its building program, enabling various areas to be refurbished, including the installation of compactus units to improve and increase storage capacity. However, very careful financial management is high on our agenda, and our Treasurer, a volunteer who is a Certified Accountant, ably assists in directing this approach.

Seeking financial support from local, state and federal government departments is extremely difficult and very time-consuming, requiring an immense amount of background information (generally for small sums between A$5,000 and A$15,000) and must be related to specific projects. Available funds are becoming less while the number of organisations seeking such funds is dramatically increasing. Consequently, many not-for-profit organisations similar to the AJM, which have limited or extremely stretched resources, are now required to deal with more extensive application guidelines and tighter criteria.

Our future challenges remain ever-present as we move towards the next decade. These are:

- *Relevance.* To survive, the AJM must remain relevant to the jazz fraternity, past, present and future. Unfortunately, many in the current younger generation of jazz musicians appear unable to acknowledge they are creating history every time they play, record or write music. Convincing them this material should be properly archived for the future is one of our major concerns.
- *Location.* The AJM is currently located in Wantirna, an outer eastern suburb of Melbourne some 28 kilometres from the city centre. It would be far too expensive to move, even if a suitable place could be found, so future plans will be to have a presence of some kind in the city centre as an introduction to the AJM for tourists and visitors.
- *Wantirna opening hours.* Currently, these are 10:00 a.m. to 3:00 p.m. on Tuesdays, Wednesdays and Fridays (except public holidays), which

can be quite restrictive for working people. We need to provide more flexible opening times. However, this is further exacerbated by our workforce being all volunteers, most of whom are senior citizens.

- *Skill base of volunteers.* As the operation of the AJM becomes more professional and businesslike, our volunteers will need to be upskilled in newly emerging archive/museum standards and protocols so our collection retains its heritage value and remains relevant for future research. This also includes developing skills in the use of cloud-based computing.
- *Carriers of sound/vision files.* This is a major challenge, for technology is constantly changing. We need to be cognisant that our jazz material should be accessible to future generations, for the electronic medium we are using today to record and store sound, images and video will be rapidly overtaken by future technological advances.
- *Lack of ensured funding.* Of major concern is the need to adequately fund the museum in the future. As large material donations continue to be received, additional storage and administration space will be required. We are a totally independent not-for-profit organisation in the art and museum sector and don't receive any local, state or federal government financial support apart from the occasional successful project-related grant applications – providing we meet the very strict criteria. Apart from increasing membership and having more fundraising events, we are considering joint ventures with local government, business sponsorships and close associations with philanthropic organisations.

The AJM hopes the information presented above will provide the reader with an insight into why the organisation was created and its general workings, and perhaps assist anyone who is thinking of setting up a similar music archive.

ACKNOWLEDGMENTS

Volunteers who provided comment in the writing of this chapter include Terry Norman, Mel Blachford, Ralph Powell, David McDowell and Mel Forbes.

REFERENCE

Museums Australia (Victoria). 2012. Museums Accreditation Programme Reaccreditation Report: Victorian Jazz Archive. Unpublished report.

18 The Australian Country Music Hall of Fame

A DIY Museum and Archive in Australia's Country Music Capital

Barrie Brennan

The story of the Australian Country Music Hall of Fame (ACMHOF) as a do-it-yourself (DIY) museum has been determined by the volunteers who work for the organisation. As a result, there are many similarities with other DIY museums and archives found in the pages of this book. The ACMHOF volunteers have been concerned about the conflict between "official/top-down" and "unofficial/bottom-up" heritage (Roberts and Cohen 2013, 3) or with "residual culture" in relation to language or customs (Williams 1965) – although, of course, their discussions may not have used such terminology. Two influences on the particular way this DIY organisation has developed have been the genre of music that is its focus – Australian country music – and the physical location of the organisation and museum in Tamworth, in rural New South Wales. Exploring these two influences provides background to the organisation's development and the ways in which these factors have impacted on the attitudes and objectives the volunteers have attributed to the ACMHOF. The chapter presents a brief history of the ACMHOF before examining the volunteers' perceptions of the short and long-term goals of the ACMHOF in more detail.

AUSTRALIAN COUNTRY MUSIC

Australian country music (ACM) has its roots in two sources. The first was the traditional songs the migrants from various parts of the United Kingdom brought with them in the nineteenth and twentieth centuries. To these were added local songs that focused on the new rather than the former homeland, the wide, brown land with gum trees rather than hedges and elms. The second source was the United States. That impact began with the gold rushes of the 1850s, continued into the twentieth century and grew with the introduction of gramophone records.

Country music – or hillbilly music, as it was often called – was very popular in the Australian capital cities before and after World War II. The advent of rock music and television in the 1950s, particularly in the cities, caused a decline in the popularity of country/hillbilly music. However, country music remained popular in rural areas and was supported by the introduction of extensive country tours by the city-based performers. The term "country and western" was also adopted for this Australian music, and its popularity was maintained in many rural communities in the east as well as the west of the country.

Two important topics have caused some controversy for ACM since the 1960s. The first was the inclusion of New Zealand with Australia, with discussions of country music represented as Australasian country music. The intensity of the debate for and against the broader term has varied from decade to decade. A second topic creating more intense argument has been a view that seeks to limit or reduce the impact of American country music on Australian country music, particularly the suggestion that American music is dominating the local product. These debates have influenced both the development of the ACMHOF and Tamworth's ACM Festival and Golden Guitar Awards.

TAMWORTH: COUNTRY MUSIC CAPITAL AND THE TURN TO HERITAGE

Before the 1970s, Tamworth's claim to international fame was that it was the first Southern Hemisphere town to have electric street lights (Milliss 1980, 127–33). In the 1960s, it did enjoy a reasonably sized group of country performers and fans. However, in the late 1960s and early 1970s, a plan developed by several people linked to the local radio station, 2TM, and businesses with an interest in ACM saw the establishment of Tamworth as Country Music Capital, a title meant to indicate Tamworth was the major city for this genre of music in Australia. This was certainly a successful bottom-up development, and was achieved without formal support from any level of government.

Symbolic of this new status, an ACM Festival was established in Tamworth in January 1973, together with a series of awards, including the Golden Guitars and the Roll of Renown. The status of the Golden Guitars was recognised nationally and in New Zealand. Gradually, the January festival expanded from a weekend to ten days and became a major tourism event in Australia.

During these developments and the ongoing focus on ACM in Tamworth from 1973 to 1990, there was little major interest in the heritage of this music and no formal recognition of this feature of the genre. However, at the beginning of the 1990s, the Tamworth City Council gained funds to repair and refurbish the 1866 Mechanics' Institute building in the CBD. In 1991, a group interested in ACM heritage was established as the Australian Country Music Foundation (ACMF) and was incorporated in 1992. A curator was employed and an exhibit on the King of Country Music, Slim Dusty, was set up in the restored Mechanics' Institute. A lack of knowledge of and experience in museum management resulted in changes in the ACMF board, the governing body elected by members, and a program was designed for volunteers to both manage a museum with changing exhibits and develop a collection. The goal of the board and volunteers in the remaining years of the 1990s was to keep the museum open. I joined the ACMF in 1996.

Around the same time, a second Tamworth ACM heritage group was formed with the goal of developing a collection, which it exhibited in Heritage Hall. This was also a volunteer group, but financial and other difficulties forced the group to close its facility.

With encouragement from the Tamworth City Council, discussions were held in the early years of the 2000s between the Heritage Hall and the ACMF. As a result, the groups merged in 2004. The Heritage Hall group possessed a larger collection than the ACMF but the ACMF had wider experience and more contacts within the museum sector. The need for a more clearly defined DIY museum and archive became evident after the amalgamation of the organisations. More substantial goals than simply remaining open were defined.

OBJECTIVES POST-AMALGAMATION

Three stages are identifiable in the progress of this new organisation. The first was linked to the development of a business plan with the aid of a state government grant and a consultant. This process was slow, with the plan not being finalised until June 2005 and the key goal being the building of a new museum. The consultant was not experienced in museum operations, the data were unreliable and the goals were unrealistic. One board member called the proposed building a Taj Mahal.

The objective of the second stage was to raise the profile of the organisation, particularly as a museum. This goal was to be achieved through four projects. They were to gain an assessment of the collection's significance; produce a report on its conservation/preservation; obtain further grants to improve the collection and its management; and, finally, to participate in the New South Wales Museums and Galleries program regarding the National Standards for Museums. The collection was assessed as being of "international and national significance" (Report from Linda Raymond 2006). Advice on conservation by Kay Soderlund in 2007 was followed up, and the Standards program was successfully completed in 2008. Additional funds were gained from the National Library's Community Heritage Grants – for example, in 2010 for the beginning of the digitisation of the collection. An outcome of this new emphasis on the museum was the new title ACMHOF being adopted to promote the organisation's activities.

In the third stage, the goal of seeking to build, from the organisation's own resources, a new and better facility was rejected and the current policy is for the collection and museum to be housed in a new facility provided by the Tamworth Regional Council. The facility will be professionally managed and the role of the current board is to move the ACMHOF towards that level of operation. Since the Tamworth Council has taken a more strategic role in the planning and management of the annual January festival, the ACMHOF's value as being a focus on Australian country music for the whole year has become more significant for the city, thus promoting the concept of ACM as a major activity throughout the year through its museum and archive.

In the current context, the ACMHOF's future is very closely linked to the short- and longer-term developments of the Tamworth Regional Council in relation to ACM. The issue of the potential influence of both American and New Zealand country music on the ACMHOF's role as custodian of ACM heritage is important, as is the importance of a home for the ACMHOF in relation to other financial demands on the council's budget. The ACMHOF is also challenged as a museum, as the ways in which potential museum visitors may choose to gain information on ACM change in response to new technologies. There is also a wider challenge regarding which collections are to be saved and which are of insufficient importance to be retained. What is the perceived value of ACM's heritage as part of Australia's broad, continuing culture?

THE VOLUNTEERS OF THE ACMHOF

The above discussion has outlined key influences on, and issues faced by, the ACMF and ACMHOF. We now explore the differing views of the volunteers, including board members, on the ACMHOF's current and future direction and goals. The comments are generalisations I have formulated from past events and recorded decisions, and are not based on specific interview data collected especially for this exercise.

The volunteer population of the ACMHOF is constantly changing. After a failed experiment with hiring staff to act as museum guides when the museum was first opened, no paid staff have been involved with the ACMF. People come and go, then sometimes return. In any given year, the volunteer group usually numbers about thirty people, with a mix of men and women. There are a number of couples, but mostly volunteers are single-family representatives. The vast majority of volunteers are middle-aged or older.

I have identified four different groups of volunteers at the ACMHOF. These groups are not identified as part of the association's policy and individuals may move from group to group over time. I imagine these groupings may be comparable with the volunteer makeup of other DIY music museums and archives covered in this book.

1 *Australian country music fans.* The first and largest group is identified as ACM fans. Like those who were around when the Country Music Capital project was being launched (1960s and 1970s), they enjoy country music, probably play it at home, and attend concerts by local and visiting artists. They support the regular monthly Country in the

Figure 18.1 Volunteers of the Australian Country Music Hall of Fame. Photo courtesy of Athol Latham and the ACMHOF.

Courtyard events held at the ACMHOF, at which a local guest and walk-up artists perform. They also support the social aspects of the ACMHOF's program that involve serving tea and coffee or selling tickets in raffles or competitions. Their activities are strongly linked to the local scene and involve entertainment and social activities. This work may be supporting the work of the ACMHOF but is not necessarily related to its heritage or conservation program. Many of these volunteers do not come for a specific period of time each week and may be involved just for certain events. They perceive the board will ensure the organisation continues and will deal with the major issues. Some members of the first group may participate in the next two groups, but only a minority.

2 *Collection work.* The next group consists of those involved with the collection. They tend to contribute weekly on a regular basis, usually at the same time, and to work on their own or with another volunteer or mentor. The work may be on the computer, recording data on collection items or preparing clothing for a new exhibit or change of exhibits. There is also the ongoing task of receiving and doing the paperwork on new acquisitions and then preparing them for, and finding them a location within, the collection at the museum or the second storage location. In association with grants gained by the ACMHOF, there are usually training sessions on aspects of the work associated with the grant, such as using new equipment or adding new types of information to the database.

3 *Running the museum*. The third group consists of those who are associated with the day-to-day running of the museum, including the office and collection areas. Tasks here include cleaning before and after the doors open/close, dealing with changes to the exhibits (such as costumes or making notes associated with a new exhibit) and checking the video machines. A major task for this group is attending to new visitors, receiving entry fees and selling merchandise. Money needs to be counted and checked after closure. These volunteers tend to become very knowledgeable about the exhibits and to develop their skills in helping visitors to enjoy and appreciate their visit.

4 *Administrative duties*. The last group comprises those with administrative tasks, and these are the jobs that have grown in number. They relate to the volunteers, computers, website, publications, public relations, research, gaining funds through grants, relationships with other organisations, membership and sponsorships, correspondence, merchandise, meeting minutes, library and so on. These volunteers usually come in on a regular basis on a particular day and gain a good deal of experience and knowledge about the workings of the organisation. They are often the source of new ideas or suggestions for different ways to do this or deal with that. Some of the members of this group become very effective as guides to our visitors to the museum.

The nine board members are also volunteers and usually have special duties or a portfolio to manage.

Most of the members of the first group comprises primarily focused on the ACMHOF as a social group and therefore are concerned with its ongoing activities. They are hopeful the organisation will continue and provide for the locals as it has in the past. They have less interest in the collection or the museum and may not enter the museum area or ever visit the collection, either at the main site or the second storage site. Their perception of the organisation is as a local facility, and they are not usually involved in its broad organisation and policy development, particularly its status at the state, national and international levels.

The work of those in the second group may be quite demanding and challenging, and often requires the use of skills gained from previous work experience or learning new skills. This possibility of new learning is attractive to some of volunteers, albeit only a limited number. Their experience working with the collection, such as digitising it, is likely to make them more interested in the collection and therefore they will tend to ask questions or be concerned about its preservation and future. The members of this group quite often have a clear preference for either working on their own or with others.

Like the second group, those working in the museum may find parts of their role demanding. Some visitors can be a problem! These volunteers tend to want to know about the exhibits, especially the new ones. There is also scope for them to explore aspects of the exhibits and especially pass on to their colleagues useful experiences they have dealing with the visitors and sharing information. Their work is quite often very individualistic, but they also tend to enjoy working with and relating to other volunteers. Quite often, those in the third group become very focused on their specific duties, whether membership or promotion. It is very important for these volunteers to be aware of changes in policy or new events or changes in routines.

From this description of the various types of ACMHOF volunteers, it may be expected there would be a wide variety of responses to the sorts of pressures, challenges and issues that face the organisation, especially the board, and the board should be aware of this wide range of responses. I expand on these responses below, but again stress that no official survey or interview data are available to support the assertions, and it is to be expected these attitudes will change over time.

The first group focuses on the ACMHOF primarily as a Tamworth institution. Members are concerned with the activities held at the ACMHOF, such as Country in the Courtyard, and fundraising activities and concerts held at other Tamworth venues. They generally have only a minor interest in the museum and its exhibits, even when new exhibits are unveiled. A similar level of interest is shown when new items are added to the collection or grant funds are acquired to extend the work on the collection. These volunteers probably support the increased role of the Tamworth Regional Council in the management of the annual January festival but would not necessarily favour a stronger American influence on the festival, though they may attend concerts at which American artists perform. The possibility of the council providing a new facility for the ACMHOF would also have their support, whatever the size, scope and facilities of the building may be, provided the project did not involve an increase in local rates, the local government tax system. Many of the volunteers in this group have been linked with the organisation since the late 1990s. They support the organisation and enjoy its social dimension and the country music it supports and provides. The development of a museum and collection that is professionally managed and supported by up-to-date technology that provides access to visitors from all over Australia and overseas through the Internet is not a central interest of these volunteers, though they support the ideas – provided the planning and execution of the work to achieve these goals is carried out by other volunteers.

The second and third groups, whose involvement includes working with the collection or in the many roles concerned with the running of the museum, either are or may potentially become interested in the stages that may move the ACMHOF from a DIY, volunteer-managed museum and archive to a professionally driven institution. The numbers of volunteers and the quality of the work contributed by the volunteers in these two groups may be a significant factor in determining the speed and degree of success the ACMHOF achieves in the process of its further development. The contribution made by these two groups of volunteers to the development of the organisation, especially since the amalgamation with the Heritage Hall, is one reason why there is confidence among many volunteers and the board that the proposed further growth of the ACMHOF is possible.

The fourth group has developed as the organisation has progressed in developing a larger collection and more effective museum.

The key factor with regard to the increased role of volunteers in these last three groups is the personal one in relation to the degree of satisfaction individuals gain from their ACMHOF volunteer experience and the extent to which they are prepared to continue to make or even increase their contribution. That is a decision for individuals to make. The differences between the various groups are illustrated by an example. Two board agenda items may be the offer of a gift to the collection of several items from a deceased person's estate and whether fat or long sausages should be used for the next fundraising barbecue. Members of the first group and some individuals from the second and third group may consider the latter issue to be very important, requiring detailed discussion. The fourth group, and hopefully the majority from the second and third groups, would see the collection issue as very significant and demanding close examination.

FINAL THOUGHTS

The ACMHOF may be able to continue as a DIY, volunteer-managed museum and archive, although there is no guarantee of this outcome. However, without a considerable increase in the contribution of volunteers in the second, third and fourth groups, the basis for progress to a professionally managed institution will be either delayed or based on less stable foundations.

The organisation's board, since the amalgamation with the Heritage Hall, has included members from the four identified groups. This has not been a specific policy objective. The groups of volunteers have not been formally identified or targeted by the organisation. But the credibility of the distinction and description of the four groups for this study is supported by the evidence of their representation on the elected board.

In the period between the submission of this chapter and its review, the Tamworth Regional Council offered the ACMHOF a new facility, the former Visitor Information Centre, and the board accepted the offer. The relocation will involve the ACMHOF in a new and different relationship with the council. In addition, the museum exhibits will change because of the new size and shape of the building, more volunteers will be required and there will be fewer opportunities for concerts within the museum. These changes cut across the activities and longer-term objectives of the four volunteer groups. However, the prime concerns in discussions with the council have been the collection and the museum. On the basis of that observation, the second, third and fourth groups may be able to recognise that their interests are being supported. If this conclusion proves to be accurate, then the future of the ACMHOF as a DIY collection and museum/archive progressing to become a professionally managed facility for Australian country music, and for Tamworth, remains a real possibility.

REFERENCES

Milliss, R. 1980. *City on the Peel*. Sydney: A.R. & A.W. Reid.
Roberts, L. and Cohen, S. 2013. Unauthorising popular music heritage: Outline of a critical framework. *International Journal of Heritage Studies* 20(3), 241–61.
Williams, R. 1965. *The long revolution*. London: Pelican.

19 Re:Muse-icology

Defining a National Landscape for the Study and Preservation of Rock 'n' roll's Built Heritage in America

Sheryl Davis

In September 2012, less than two weeks after graduating with an MA in Historic Preservation from the Savannah College of Art and Design in the United States, I founded Re:Muse-icology to create a platform for discourse on music heritage sites and establish a brand identity to represent my efforts in reframing musicology for scholarship of the built environment and the practice of historic preservation. Re:Muse-icology is a play on words, combining the prefix "re" with "muse" and "musicology" to represent my work as a DIY practitioner in preserving and reimagining music heritage sites for cultural, economic and environmental sustainability.

Re:Muse-icology emerged from my MA study, which focused on the preservation of American popular music heritage sites including the Buddy Bolden house in New Orleans, Louisiana, the Hurricane East club and Doo Wop architecture of Wildwood by-the-Sea, New Jersey, and Johnny Cash's boyhood home in Dyess, Arkansas. This culminated in a project entitled "State of Rock 2012: A Current Look at the Built Heritage of Rock 'n' Roll in 1950s America," in which I documented 100 buildings that influenced early rock 'n' roll on the national stage and behind the scenes. With this background, Re:Muse-icology involves self-directed activities in social media (Facebook and Twitter, specifically), pro bono volunteer consulting, and research and documentation, all of which contribute to my overarching goal of developing the subject of music history as a thematic study and typology in the field of historic preservation.

Specifically, in reimagining popular musicology for the world of architecture and the American preservation movement, Re:Muse-icology introduces a new kind of conscious architectural historicism that actively engages the intrinsic value of music's built heritage (embodied energy and design intelligence) and the synthesis of musicology, architectural history and phenomenology. This confluence of human circumstance, artistic will and architectural environment shaped the course of American popular music history and, with the exception of age and architectural style, remains peripheral to or unacknowledged by American institutional standards of evaluating and determining a building's historic significance. I established Re:Muse-icology with the aim of addressing this absence.

THE STATE OF ROCK 2012 PROJECT

My current efforts to survey buildings significant to the birth and development of rock 'n' roll are done with broader consideration for the architectural legacy of American popular music (1900s–1960s), including the contributions of other genres and sub-genres of American roots music such as ragtime, jazz, blues, rockabilly, folk, country, rhythm and blues (R&B), soul, gospel and bluegrass. Because the methodology that informs my work with Re:Muse-icology draws on my MA research, it is worth recounting that project here.

The project was underpinned by a recognition that many historic resources significant to our recent past remain undocumented and therefore underrepresented in the practice of historic preservation in the United States. Among them are the places that tell the story of rock 'n' roll music, an American art form that emerged in the 1950s. My research was a preliminary effort to identify and record buildings associated with the history and development of rock 'n' roll in 1950s America (see Table 19.1 for decade highlights,1950–59). As both a historic resources inventory and preservation activity survey, the resulting report provides the first comprehensive resource of its kind, establishing a foundation for more intensive research.

Table 19.1 Rock 'n' roll American decade highlights, 1950–59.

Year	Highlight
1950	Sam Phillips opens the **Memphis Recording Service** on Beale Street in Memphis, Tennessee.
	Leo Fender introduces the Precision bass and reissues the Broadcaster (first introduced in 1948) as the Telecaster, produced at his **original guitar factory** in Fullerton, California.
1951	Jackie Brenston & His Delta Cats (Ike Turner's band) record "Rocket 88" at the **Memphis Recording Service** in Memphis, Tennessee, later released on **Chess Records** label in Chicago, Illinois. It acknowledged as one of the first rock 'n' roll records.
	DJ Alan Freed ("Moondog") introduces the term "rock 'n' roll" on air at **WJW Radio** in Cleveland, Ohio.
	Jackie Brenston & His Delta Cats release "Rocket 88" on **Chess Records** in Chicago, Illinois, one of the first rock 'n' roll records.
1952	Sam Phillips launches his own label, **Sun Record Company**, in Memphis, Tennessee.
	Johnny Ace makes his debut at the **Hippodrome** in Memphis, Tennessee, with "My Song," which hits #1 on the R&B charts the next month. He achieved success that was rare for black artists at that time.
	Alan Freed's "Moondog Coronation Ball" takes place at **Cleveland Arena** in Cleveland, Ohio, known as the first rock 'n' roll concert.

(Continued)

Year	Highlight
1953	The Orioles of **Jubilee Records** in New York City are the first black group to reach the white market with "Crying in the Chapel." The R&B charts begin to reflect an emerging dominance of rock 'n' roll and a growing interest among the young white population.
1954	The Treniers appear in New York City on NBC's Colgate Comedy Hour at the **Colonial Theater**, one of the earliest rock 'n' roll performances on TV.
	Bill Haley and the Comets give their first public performance of "Rock Around the Clock" at the **Hofbrau Hotel** in Wildwood, New Jersey.
	Leo Fender introduces the Stratocaster that was first made in his **original guitar factory** in Fullerton, California.
	Elvis Presley's first commercial release with **Sun Records**, "That's All Right," is being played endlessly to rave reviews on Dewey Phillip's "Red, Hot & Blue" show at **WHBQ Radio** in Memphis, Tennessee. Elvis is at the **Suzore Theater** watching a movie with friends when his parents arrive to tell him the news and send him to the station to do an on-air interview.
	Elvis Presley performs at **Overton Park Shell** in Memphis, Tennessee, widely recognised as the first rock'n'roll concert.
	Rising star Johnny Ace dies from a gunshot wound backstage at the **City Auditorium** in Houston, Texas, and is referred to rock 'n' roll's first casualty.
1955	Bo Diddley appears on *The Ed Sullivan Show* (**CBS-TV Studio 50**) in New York City.
	NBC Color Studios open at **NBC West Coast Radio City** in Hollywood, California, as the first television studios designed specifically for colour television broadcasting.
	"Bob & Buddy" (Bob Montgomery and Buddy Holly) open for Elvis Presley at the **Fair Park Coliseum** in Lubbock, Texas, in February and again with Larry Welborn in October. The trio also open there for Bill Haley & The Comets in October, where talent scout Eddie Crandall first takes notice of Buddy, leading to his first record deal with Decca.
	Elvis Presley performs his first concert north of the Mason-Dixon Line at **Brooklyn High School** in Brooklyn, Ohio.
1956	The Teen Kings, including Roy Orbison as vocalist, hold the first rock 'n' roll session at **Norman Petty Recording Studios** in Clovis, New Mexico, recording "Trying to Get to You" and "Ooby Dooby."
	Elvis Presley makes his first TV appearance on the *Dorsey Bros "Stage Show"* at **CBS-TV Studio 50** in New York City.
	Capitol Records Building in Los Angeles, California, opens as the first major record label on the West Coast. It is the world's first circular office building.
1957	Elvis Presley buys **Graceland** in Memphis, Tennessee.
	Dick Clark's first national telecast of *American Bandstand* takes place from the **Starlight Ballroom** in Wildwood, New Jersey. The show finds a permanent home at **WFIL-TV Studio B** in Philadelphia, Pennsylvania.

Year	Highlight
1957–58	Buddy Holly and The Crickets record songs such as "That'll Be The Day," "Maybe Baby," "Not Fade Away," "Peggy Sue," "Oh Boy!," and "Well, All Right" at **Norman Petty Recording Studios** in Clovis, New Mexico.
1958	Elvis Presley is drafted into the US army and is given his famous GI haircut at **Fort Chaffee Barbershop** in Fort Smith, Arkansas.
	Elvis Presley makes his final recordings of the 1950s at **RCA Victor Studio B** in Nashville, Tennessee.
	Bob Keane of **Del-Fi Records** in Los Angeles, California discovers Richard Steven Valenzuela (Ritchie Valens) and records "Come On Let's Go," "Donna" and "La Bamba" at **Gold Star Recording Studios** down the street.
1959	Buddy Holly, Ritchie Valens, and JP "The Big Bopper" Richardson give their final career performances on the Winter Dance Party Tour at the **Surf Ballroom** in Clear Lake, Iowa. They are killed in a plane crash later that night.

In this project, subject buildings were determined based on the following criteria for significance:

- *National Register of Historic Places (NRHP):* Criterion A: "Property is associated with *events* that have made a significant contribution to the broad patterns of our history" (National Park Service, 2002, Section II); Criterion B: "Property is associated with the lives of *persons* significant in our past" (National Park Service, 2002, Section II). Although not limited to these criteria, subject buildings are deemed significant under the NRHP's Criteria A and/or B for local and national significance in the areas of *performing arts* and *entertainment/ recreation*.
- *Rock 'n' roll Hall of Fame and Museum (RRHOFM):* inductees are recognised for their significant contributions to rock 'n' roll in the 1950s and "Songs that Shaped Rock and Roll," a list developed by the RRHOFM that identifies the recordings, artists and record labels that defined the rock 'n' roll movement.

The survey excluded lyrical landmarks, memorials, religious buildings and gravesites, unless a gravesite shared the location with a subject building, but included extant and non-extant buildings. Each building was investigated for the following data fields:

- *Property name:* historic name of resource
- *Location:* physical address
- *Built:* year of construction and architect and/or builder, if known
- *Significance:* historic function of resource as associated with recognised artists, record labels and/or events per the above criteria

- *Property status:* current function of resource, condition where not in use, common name if different from historic name, preservation activity such as historic designations, interpretive historical markers, heritage trails, grants etc.

The 100 subject buildings surveyed in my study are divided into the four major regions as recognised by the United States Census Bureau: Northeast, Midwest, South and West. These sites do not represent an exhaustive list of historic resources or related information but rather a first effort to recognise and record subject buildings and strategies in music heritage management for further exploration and assessment. The locations and number of historic resources by region were as follows:

- *Northeast* (19): Boston, Massachusetts; Wildwood, New Jersey; New York, New York; Philadelphia, Pennsylvania
- *Midwest* (12): Clear Lake, Iowa; Chicago, Illinois; Detroit, Michigan; Duluth, Minnesota; St Louis, Missouri; Brooklyn, Cincinnati, Cleveland, Ohio
- *South* (54): Dyess, Fort Smith, and Kingsland, Arkansas; Jacksonville, Florida; Ferriday, New Orleans, Shreveport, Louisiana; Baltimore, Maryland; Jackson, Tupelo, Mississippi; Memphis, Nashville, Tennessee; Houston, Killeen, Lubbock, Wichita Falls, Texas; Washington, DC; Bluefield, West Virginia
- *West* (15): Clovis, New Mexico, Fullerton, Compton, Los Angeles, Hollywood, West Hollywood, Oakland, California; Las Vegas, Nevada.

The building types included residential, commercial, institutional, civic and recreational, encompassing the following functions during their period of significance: single-family dwelling/detached house, apartment building, hotel, hotel/casino, auditorium-arena, club, clothing store, coliseum, roller-rink ballroom/hippodrome, ballroom, band shell, barber shop, quonset hut, hardware store, inn, courthouse, theatre, armory, record-company office, radio station, recording studio, music-publishing office, television broadcasting studio, town hall, fraternal temple, school, record store, warehouse, shopping centre, manufacturing centre. These places were constructed between 1870 and 1956 by the following architects and builders:

- *Architects:* George Keister, Victor A. Bark, Jr., Herbert J. Krapp, Rapp and Rapp, Horatio R. Wilson, Townsend and Weiner, Philip Bettenberg, Clyde Kelly, Owen Williams, Thielbar and Furgard, Giaver and Dinkleberg, Harry P. Hansen, Karl Marshall Waggoner, Roy Benjamin, R.E. Hall, Max Furbringer, Merrill Ehrman, Howard Eichenbaum, J. Frazer Smith, Walk C. Jones, Sr., George Awsumb, Edwin B. Phillips, E.L. Harrison, Samuel Weiner, Raymond B. Spencer, John L. Donovan, Welton Becket

- *Builders:* Henkel Construction, Vernon, Jessie and Vester Presley, Dan Maddox.

Property status, including the level of preservation activity, varied and can be characterised as follows:

- *Condition:* demolished, vacant/not in use, threatened due to neglect or development, preserved and maintained, restored or being restored, rehabilitated (adaptive use) or being rehabilitated, reconstructed, renovated or being renovated for new use incompatible with historic use and function (loss of historic integrity)
- *Functions that utilise historic significance:* historic function retained, operations as a museum, heritage tourism site, classroom, not-for-profit arts organisation
- *Historic interpretation of sites, extant or non-extant:* exhibits, murals, historical markers, heritage trails, historical tours, original cornerstones
- *Awareness campaigns:* historic designations, endangered lists
- *Funding:* grants for restoration, endowments for preservation and maintenance.

The artists associated with these historic resources are Bill Haley & His Comets, Buddy Holly & the Crickets, The Orioles, The Shirelles, Little Anthony and the Imperials, Ray Charles, Clyde McPhatter, The Drifters, LaVern Baker, "Big" Joe Turner, Elvis Presley, Bo Diddley, James Brown, Frankie Lymon, The Dominoes, The Coasters, Johnny Ray, Ruth Brown, The Clovers, The Cardinals, Chuck Berry, Jerry Lee Lewis, Jo-Anne Campbell, Paul Anka, The Treniers, Neil Sedaka, Jackie Wilson, Billy Ward & His Dominoes, The Cadillacs, Bobby Freeman, The Royaltones, Mickey & Sylvia, Lee Andrews & the Hearts, The Five Crowns, The Duvals, The Swans, DJ Fontana, Bill Black, Scotty Moore, The Jordanaires, Howlin' Wolf, Muddy Waters, Ike Turner, Jackie Brenston & His Delta Cats, Willie Dixon, Little Walter, Etta James, Ritchie Valens, JP "The Big Bopper" Richardson, The Four Lads, Priscilla Wright, Pat Boone, John Lee Hooker, The Moonglows, The Flamingos, Paul Williams & His Hucklebuckers, Danny Cobb, Tiny Grimes & the Rockin' Highlanders, Varetta Dillard, Johnny Otis, The Platters, Dinah Washington, The Penguins, Earl King, Frankie Ford, Jimmy Clanton, Huey "Piano" Smith, Joe Tex, Scotty McKay, Bobby Marchan, B.B. King, Nat "King" Cole, Elmore James, Louis Jordan, Sam Baker Jr, Fats Domino, Little Richard, Bill Doggett, The Five Keys, Faye Adams, The Five Satins, Tommy Brown, The Robins, Johnny Torres, Big Jay McNeely, Johnny Ace, Memphis Slim, Dave Bartholomew, Bobby "Blue" Bland, Little Junior Parker, Hank Ballard & the Midnighters, Smiley Lewis, Professor Longhair, Shirley and Lee, Don Guess, Johnny Cash & The Tennessee Two, Carl Perkins, Sonny Curtis, Christine Kittrel, Milt Jackson, T-Bone Walker, Willie Mae "Big Momma" Thornton, Rosco Gordon, Larry Welborn, Bob Montgomery, James Cotton, Lloyd Price,

Guitar Slim, Mississippi Slim, Patsy Cline, Brenda Lee, Gene Vincent, Slim Whitman, Billy Walker, Carter Sisters and Mother Maybelle, Chet Atkins, Sonny Boy Williamson, Huddie "Leadbelly" Ledbetter, Aretha Franklin, Joe Willie Wilkins, James Waller, Little Milton, Wynonie Harris, Little Esther Phillips, Lionel Hampton, Duke Ellington, Ivory Joe Hunter, The Teen Kings (Roy Orbison, vocalist), Ricky Nelson, Eddie Cochran, The Teddy Bears, The Champs, Charles Brown, Lil Green, Little Miss Cornshucks, Calvin Boze, Lightnin' Hopkins, Helen Humes, The Teen Queens.

KING AND COUNTRY: SAVING ELVIS PRESLEY'S CIRCLE G RANCH

Since its establishment, a key project for Re:Muse-icology has been advocating for the preservation of Elvis Presley's Circle G Ranch. In August 2012, while conducting research for my MA final project, I discovered the Circle G Foundation and contacted the CGF's founder to volunteer my assistance. The Circle G Foundation (CGF) was established in January 2012 by Lesley Pilling of Cheshire, England. It is an all-volunteer, fan-based international non-profit organisation dedicated to reviving Elvis Presley's former Circle G Ranch in Horn Lake, Mississippi. Born out of the informal Facebook campaign "Friends of Elvis – Save the Circle G," which was begun in August 2010 by Pilling after her first visit to the ranch, its organisational framework, the Circle of Friends, now consists of six management team members and fifty ambassadors representing fan clubs in the following sixteen countries: Argentina, Australia, Belgium, Brazil, Canada, Denmark, France, Germany, Italy, the Netherlands, Norway, the Philippines, South Africa, Sweden, the United Kingdom and the United States. The growing volume of messages and letters of support comes not only from legions of Elvis fans worldwide but from state and local politicians, businesses and personal friends who spent time with Elvis at the ranch. Advocacy is mobilised not only through the CGF's fan club affiliates but via the foundation's website and social media network (Facebook and Twitter) that appeal to the wider public interest.

In its mission statement, the CGF aims to generate public awareness and support for the preservation of Circle G Ranch while actively documenting the property's history and working to secure the necessary funding ($3.65 million) to acquire it. The foundation's vision is to save and restore the Circle G's existing historic resources, prioritising those from the Elvis Presley period of ownership, and to sensitively adapt the ranch as a heritage tourism site where his charitable legacy will continue. In an unprecedented grassroots effort by Elvis fans, the CGF's tagline, "Where the King Became a Cowboy," and an Elvis-inspired cowboy silhouette featured in its circled G logo, symbolise the unique story of Elvis Presley's life at Circle G Ranch that the foundation aspires to tell. When I contacted Pilling in August 2012, the foundation did not have a preservation specialist on its management team and Pilling welcomed me to fulfil that role in September 2012 after graduation.

My work with the CGF sees me implement and manage all preservation-related activity in support of the foundation's vision, including research and documentation of the ranch, nominations for historic designations and endangered lists, the interpretation and installation of the Mississippi state historical marker, and opportunities to inform and educate the public on the property's historic significance and the importance of its preservation and reuse. As the foundation's preservation consultant and only American management-team member, I also educate the CGF on the principles and practice of preservation in the United States.

On May 30, 2014, after nearly four years of collective campaigning by Pilling and fellow Elvis fans, Real Estate International (REI) acquired Circle G Ranch for $3.65-million. The official press announcement was released on June 3, 2014, on the Circle G Ranch website:

> *Horn Lake, Miss. (June 3, 2014)*–The Circle G Ranch in Horn Lake, Mississippi, has been purchased and is now officially under new ownership. The 231-acre tract, of which 163 acres is well known for once being owned by Elvis Presley and his wife, Priscilla, sits on the corner of Highway 301 and Goodman Road. The property is rich in historical features including the Honeymoon Cottage shared by Elvis and Priscilla, the stable where Elvis kept his horses, a 14-acre lake and a prominent 55-foot cross.
>
> The property has been purchased by a group of investors led by Mississippi native, Davage "Buddy" Runnels Jr., the founder and owner of Real Estate International, Inc. (REI). REI, based in Destin, Florida, is a commercial and residential development group established over 47 years ago.
>
> Specific plans for the restoration of the property will be announced in the future. For more information, visit www.circlegranch.com.
>
> (Circle G Ranch 2014b)

On that same day, the CGF also made an official announcement to Elvis fans and followers on Facebook and Twitter, revealing the foundation had been in discussions with REI for well over a year while the company had Circle G Ranch under land contact. During that time, I had been advising the CGF and REI on cultural heritage management-related issues and inquiries.

The CGF is leading the way and making history with unprecedented fan involvement in the preservation of an Elvis Presley heritage site. In addition to serving as the conduit between the international fan community and REI, the foundation is also sponsoring a Mississippi state historical marker to be erected at Circle G Ranch, and will be partnering with REI on fan-led charity activities at the ranch as well as interpreting the organisation's history on site.

Figure 19.1 Elvis and Priscilla Presley's honeymoon cottage at Circle G Ranch. Photo by Sheryl Davis.

Phase 1 of restoration began in August 2014 and is slated for completion in August 2015 (Circle G Ranch, 2014a). The effort will include various rehabilitation and preservation treatments of Elvis-era historic resources, including Elvis and Priscilla's honeymoon cottage (see Figure 19.1), horse stables, 55-foot cross, footbridge and EP-monogrammed barbecue pit. New additions for Phase 1 will include a parking area and walking paths, a riding arena near the restored stables, a dynamic multimedia water feature in the 14-acre lake, and a stage and lawn terrace seating situated nearby for live entertainment.

THE ADVOCACY WORK OF RE:MUSE-ICOLOGY

Although Re:Muse-icology is still in its infancy, it has been involved in a number of projects in addition to the pro bono volunteer consultancy with the CGF. For example, in February 2014 I reached out to the National Association for the Preservation of African-American History & Culture (NAPAAHC), a newly established organisation spearheading the inaugural "America's 10 Most Threatened African-American Historic Properties 2015." The list is a vehicle to help generate awareness and preservation assistance for endangered African-American historic properties of national importance.

I volunteered to assist with facilitating the call for nominations and, consulting my growing inventory of research findings, identified several endangered African-American popular music heritage sites as potential candidates. In the capacity of liaison, I initiated communication with representatives of identified properties and invited them to participate in this unique first effort to achieve greater visibility for African-American and music heritage properties in the American preservation movement. I also provided general support in the application process where needed.

Nominated sites represented significant associations with nationally recognised African-American music artists ranging from ragtime to soul. The NAPAAHC board will determine its selections in December 2014, and the list will be announced in January 2015:

- Club Plantation/Bobbin Records (St Louis, Missouri)
- Cotton Club (Gainesville, Florida)
- Dew Drop Inn (New Orleans, Louisiana)
- John Coltrane house (Dix Hills, New York)
- Nina Simone birthplace and childhood home (Tryon, North Carolina)
- Trumpet Records (Jackson, Mississippi)
- United Sound Systems (Detroit, Michigan).

In September 2014, I was named Music Heritage UK's first ambassador. In my official role, I assist in furthering the charity's mission to promote, protect and preserve the United Kingdom's popular musical heritage while keeping the organisation current on Stateside campaigns and related strategies.

CHALLENGES AND THE FUTURE OF RE:MUSE-ICOLOGY

As a DIY practitioner, having a lack of financial resources represents both my greatest challenge and my biggest opportunity. While I have continued to make what I believe are small but significant strides in successfully developing a specialisation in music heritage preservation, the rate and scope of progress have thus far been limited to remote consulting (pro bono volunteering), social media curation (Facebook and Twitter) and independent research. Now, having built up over two years' worth of contacts, fieldwork and intellectual property, the priority for the future is to make that existing knowledge and experience commercially viable, to disseminate it within the historic preservation community and to mobilise the Re:Muse-icology platform beyond its largely virtual confines into the realm of direct engagement and productive, on-the-ground involvement with grassroots campaigns in the United States and abroad. At this juncture, producing a livable income is essential to the immediate sustainability of Re:Muse-icology, as well its expansion and longevity.

To me, the future of Re:Muse-icology is truly exciting as I pursue new possibilities for revenue streams and collaboration with allied fields. Some specific examples include publishing in major music and travel and tourism magazines, historical consulting for film and television (location scouting, cinematic interpretation and site management of music landmarks), and curating special exhibitions at music heritage-focused cultural institutions. I will also continue to be enterprising in the effort to gauge potential employment opportunities with the many non-profit organisations and other DIY groups representing music heritage sites identified in my MA final project and ongoing research.

In addition to seeking grants and fellowships to support my study and documentation of new and existing subject buildings, I will be introducing the concept and application of phenomenology, specifically as it pertains to the emotional impact of experiencing interpreted music heritage sites. I will also be creating a tourist/visitor exit survey to be administered at several destinations, and new avenues will be explored to utilise the creative utility and cultural capital of these special places in order to promote music education and related arts-based philanthropy, sustainable design and community revitalisation efforts.

With the same democratising spirit of independence that built the American musical ethos and its architectural legacy, I am proud to have realised my vision as a DIY practitioner. It is my hope the Re:Muse-icology platform will serve as a substantial contributor in not only creating a new specialisation but in further diversifying the appreciation, study and preservation of our built environment and popular music heritage.

REFERENCES

Circle G Ranch. 2014a. Circle G Ranch, previously owned by Elvis Presley, commences Phase 1 of restoration. Media release, August 12. http://circlegranch.com/circle-g-ranch-phase-one.

Circle G Ranch. 2014b. Circle G Ranch, previously owned by Elvis Presley, is officially under new ownership. Media release, June 2. http://circlegranch.com/circle-g-ranch-previously-owned-by-elvis-presley-under-new-ownership.

Davis, S. 2012. State of rock 2012: A current look at the built heritage of 1950s rock 'n' roll in America. Unpublished MA thesis, Savannah College of Art and Design.

National Park Service 2002. How to apply the National Register criteria for evaluation. U.S. Department of the Interior. Accessed December 14, 2014. http://www.nps.gov/nr/publications/bulletins/nrb15.

20 Editions of You

A DIY Archive of DIY Practice

Lisa Busby

I never wanted to be an archivist. I've wanted to be a veterinarian (practical childhood), riot grrl heroine (awkward teens) and a curator (over-ambitious episodes in my twenties). And it is this last ambition – specifically to curate an exhibition that shoved a personal interest in subversive DIY musical practices under the noses of a mainstream, conservative and principally visual arts demographic – that has seen me stumble into the role.

Abreu (2013), among others, posits that collecting and collections on an individual and social scale serve as counter-hegemonic strategies, challenging dominant narratives and offering new standpoints for understanding social history as well as preserving history that would otherwise be lost. While I am proud to say Editions of You certainly fits the remit of what has become known as the radical or activist archive, I'd suggest at its inception that a different term might more accurately fit the bill.

Editions of You is an accidental archive. I am most certainly an accidental archivist. This chapter looks at how the project Editions of You emerged, its contents, day-to-day practical problems of its running and the larger curatorial issues it presents, and finally how its value as a resource or network might be accessed and shared. While I consider the currency and cultural worth of the project, the purpose of the chapter is not to argue for the legitimacy of either the practices contained therein or its existence. Rather, it is to present a series of honest and applicable observations of the aspirations and struggles of what might legitimately be called a micro archive and its archivist as a contribution to the growing acknowledgment of self-authorised and unauthorised heritage-as-praxis (Roberts and Cohen 2014). In short, I argue that not knowing the right stuff or doing things the right way does not mean your work is not valuable.

AMBITIOUS BEGINNINGS, HUMBLE ONGOINGS

Like countless other singer-songwriters, bedroom producers, bands, sound artists, DJs and frankly anyone who finds themselves in the position of having made some recordings but is not in a position to have them mass produced, I developed my own cottage industry approaches to sharing and releasing my musical output. It was nothing earth-shatteringly original. To begin with, illustrated wraps or collaged inserts housed manually duplicated cassettes and CDs. Over time, and in no small part intensified by academic research into the interdisciplinary practices of pop musicians, my approach became bolder and more elaborate, involving vintage textiles, stamps and wax seals, book binding, found objects and more. I released a single on 3-inch CD encased in a handspun ball of wool (Sleeps in Oysters 2010). I released an album accompanied by a cross-stitch kit and thimble (Sleeps in Oysters 2011). These practices were not sales-boosting gimmicks; the underground economy my music inhabits will never earn me a living. Rather, they provided me with a way to reflect the process or meaning of the soundwork in physical form and to explore skills and interests in other crafts and practices – to rejoice in other forms of making.

While making these works, I was aware of a world of musicians and artists exploring similar territory, and felt this culture should be celebrated, provided with a public arts forum and acknowledged status similar to that enjoyed by zines, artists' books, and poster and flyer art. In 2011, I successfully secured a modest amount of funding from Arts Council England and Oxford Brookes University as part of a joint bid that aimed to bring new audio cultures to Oxford. In conjunction with partners Oxford Contemporary Music, Oxford Castle and O2 Gallery, this funding allowed me to curate a four-week exhibition with associated gigs, talks, and a record and zine fair, raising the profile of and broadening public engagement with this type of underground work. As well as providing financial support for new artworks, musical releases and workshops, the funding allowed me to purchase a significant proportion of what is now the archive – the original selection of work that made up the exhibition. The festival is documented in full online (Editions of You 2011b).

When the month-long festival was over and the excitement of its success was fading into memory, all of these things were still there and I realised I was responsible for them. Together they represented something, and once I started to perceive them as a collection – a record of a current movement or a phenomenon – I also knew this assemblage could not be static and must be "porous to societal processes and discourses" (Hamilton, Harris and Reid 2002, 7), reflecting the living creative scenes it sought to represent by growing and changing. Burton (2005, 6) observes "archives do not arrive or emerge fully formed." Despite the fact this one arguably did, I was determined to never allow it to stay that way.

THE ARCHIVE AT A GLANCE

Finding a way to describe the collection was (and is) not easy, as the range of work is vast. The Editions of You website summarises the project as "celebrating and showcasing self-publishing and self-releasing musicians and the handmade editions and releases they create" (Editions of You, 2011a). The core of the project is a collection of approximately 200 items that in one way or another fit my own rather loose definition of handmade editions and releases. In the main, these are releases by autonomous, unsigned artists or independent micro-labels and have one or more of four defining characteristics:

- handmade sleeves and packaging
- limited, special-edition short runs
- unusual or obsolete physical formats
- a focus on design (2D and 3D).

The best way to understand how these rather open descriptors can form a coherent (or perhaps incoherent) narrative within the archive is to briefly discuss some individual objects. They broadly fall into three categories:

1 those perceived as traditional or familiar modes of DIY or homemade releasing: the screenprinted cardboard covers of Julie La Rousse's *L'année de l'empereur* (2008) or the spray-painted, stickered, collaged or otherwise decorated tapes and inserts of They Live We Sleep records (Video Nasties, 2010)

Figure 20.1 Clockwise from top left: Sleeps in Oysters: *The Brambles in Starlight*, various releases by They Live We Sleep Records including Video Nasties: *No 3*, Luz Alibi: *Warm Marrow*, Rachael Dadd: *Balloon/ Sticking in Pins* and *Claw &Tooth/Window*. Photo by Lisa Busby.

Figure 20.2 Clockwise from top left: Various releases by Diskette Etikette Records
including various artists: *Now that's What I Call Retro-futurism
Vol. 3*, Lustrous Chemist: *Pop Mantra*, Various releases by Earjerk
Records including The Grass Magic: *The Grass Magic*, Felicity Ford:
Soundwalk Stationary. Photo by Lisa Busby.

2   releases that focus on the unique crafted object, with each edition often
different from the last: each *Warm Marrow* cassette from Luz Alibi
(Resipiscent, 2009) comes with an accompanying tape stand made from
piano hammers, and Frenchbloke & Son enclosed the recordings of
*Société de Radiodiffusion de l'homme et du fils Français – Bruit dans
l'internet de Musique* on cassette (Seed, 2010) inside hollowed-out,
secondhand books
3   works that dispense with a physical music format altogether: Rachael
Dadd's double A-side releases *Balloon/Sticking in Pins* and *Claw &
Tooth/Window* (Broken Sound, 2011) both come as multimedia download bundles with handmade art badge, and Alcopop records, well
known for their innovative physical packaging (Cooke, 2012), released
label compilation *Alcopopular Vol. 3* (2009) as a treasure map and message in a bottle, several of which they did throw into the sea (*The Great
Bottle Launch*, 2009).

Even within these categories, sub-sets emerge. I hold various releases on
unusual, obsolete or difficult-to-access formats: the floppy-disc output of
Diskette Etikette Records (for example, their compilation *Now That's What
I call Retro Futurism 2*, 2011) or Exotic Pylon's miniature A/V release on

SD card (*Works on Foil*, 2014). There are works that utilise recycled materials: Graham Dunning's "Music by the Meter" series dubbed to recycled tapes (a good example being the short run of four, *Winning in Negotiations*, 2014); the work of Lustrous Chemist that repurposes torn pages from 1980s *Smash Hits* magazines as origami sleeves (*Pop Mantra*, 2009); or Earjerk Records's thrift-shop record sleeve finds turned inside out and screen printed with new artwork to house their own LP releases (for example *The Grass Magic*, 2008). Some artists choose to focus on high-spec or innovative design: the bran(...) pos CD sleeve that is also a functional pinball game (*Quaak Muttar*, 2005) or the L.O.A.F and Non Format EP series that aimed to make CD packaging that could be housed in LP racks, winner of a D&AD Yellow Pencil international design award (Non-Format, 2009).

Given the historical links between music and other forms of making that are prominent in, for example, the punk, post-punk and riot grrrl scenes (Duncombe 1997), there is inevitable crossover with work produced by zine makers and other self-publishing artists, writers and activists. Even though extensive zine archives already exist,[1] to preclude the inclusion of this type of work on the basis that they are not strictly music releases would be a mistake as it would fail to acknowledge the crossover practices of the artists it seeks to represent. The archive therefore includes music zines (for example, *Raw Pogo on the Scaffold*, 1992–97; *Angry Violist*, 2009–11) but also music releases presented in zine form with download code from cross-media collectives, including Crumb Cabin (*Briscuits/Animales*, 2013) and Monster Emporium Press (*The Duchess, The Demon, The Double: A Book of Songs*, 2011).

Finally, we have work that is difficult to categorise at all. The archive holds various editions by field recordist and sound artist Felicity Ford; *Soundwalk Stationary* (2010) is a good example of a sound object that does not include any recorded audio. *Dr Roger Glass Appointment Card* (2013) by James Marples is an artefact from a live performance installation. We also hold various record-label and band ephemera – stickers, badges, handwritten letters and illustrations, and more – that have been sent to accompany releases in some cases and in others produced as works in their own right.

A SMALL NOTE ON "PHYSICAL," "VIRTUAL" AND THEIR SUPPOSED DISPARITY

A defining feature of all items in the archive is their tangibility – their physical nature. Despite the retrospective focus this might imply, as an archivist and researcher in this field I am neither a luddite nor a technophobe. Music journalist Joe Muggs (2011) astutely observes:

> Whether it ever proves to be economically viable or not, we are certainly in a period where the digitisation of music, far from disembodying it, seems to make the carrying object more and more important. The

love of and engagement with musical formats from the past is about tapping into historical technological streams as they flow through the present moment, not about trying to recover or recreate the past. Listeners create new relationships to the music as much as they hanker after old ways of hearing.

The continued engagement with and demand for music on physical media is more complex than simple nostalgia or even Simon Reynolds's more nuanced notions of "retromania" (2011). Listeners and consumers are not neatly divided into tribes of vinyl junkies vs. digital evangelists for multi-faceted (and differing) reasons beyond "reductive questions of old vs. new, retro vs. modernist, or analogue vs. digital" (Muggs 2011).

Editions of You is not an attempt to sanctify arguably outdated formats and ways of dissemination. Rather, it was born from an interest in inter-disciplinarity and the phenomenon of generalist practitioners in the arts, those working and collaborating freely across media. This archive is neces-sarily non-comprehensive, collecting the artefacts of short-lived, small-scale modes of creation that occur on a massive canvas. The vast majority of these practices originate with DIY artists in underground scenes who can make whatever they want and sell for whatever they want (in my experi-ence, often at a substantial loss on materials and labour) because economic considerations – the pressure to sell and ultimately turn a profit – are not necessarily a central motivating factor. However, these trends in making and releasing are filtering across the industry at all levels and the recent increase in limited-run and high-priced editions of records by established artists,[2] hailed as revolutionary by some and simply exploitative by others, have sparked debate about to what model really is best for musicians and fans (Barry 2014). This modest archive provides a way of documenting at least some of the practice that would normally be omitted from such mainstream debates in what is an interesting period of rapid change in the post-virtual music climate where the physical and virtual collide.

EVERYDAY PROBLEMS AND ENCOUNTERS

My decidedly amateur status as collector-as-archivist presents practical challenges in the day-to-day running of Editions of You.

- *Time.* As the majority of time given to Editions of You is on a voluntary basis, it is necessarily limited. Consequently, there is always a backlog of jobs or limitless research to be done: cataloguing new acquisitions and responding to queries, keeping up to date with emerging scenes, seeking out new artists, labels and works.
- *Funding.* The process of acquiring new items has been financed in vari-ous ways: the initial public funding secured for the exhibition, tapping

into small research pots from the institutions with which I have worked and in no small part from my own pocket. This position, which I affectionately term the "scrabbling around for change" model, does not allow for healthy growth of the archive. I have no doubt this position could be improved if I had more time.

- *Space.* I have a less than secure climate for the collection's storage, namely cardboard boxes on some shelving in my office. There is no temperature or humidity control; there are no non-destructive fire-suppression measures. Appropriate viewing conditions for the collection are also a problem, given the lack of physical space. I have no doubt this position could be improved if I had more funding.
- *Access.* There is no formal means of public access to the collection. Students, researchers and the public are openly welcomed on the project website to book an appointment and peruse the collection, but few have taken up this offer. I have no doubt this position could be improved if I had a better location for its housing.
- *Training and skills.* I have limited knowledge of proper procedures of archiving or librarianship and am constantly learning by making a lot of mistakes. For preservation purposes, everything should be individually wrapped so as not to get torn or damaged, so ink or paint doesn't bleed from one work to the next or just so items don't get grubby or creased. I found this out the hard way. I must be mindful of this, but also develop ways of wrapping and storing items using the free, recycled materials available. In my record keeping, I frequently realise I am not retaining crucial information about items, because what seems crucial when you start a project is perhaps not the same as what seems crucial three years in, and my spreadsheets often don't tell me the information I want to know. Therefore I am perpetually re-researching older acquisitions, rebuilding spreadsheets to add new data or attempting to add new formulae to generate new statistics I didn't realise I needed. Every so often, you'll stumble across another archive or database that makes you want to start all over again but inevitably this is impossible.

But by far the biggest headscratcher was how the collection should be catalogued and organised. For ease of navigation, alphabetising any collection is helpful. It took me longer than you'd expect to work this out, but even this is more complicated than you'd first imagine. We all have awkward, oversized records or books in our collections that won't fit into their proper alphabetical place and if I tell you in the archive that I have a CD housed inside a 12-inch ceramic ball you'll appreciate this problem affects the Editions of You collection more than most home collections. I could alphabetise by label or artist; I could sub-categorise by release format or type of work (i.e. release, zine, label ephemera, project artefact), but even this presents difficulties. Some artefacts would be in a category all of their own, some items are intrinsically linked to others and are inseparable, and others fall into more than one category. How do I categorise a collection of items designed not to fit into categories? In the end, I've chosen a system that is certainly not perfect and not necessarily always consistent. It is one that is functional, that gives some semblance of order while allowing flexibility for groups of linked items when necessary.

I'd speculate these five issues will be familiar to others undertaking DIY heritage practices. I have rather lightheartedly nodded to how these problems are interconnected, but the truth is that while my archivist status is DIY, I am extremely fortunate to be in a position that allows me to undertake some work on this project as a small part of my role as an academic, and furthermore tap into funding streams from an acknowledged position and institution. Working without this support framework, as most DIY heritage practitioners undoubtedly do, would be much harder.

CURATION, SUBJECTIVITY AND VALUE

These small-scale, domestic trials and tribulations exist alongside larger curatorial questions. The central issue I face is what is appropriate for this collection and how I navigate the terms and scenes "DIY," "self-releasing," "independent" and "handmade." Thomas Bey William Bailey (2012, 16) rightly points out:

> It really can't be stressed enough that "do-it-yourself" audio was never wholly synonymous with "handmade" or "unofficial" audio. While much of DIY music is still recorded and produced using makeshift means, and does not involve the presence of mediating personae during these same processes, it can still take full advantage of other forces of mass production. It's not uncommon these days to find music recorded in one's bedroom with the most humble of tools, and yet released in large unit runs on deluxe formats.

My collection contains works where all three stages of recording, production (of format and artwork) and release/distribution are handled completely independently. Equally, though, many artefacts have a mixed methodology, with some processes professionally handled and others more DIY in their manufacture. Some artists are working without record labels while others are part of small labels or collectives so are arguably not truly self-releasing or self-publishing at all. From another angle, DIY as a term or rationale for self-release is, for many artists, intrinsically linked with a protest stance, a deliberate opting out of the mainstream industrialised system for political reasons. But for others the rationale is different. The Editions of You artists speak variously of political concerns but also of a desire for intimacy or closeness with their audience; for the fulfillment of crafting and making things; for non-audible aspects of the musical release to be as carefully attended to as the music; and for physical presentation to reflect the themes or concepts of the music or be a constituent element of a holistic artwork.

My curatorial policy, then, is exceptionally open for two reasons. First, if this archive is to even attempt to capture a snapshot of a cultural phenomenon that pervades the industry at various levels, then over-rigidity in the gatekeeping of its acquisitions would simply be counter to its aims. Second, this archive relies on donations, and if an artist is kindly offering their work, I do not refuse it. This is not simply a practical concession. The definitions DIY, self-releasing, independent or handmade music mean different things to different artists. Why should my definition or any one definition of these terms take precedence? Although its content is shaped by the limited field of my awareness as archivist and conscious/unconscious predispositions as curator – oppositional and counter-hegemonic collections like my own are as influenced by the role of the archivist as any other, and even alternate recordings of history are subjective (Hamilton, Harris and Reid 2002) – the archive is intrinsically diverse given the diversity of the practices of donating artists.

Although, for many scholars and archivists, this deliberate lack of screening, and the refusal to edit or define on my part, may quite reasonably appear to be a methodology without focus and with little regard to what might be of preservation value, I would vehemently disagree. A recent, illuminating discovery for me was Ursula Marx et al.'s (2007) beautiful book *Walter Benjamin's Archive*, which presents thirteen of Benjamin's collections in image form with accompanying critical discussion by the editors. Most pertinent was Benjamin's interest in keeping material mobile within a collection and the idea of a scholarly book being an outdated mode of communicating knowledge. He states: "Everything that matters is to be found in the card box of the researcher who wrote it, and the scholar studying it assimilates it into his own card index" (Benjamin 1979, 62). So Marx's (2007, 32) editorial observation that "at the outset all material is of equal value, knowledge that is organized in slips and scraps knows no hierarchy" is crucial to understanding the potential of Editions of You in its current form. The unedited collection as a montage of fragments does not seek to create totality or continuity (Mbembe 2002). Rather, it offers multiple narratives, each one unique to those different people who encounter it.

Digitisation of the archive is another pressing issue. Despite only ever providing a snapshot, the physical archive is exceptionally important as the only concrete and historically reliable record of many of these activities by mostly underground artists. It exists within a changing landscape where scenes come and go, expand and fade, and while it has become easier to locate these pockets of creativity using the Internet, without the objects themselves, records of them can become more transient and unreliable. I have works in the collection from limited runs as small as five or ten, works only released in an analogue format and never simultaneously as a download, works where the artist has moved on or the label has dissolved and all traces have disappeared from the Internet – most makers at this level will not keep up a website for a band or project that is no longer active for artistic or financial reasons. It is also worth remembering that, while many artists use digital means as one constituent part of their work, some artists oppose their work being reduced to a digital form, with a few artists not disseminating their work on the Net at all. If the physical archive didn't exist, we would have no record of these activities and I would receive far fewer donations as I'd be fundamentally out of touch with the intentions of many artists and their work.

All of this said, I believe that for collections like Editions of You, a best-case scenario is for physical and digital archiving and dissemination to work in productive symbiosis. The physical archive presents problems as well as benefits – it is not securely stored, so a fire or a burst pipe could destroy it quite easily. Acts of God notwithstanding, many of the items are very fragile and in some cases perishable. From an access point of view, much of the music in its physical form is unplayable to those without the relevant, and sometimes hard to come by, playback technologies. A virtual platform that contained high-quality image documentation of the artefacts and digital audio records of the music (with artists' permission only) would make the archive far more accessible to researchers and other interested parties. Unfortunately, in order to do this, even for a small volunteer archive like my own, time and funding are required. Amid rapid change in digital audio technologies, is this investment for the small-scale archivist of physical artefacts really justified if current digital archiving formats may be in danger of becoming obsolete in the near- to mid-term?

THE ARCHIVE COMMUNITY

In conclusion, I'd like to address how we might successfully value and codify work that is intended to sit outside cultural systems that exist for that purpose. I'd suggest the challenge for Editions of You, as for many similar heritage projects, is sensitively balancing its importance as a site for resistance with formal strategies for highlighting and sharing its broader cultural significance, given the practical limitations already outlined.

Over its three-year lifespan, Editions of You has evolved in response to this challenge in a number of ways. First, the activities of the project have expanded to incorporate, as one might expect, public exhibitions and talks but also fundraising to support independent releases; running a not-for-profit distro[3] to provide a wider network of dissemination for the artists; running workshops and live gigs; DJing the archive; and the creation of promotional mixtape compilations. In undertaking these diverse activities, it has become apparent that Editions of You has much in common with some of the independent labels and collectives with which the project engages. Similarly, the ethos of these small labels is often curatorial and archival as much as it is concerned with the sale, distribution or promotion of products. United Kingdom labels Eyeless Records and RHP CDRs, for example, keep comprehensive archives of their releases, events and other outputs/activities. The latter, describing itself both as a limited edition record label but also a research, production and event programming unit, is an excellent example of a project whose new work (live events, talks, exhibitions, publications) is in dialogue with its artist roster and archive. So as we see the boundaries between creative practice and the documentation of that practice become fluid (Mereweather 2006; Osthoff 2009), we also see commercial activity and heritage activity arriving at similar destinations. The expanding activities of projects like Editions of You in an environment where perceptions of economic value or profitability in music are changing rapidly – as are the boundaries around who and what can be considered curator, researcher and more – suggest the possibility of a new common understanding of the value of musical activities and artefacts.

Second, as well as an open stance on the terms DIY, self-releasing, independent and handmade, there is an equally deliberate open policy on music type or genre. Not being limited by considerations of style, and setting aside subjective measures of personal taste or so called quality, means inclusivity becomes one of the defining features of the project. Editions of You is a place where anyone is welcome: a site of empowerment and support. A glance at the blog will show it is as much a community noticeboard for the network of artists it represents as it is a document of the project. So what becomes valuable about the archive, the distro and all the project's activities to the practitioners with whom I am working is centrally that the project exists and ascribes a value to what they do.

As a result of these characteristics, the archive exists within and contributes to the flow of both creative and commercial activity. It is not simply preservationist but an active site for the support and generation of new creative work.

NOTES

1. In the United Kingdom, we have physical zine collections housed in national institutions (the British Library), academic institutions (London College of Communication) and community or volunteer-run centres – for example, the Salford Zine Library or the 56a Infoshop (London).
2. The growth in exclusive luxury releases, deluxe reissue box sets and 180-gram vinyl pressings in the mass-produced and mainstream industry since the start of the twenty-first century has yielded some extreme examples of so-called special editions. In 2011, Björk famously released Apple's first official app album, *Biophilia*. Possibly less widely known is the Ultimate Art Edition of the album, featuring exclusive audio, a book and a set of tuning forks, all housed in an oak case, priced at the not insignificant US$800 on release. Perhaps the ultimate exclusive edition was announced by Wu-Tang Clan in Spring 2014. The double

album *Once Upon a Time in Shaolin* (which comes in a hand-carved silver box) is to be toured, made available for listening in galleries, museums and venues before being auctioned off to the highest bidder as a private collector's item. Fan groups responded by instigating an unsuccessful crowd-funding campaign to buy the album collectively and release it for free.

3. In this context, the term "distro" (derived from the word "distributor" or "distribution") refers to a person or group who most commonly assists the promotion, distribution and sale of independent publications but also music and crafts. The organisation and running methods of distros vary enormously, given they are DIY labours of love endeavours, but it is fair to say the relationship between artist and distro is much less formal than that between, for example, artist and publisher or manager (Wrekk 2009).

REFERENCES

Abreu, A. 2013. Collaborative collecting: A literature review. *InterActions* 9(1). Accessed December 1, 2014. http://escholarship.org/uc/item/43h2342f.

Bailey, T.B.W. 2012. *Unofficial release: Self released and handmade audio in post industrial society.* Belsona Books. Accessed December 4, 2014. http://www.tbwb.net.

Barry, R. 2014. Why the music business shouldn't turn into the art business. *The Quietus.* Accessed November 13, 2014. http://thequietus.com/articles/14940-wu-tang-clan-music-industry-art-world.

Benjamin, W. 1979. *One-way street and other writings.* London: NLB.

Big Scary Monsters YouTube 2009. *The Great Bottle Launch.* Video. Accessed November 15, 2014. https://www.youtube.com/watch?v=67TdHUKzaZs.

Bjork 2011. *Biophilia: The ultimate art edition.* Accessed November 15, 2014. http://bjork.com/special/biophilia_ultimate_edition.html.

Burton, A. 2005. *Archive stories: Facts, fictions and the writing of history.* Durham, NC: Duke University Press.

Cooke, C. 2012. Q&A: Jack Clothier, Alcopop! Records, Complete Music Update. Accessed November 23, 2014. http://www.thecmuwebsite.com/article/qa-jack-clothier-alcopop-records.

Duncombe, S. 1997. *Notes from the underground: Zines and the politics of alternative culture.* New York: Verso.

Editions of You. 2011a. About. Accessed November 25, 2014. http://editionsofyou.com/aboutandcontact.

Editions of You. 2011b. Editions of You Festival 2011. http://editionsofyou.com/festival2011.

EZCLZIV SCLUZAY 2014. EZCLZIV introduces The Carmen Clandestine Experience, the world's first private music service. Accessed December 5, 2014. http://scluzay.com.

Fans of Wu Tang the World Over Kickstarter Campaign. 2014. *Once upon a time in Shaolin – for Wu fans, for Wu people.* Accessed November 25, 2014. https://www.kickstarter.com/projects/1308696559/once-upon-a-time-in-shaolin-for-wu-fans-for-wu-peo.

Hamilton, C., Harris, V. and Reid, G. 2002. Introduction. In C. Hamilton, V. Harris, J. Taylor, M. Pickover, G. Reid, G. and R. Saleh (eds.), *Refiguring the archive.* Dordrecht: Kluwer, 7–17.

Marx, U., Schwarz, G., Schwarz, M. and Wizisla, E. (eds.). 2007. *Walter Benjamin's archive: Images, texts, signs.* New York: Verso.

Mbembe, A. 2002. The power of the archive and its limits. In C. Hamilton, V. Harris, J. Taylor, M. Pickover, G. Reid, G. and R. Saleh (eds.), *Refiguring the archive.* Dordrecht: Kluwer, 19–26.

Mereweather, C. (ed.). 2006. *The archive: Documents of contemporary art.* London: The Whitechapel Gallery and MIT Press.

Muggs, J. 2011. The medium is the message. *Red Bull Music Academy.* Accessed November 25, 2014. http://www.redbullmusicacademy.com/magazine/medium_is_the_message.

Non-format. 2009. Non-format music packaging for the LOAF label. Accessed November 25, 2014. http://non-format.com/loaf.

Osthoff, S. 2009. *Performing the archive: The transformation of the archive in contemporary art from repository to documents to art medium.* New York: Atropos.

Reynolds, S. 2011. *Retromania: Pop culture's addiction to its own past.* London: Faber and Faber.

Roberts, L. and Cohen, S. 2014. Unauthorising popular music heritage: Outline of a critical framework. *International Journal of Heritage Studies* 20(3), 241–61.

Wrekk, A. 2009. *Stolen Sharpie revolution 2: A DIY resource for zines and zine culture.* Portland, OR: Lunchroom.

DISCOGRAPHY

Björk. 2011. *Biophilia* (Ultimate Art Edition). London: One Little Indian.

Wu-Tang Clan. 2014. *Once upon a time in Shaolin* (Double CD). EZCLZIV Scluzay-Archive artefacts and artist links.

Anon. 1992–97. *Raw pogo on the scaffold box set.* Nos 10–14. Zinc. http://www.easysubcult.bigcartel.com.

Anon 2009–11. *Angry Violist*, Nos. 1–5. Zine. Cambridge https://angryviolist.wordpress.com.

Beta blocker and the body clock/Ines Estrada. 2013. *Briscuits/Animales.* Zine. London: Crumb Cabin. http://www.crumbcabin.com.

bran(...) pos. 2005. *Quaak Muttar* (CD). San Francisco: Resipiscent http://soundcrack.net/branpos/.

H. 2011. *The duchess, the demon, the double: A book of songs.* Download, zine. London: Monster Emporium Press. http://www.monsteremporiumpress.co.uk/ddd.

Dadd, Rachael. 2011. *Balloon/sticking in pins.* Download, badge. London: Broken Sound.

Dadd, Rachael. 2011. *Claw and tooth/window.* Download, badge. London: Broken Sound http://www.rachaeldadd.com.

Dunning, G. 2014. *Winning in negotiations.* Cassette. http://grahamdunning.com.

The Grass Magic 2008. *The grass magic.* LP. Wisconsin: Earjerk. http://earjerkrecords.blogspot.co.uk.

Ford, F. 2010. *Soundwalk stationary.* (Map, envelopes, cards to accompany and facilitate soundwalk. http://www.felicityford.co.uk.

Frenchbloke & Son. 2010. *Société de Radiodiffusion de l'homme et du fils Français – Bruit dans l'internet de Musique.* Cassette. London: Seed Records. http://www.seedrecords.co.uk.

La Rousse, J. 2008. *L'année de L'empereur*. CD. http://julie.la.rousse.free.fr.
Lustrous Chemist. 2009. *Pop mantra*. 3 in. CD. http://www.lustrouschemistry.com.
Luz Alibi. 2009. *Warm marrow*. Cassette. San Francisco: Resipiscent. http://www.lizallbee.net.
Madden/Dylewski. 2014. *Works on Foil*. SD card. London: Exotic Pylon Records. http://exoticpylonrecords.com.
Marples, J. 2013. *Dr Roger glass appointment Card*. Installation ephemera. London.
Sleeps in Oysters. 2010. *The brambles in starlight*. 3 in. CD. London: Seed Records.
Sleeps in Oysters. 2011. *Lo!* CD. London: Seed Records. http://www.sleepsinoysters.com.
Video Nasties. 2010. *No. 3*. Cassette. Montréal: They Live We Sleep Cassettes. http://theylivewesleepcassettes.bandcamp.com.
Various Artists. 2009. *Alcopopular Vol. 3*. Download, bottle, map. Oxford: Alcopop! http://www.ilovealcopop.co.uk.
Various Artists. 2011. *Now that's what I call retro futurism 2*. Floppy disc. London: Diskette Ettikette Records. http://www.disketteetikette.tk.
Various Artists 2006–07. *L.O.A.F. 1–15*. CD, 3 in. CD. London: L.O.A.F. http://www.lorecordings.com.

LABELS

Eyeless Records. http://www.eyelessrecords.net.
[RHP CDRs]. http://rhpcdrs.wordpress.com.

List of Contributors

Dave Allen PhD is a recently retired academic who has specialised mostly in visual arts and pedagogy. However, his first career in the late 1960s was as a professional pop musician and he has performed semi-professionally ever since. In the final phase of his academic career, he taught, researched and wrote about popular music.

Sarah Baker PhD is an Associate Professor in Cultural Sociology at Griffith University, Queensland, Australia. She is the co-author of *Creative Labour: Media Work in Three Cultural Industries* (with David Hesmondhalgh, 2011) and *Teaching Youth Studies Through Popular Culture* (with Brady Robards, 2014), and co-editor *of Redefining Mainstream Popular Music* (with Andy Bennett and Jodie Taylor, 2013) and *Youth Cultures and Sub-cultures: Australian Perspectives* (with Brady Robards and Bob Buttigieg, 2015). Her current research focuses on DIY popular music archives and museums, and other aspects of popular music heritage and cultural memory.

Amanda Brandellero PhD is a Lecturer in the Department of Sociology and Anthropology at the University of Amsterdam. She previously held a post-doctoral research position at Erasmus University, where she worked on the HERA-funded project Popular Music Heritage, Cultural Memory and Cultural Identity (POPID). Her research focuses on local and global dynamics of production and consumption within the popular music industry and the market for contemporary art.

Barrie Brennan was previously an academic in adult education at the University of New England, Armidale, where he was recently awarded his PhD. Since 1972, he has lived in Tamworth, Australia's Country Music Capital, where he volunteers at the Australian Country Music Foundation Hall of Fame.

Lisa Busby is Lecturer in Music at Goldsmiths, University of London and a practising musician, artist and researcher. She plays in various musical outfits and creates work in installation and performance. Lisa leads two research projects at Goldsmiths: Editions of You, celebrating self-releasing musicians and handmade editions, and Shit! I Can DJ, exploring experimental and crossover DJ practices.

Oliver Carter PhD is a Lecturer in Media and Cultural Theory and a member of the Centre for Media and Cultural Research at Birmingham City University. His research focuses on alternative economies of media production, particularly fan production, and he recently completed his doctoral thesis, "Making European Cult Cinema: Fan Production in an Alternative Economy." He has published work on cult cinema fandom that appears in *Murders and Acquisitions: Representations of the Serial Killer in Popular Culture* (A. MacDonald, ed., Bloomsbury, 2013) and *The Piracy Effect* (R. Braga and G. Caruso, eds., Mimesis, 2013). He is also a contributing author to the book *Media Studies: Text, Production and Consumption* (P. Long and T. Wall, eds., Prentice Hall, 2009).

Jez Collins is a researcher and research developer in the Centre for Media and Cultural Research at Birmingham City University, where his interests are the music industries and popular music as heritage. He is currently studying for his PhD at the University of Liverpool. Jez is the founder of the Birmingham Music Archive and the executive co-producer for the award-winning documentary *Made in Birmingham: Reggae Punk Bhangra*.

John Collins has been active in the Ghanaian/West African music scene since 1969 as a guitarist, band leader, music-union activist, journalist and writer. He obtained his PhD in ethnomusicology from SUNY Buffalo in 1994. He began teaching at the Music Department of the University of Ghana in 1995, obtained a Full Professorship there in 2002 and between 2003 and 2005 was Head of Department. He is currently on a post-retirement contract with the university, is the manager of Bokoor Recording Studio, chairman of the BAPMAF Highlife-Music Institute and archives, a patron of the Ghana Musicians Union MUSIGA and co-leader of the Local Dimension highlife band.

Sheryl Davis holds an MA in historic preservation from Savannah College of Art and Design. She served as Circle G Foundation's first and only historic preservation consultant in its advocacy of the Elvis Presley Circle G Ranch restoration project in Horn Lake, Mississippi, and advised the National Association for the Preservation of African-American History & Culture on prioritising music heritage in its inaugural list of America's 10 Most Threatened African-American Historical Properties 2015. In September 2014, Sheryl became Music Heritage UK's first ambassador. Through her Re:Muse-icology platform, she provides the only social-media news source dedicated exclusively to music heritage sites.

Mark Duffett PhD is Senior Lecturer in Media and Cultural Studies at the University of Chester, United Kingdom. In 2013 he published *Understanding Fandom* (Bloomsbury), a textbook on media fandom, and the edited volume *Popular Music Fandom* (Routledge).

Stephanie Fremaux PhD is a Senior Lecturer in Media Studies at Teesside University in Middlesbrough, United Kingdom. She completed her PhD thesis on issues of image and performance in The Beatles' films in 2009 at the University of Exeter and is currently exploring interdisciplinary research on popular music, tourism and new modes of fandom.

Gérôme Guibert is a Doctor in Sociology and Associate Professor at the Paris 3 Sorbonne Nouvelle University. He has published many books including *La Production de la culture: le cas des musiques amplifiées en France* (2006) and *Ça Part en Live* (2013), cowritten with Pr D.S. Sagot-Duvauroux. He is also editor-in-chief of *Volume!*, the French journal of popular music studies.

Susanne Janssen PhD is Professor of Sociology of Media and Culture and Chair of the Department of Media and Communication in the Erasmus School of History, Culture and Communication at Erasmus University, Rotterdam. She is also an Honorary Professor in the Griffith Centre for Cultural Research at Griffith University, Queensland, Australia. Susanne is editor-in-chief (with Timothy J. Dowd) of *Poetics: Journal of Empirical Research on Culture, Media and the Arts*.

Coromoto Jaraba works in Caracas, Venezuela for a project on information-technology literacy. She holds a Bachelor of Arts in Modern Languages in the area of translation from Universidad Central de Venezuela. Coromoto is the founder of Proyecto Caracas Memorabilia.

Marion Leonard PhD is a Senior Lecturer in the Department of Music at the University of Liverpool. She is author of *Gender in the Music Industry* (Ashgate, 2007) and co-editor of *Sites of Popular Music Heritage* (Routledge, 2014). She has published on a range of topics about popular music and has particular interest in issues connected with gender, collecting and museum practice.

Anja Löbert studied sociology, media and popular music in Halle/Saale and Liverpool. Since 2005, she has worked as a journalist specialising in British and American popular culture for German newspapers such as *Frankfurter Allgemeine Zeitung* and *ZEIT Online* while simultaneously carrying out independent scholarly research as an affiliate of the University of Salford. Her research into fan communities, Cliff Richard and boy bands has been published in *Popular Music*, *Popular Music History*, and various German books and journals.

Paul Long is Professor of Media and Cultural History at Birmingham City University. He has written about class, culture, radio and popular music, as well as the cultural politics of the City of Birmingham. He is the author of *Only in the Common People: The Aesthetics of Class in Post-war Britain* (Cambridge Scholars Publishing, 2008) and is currently researching aspects of cultural intermediation and community.

Bill Odidi is a senior radio producer at the Kenya Broadcasting Corporation. He is a creative consultant and researcher for Ketebul Music, and writes on art and culture for a wide range of newspapers in Kenya, including the *Daily Nation*, the *East African* and the *Business Daily*.

William "Tabu" Osusa, the founding executive director of Ketebul Music, has been involved in Kenyan music as a producer and band manager for over thirty years. He has also been the project coordinator for the Retracing Kenyan Music series, a research-based documentary project with the primary aim of archiving and documenting the musical culture of Kenya.

Emmanuel Parent holds a PhD in anthropology of music (EHESS, Paris, 2009). His thesis on Ralph Ellison, jazz and black modernism is to be published in Spring 2015 by CNRS éditions. After some years working in the music industry in Nantes (Le Pôle régional musiques actuelles des Pays de la Loire), he is now Associate Professor in the Music Department at the University of Rennes, where he teaches ethnomusicology and popular music studies.

Rosa Reitsamer PhD is a Senior Scientist in Sociology at the University of Music and Performing Arts Vienna. She has published the monograph *Die Do-It-Yourself-Karrieren der DJs: Über die Arbeit in elektronischen Musikszenen* (transcript, 2013) and several articles on popular music, such as "'Born in the Republic of Austria': The Invention of Rock Heritage in Austria" (*International Journal for Heritage Studies*, 2014).

Toni Sant PhD is Director of Research at the University of Hull's School of Arts & New Media in Scarborough, United Kingdom. He is the author of the book *Franklin Furnace & the Spirit of the Avant Garde: A History of the Future* (Intellect, 2011) and is the Digital Curation & Innovation Consultant for the Routledge Performance Archive.

Ray Sutton is the General Manager of the Australian Jazz Museum, incorporating the Victorian Jazz Archive Inc., where he has been a volunteer for more than ten years, nine as GM. While a keen lover of jazz, he doesn't play an instrument. However, he recognises the importance of preserving the heritage of Australian jazz for future generations.

Arno van der Hoeven is a Lecturer in the Department of Media & Communication at Erasmus University, Rotterdam. In 2014, he defended his dissertation "Popular Music Memories: Places and Practices of Popular Music Heritage, Memory and Cultural Identity." Arno's main research interests include media studies, identity and cultural heritage.

Index